Resource Management
for Colleges and Universities

Resource Management for Colleges and Universities

William F. Massy

Johns Hopkins University Press
Baltimore

Johns Hopkins University Press
2715 North Charles Street
Baltimore, Maryland 21218-4363
www.press.jhu.edu

Library of Congress Cataloging-in-Publication Data

Names: Massy, William F., author.
Title: Resource management for colleges and universities / William F. Massy.
Description: Baltimore : Johns Hopkins University Press, 2020. |
    Includes bibliographical references and index.
Identifiers: LCCN 2019033938 | ISBN 9781421437859 (hardcover) |
    ISBN 9781421437866 (ebook)
Subjects: LCSH: Universities and colleges—United States—Finance. |
    Universities and colleges—United States—Administration—
    Decision making.
Classification: LCC LB2342 .M364 2020 | DDC 378.1/06—dc23
LC record available at https://lccn.loc.gov/2019033938

A catalog record for this book is available from the British Library.

Special discounts are available for bulk purchases of this book. For more information, please contact Special Sales at specialsales@press.jhu.edu.

To Mary Katherine (Kay) Klippel
Beloved

Contents

Preface

American colleges and universities remain the gold standard for worldwide higher education, but flaws in their decision-making cultures and business models are becoming ever more apparent. I have been concerned about these flaws for many years. Recent trends are driving observers both inside and outside the academy to speak, write, and, where possible, act on these concerns.

My own assessments, diagnoses, and recommendations for change were stimulated by collaborations with Robert Zemsky beginning in the late 1980s. I summarized my early thinking in *Honoring the Trust: Quality and Cost Containment in Higher Education* (2003) and presented more specific proposals for change in *Reengineering the University: How to Be Mission Centered, Market Smart, and Margin Conscious* (2016). Now, this book connects the conceptual dots and describes how colleges and universities in the United States and Australia are developing new decision-making tools and methods for reducing these proposals to practice.

I have found it useful to use the term "academic resourcing" (AR for short) when referring to the new tools and methods. AR deals with resource allocation writ large: not just the university's budget and associated processes but everything that involves the application of money, human resources, and physical resources such as facilities and equipment to the furtherance of academic goals. This applies both to so-called direct activities like teaching, research, and service and to indirect ones like academic and institutional support. In other words, the ideas expressed in this book have the potential to impact everything and everyone. This is as it should be, because better decision-making is needed all across the university.

All colleges and universities are governed by their "internal economies." I define this idea in chapter 1, but for now it is enough to say that an institution's internal economy consists of the information, incentives, and so on that determine what gets done in the academy's decentralized decision-making environment. Organizational psychologist Jim March has described decision-making in universities as organized anarchy. I believe this stems from deep flaws in the university's internal economies as well as from clashing cultures, faculty politics, and the cacophony of opinions and values one finds within academic organizations.

The tools and methods described in this book will make the internal economies perform better, which is a necessary condition for fixing the flaws called out earlier. I present the models in enough detail for presidents, provosts, deans, and other academic leaders to evaluate their contributions and understand what is required to install them at their institutions. Most importantly, I describe situations where the models can be applied and why these applications are so important for institutional success.

But making the proposed tools and methods available is not enough. Equally important is to surmount the cultural barriers that stand in the way of improved decision-making. Therefore, this book is about academic culture as well as the models per se, and about the ways to transform the culture without damaging the institution or its core values. That is the main reason for my focus on decision-making *conversations* (beginning in chapter 1), which are a key vehicle by which such transformations are effected. I also elaborate on the point, made in *Reengineering the University*, that the use of the proposed tools and methods will further rather than undermine academic values—a conclusion that is crucial for overcoming cultural barriers.

I concentrate on academic decision-making and culture, but the same principles apply to the rest of the university. This is because nonacademic decisions are deeply intertwined with academic ones, and also because the academic culture tends to carry over to decision-making in the administrative and support areas. I discuss nonacademic issues to some extent, but it should be understood that the ideas are less well developed in this arena. The priorities are clearly on the academic side, but success there surely will lead to nonacademic solutions in a relatively short time.

My work with model developers and interviews with model adopters allows me to share new insights about how AR models are, in fact, being constructed and used, as well as the kinds of cultural and organizational barriers they must overcome during adoption. These insights have been informed by the recent work of others as well as the maturation of my own thinking. The result has been a reaffirmation of my belief that the time has come to fix the flaws in the university business model, and that methods' and tools' potential for transforming institutional processes is clear and present. I believe we are looking at game changers here, and I am optimistic that traditional colleges and universities will, by using these or similar tools and methods, succeed in renewing themselves.

Three kinds of AR models are addressed in this book. The first (internal economic) model provides decision makers with information about the details of their institution's activities (especially as they relate to teaching), plus what the activities cost, the revenues they earn, and the margins they generate. This model knits together the university's activities and provides a platform to support tasks that range from operational choices within departments to strategic decisions about which academic programs to offer and at what scale. The second (external economic) model extends the range of marketplace information that is available to program reviewers and strategic planners. The third (mission-market-margin) model addresses a specific problem in budgeting that I first considered in *Reengineering the University*: how to choose among submitted proposals for funding in a way that systematically furthers consideration of the institution's academic mission as well as financial and market factors. The new version of this model is more powerful and easier to understand and use than the previous one.

The book is organized into three parts, each of which consists of three chapters. Two of the parts are on the internal economic tools— which I often refer to simply as AR models. Part I provides an overview of this kind of model. The conversations mentioned earlier are described in chapter 1, along with an introduction to the aforementioned academic cultural issues and how to address them by using a combination of "hard" and "soft" resource management approaches. Chapter 2 describes an internal economic model of intermediate complexity, provides a road map for models of this genre and how they are being used by colleges and universities, and offers advice about how to get started. Chapter 3 defines internal economic models as "prediction machines," summarizes their evolution, describes the benefits achievable through their use, and addresses the all-important question of building trust in the models.

Part II takes a deep dive into the most robust type of internal economic model, the one that provides for the full spectrum of decision-making support discussed in the book. Chapter 4 explains this model's structure and the kinds of information that it produces. Chapter 5 elaborates on the model's "historical" version and the range of decisions to which it contributes. Chapter 6 looks at how the model's "predictive" version can be used to do what-if analyses, including its role in enabling effective scenario planning. Some readers may wish to skim the details in these three chapters, but I include them in order to provide a good picture of what models of this genre can do and how they do it. (Additional details are provided in the appendices.) In my experience, anyone seriously interested in using the models will, sooner or later, come up with questions that are answered by these chapters.

Part III addresses the other two AR models, plus certain additional topics relevant to their use. Chapter 7 describes the new marketplace (external economic) models and how they can be used to improve program review. It also addresses the important matter of teaching quality, which is latent in all AR models. Chapter 8 discusses the third (mission-market-margin) AR model and the problem that gives rise to it. This is the need for trade-offs among subjectively determined missions, semiquantified market considerations, and quantitatively defined contribution margins.

The conclusion, "The Way Forward," offers some suggestions about where the models and processes of AR should go from here. After reviewing takeaways from the previous chapters, we take another look at the achievement of AR model adoption by individual universities. This includes discussions of the barriers that need to be overcome, strategies for overcoming them, five principles for achieving the needed changes, and eight ways of accelerating the change process. Next come suggestions about how people outside universities (e.g., in foundations, governments, and so on) can help propagate AR modeling. Basically, this involves building what might be called an "infrastructure" for diffusing information about AR and facilitating the development of trained cadres of implementers and facilitators. (It's worth noting that the National Association of College and University Business Officers [NACUBO] recently launched an Economic Models Project to further these objectives.) The book ends with a call for action by college and university leaders, governing boards, and other higher education stakeholders.

It occurred to during my writing that the descriptions of university operations and decision-making needed to describe the models also can be valuable for people who seek in-depth knowledge about universities generally. Such knowledge is complicated, and the material in this book provides a good framework for assimilating it. Therefore, the book may be a good reference for courses and seminars on academic administration.

I am grateful to many people and organizations for their assistance in thinking through the issues and providing examples for use in the book. The most instrumental of these is my friend Lea Patterson, chief executive officer of the Pilbara Group, with whom I have shared many thoughts and aspirations about AR modeling. He and his colleagues endorsed the thinking I presented in *Reengineering the University*, to the point of incorporating the core ideas in their university-wide, activity-based costing platform and then working to stimulate their adoption in Australia and the United States. Pilbara's platform, upon which chapters 3 through 6 are largely based, represents the state of the art in full-function AR economic modeling. Let me disclose here, as I do in multiple places throughout the book, that I have partnered with Pilbara in furthering this work. Their support has helped me in uncountable ways.

Among the other staff at Pilbara, my special thanks go to Michelle Brooke, Andrew Faulkner, Mike Skopal, and Michael Gerding. Anthony Pember, now of Grant Thorton LLC, belongs in this group as well. All have been delightful colleagues and most generous with their time, and I have learned a great deal from them.

I am grateful, too, for Pilbara's support of my extended visit to Australia during the winter of 2018, where I participated in meetings with five of their AR modeling clients, and to two such clients in the United States. For the record, these were Deakin University, Royal Melbourne Institute of Technology, Australian National University, University of Adelaide, James Cook University, New York Institute of Technology, and the University of Maryland, College Park. (I also consulted on Pilbara's installation at the University of California, Riverside.) My thanks go to everyone with whom I met, and especially to Chris Grange (chief operating officer at Australian National University), who reviewed my description of his university's budget redesign plans as presented at the end of chapter 6. I am also grateful to Adam Rabb of Embry-Riddle Aeronautical University, who advised me on the model described in chapter 1.

My deep thanks also go to Bob Atkins and his team at Gray Associates, who gave me unfettered access to their models and provided a number of important tables and figures for use in the book. They hosted my visit to their corporate headquarters and an exciting day of conversation about both internal and external AR models, and I have worked with them on a number of presentations and webinars.

Another special thank-you goes to Grace Royal, at the time with Academic Impressions, a company that specializes in building the capacity of staff members and developing the next generation of leaders in colleges and universities. Like her colleagues at Academic Impressions, Grace develops programs that help institutions control their costs and thereby improve student accessibility. She has been instrumental in propagating the concept of activity-based costing and, more recently, all three of the AR models discussed in this book. Her keen sense about how program participants can assimilate complex materials about these subjects has been enormously valuable.

Matt Crellin of the Bill and Melinda Gates Foundation provided great encouragement at certain stages of my work, and my longtime friend Bob Zemsky offered his usual sage advice on some critical issues. I also am grateful for the continuing interest of Joel Meyerson of the Forum for the Future of Higher Education. Finally, my editor Greg Britton and his colleagues at Johns Hopkins University Press have been a joy to work with on both this and my previous book.

I dedicated *Reengineering the University* to my late wife, Suzanne May Massy, who died in 2017 after a short and unexpected illness. I am grateful to her for many things, not the least of which was her commitment to always move forward when times get tough. Her death was a catastrophe, but moving forward after her passing led to the renewal of my research and writing, and hence to the genesis of this book.

This preface would not be complete without deep thanks to Kay Klippel, who became my partner during the past year and has been wonderfully supportive both personally and professionally. The dedication page says it all.

Preview of Applications

Decision-making in the area of academic resourcing (AR)—the application of money, human resources, and physical resources to the furtherance of academic goals—involves a trifecta of issues. I shall illustrate them in terms of the teaching function. The first issue involves values and priorities, many of them academic in nature, which derive from the university's *mission*. What is the relative priority of fields and programs, for example? How important are small classes to the teaching mission?

The second issue involves detailed knowledge about the *activities* in which each part of the university is currently engaged: the initial conditions for the decision-making process. This knowledge must be sufficiently granular and up-to-date to provide a baseline for the choices being made. For example, how many courses are offered in each field, who teaches each type of section, and what are the class sizes? Context is helpful as well, which means that similar information should be available for a number of recent years and, if possible, for other institutions, schools, fields, and so on.

The third element of the trifecta concerns the *economics* of the various activities. What resources does each activity consume? How much do the resources cost? How many students are enrolled, and how much revenue do they generate? What is the activity's margin: that is, the difference between the revenue generated and the costs incurred? (Revenues can be measured both gross and net of financial aid, and margins may reflect indirect as well as direct costs.) Decision makers need these data on both an "average" and "incremental" basis, an example of the latter being the result of adding some number of enrollments to a course or program.

The AR models discussed in this book provide meaningful data on the second and third issues. The first issue is and must remain the province of academic judgment. That's why the book is oriented toward academics: presidents, provosts, deans, department chairs, and even individual faculty members. Financial staff certainly have an interest in the economic issues, but because the trifecta must be viewed holistically, their interest cannot dominate. In other words, it is the academics who must bring the elements of the trifecta together.

AR decisions extend from the very top of the institution, where program portfolio and similar choices are made, right down to the grassroots, where courses and course sections are planned and implemented. Therefore, AR models must provide activity and economic data down to the course level—or perhaps even to the level of individual class sections. Otherwise, the trifecta of decision-making information will be built on sand: that is, without data about what's happening at the core of the teaching enterprise. What's different about AR models is that they bring together elements two and three of the decision trifecta, and that they begin with detailed data at the course level and then roll up the institutional hierarchy rather than approximating the higher-level data by using accounting allocations.

The following narratives describe some of the ways that AR models and their associated decision-making processes can be applied to mainline academic decisions. Unless otherwise noted, they refer to the internal economic AR model introduced in chapter 1. Don't worry if the details of an application aren't entirely clear. I will explain them in the body of the book.

Narrative 1: Adjust to Changed Enrollments

Suppose the budget staff of a university or one of its schools is considering the impact of admitting more students. Other things being equal, they know this action will increase class sizes. Some elements of teaching (e.g., feedback and grading of essays) would require more time or else get shortchanged. Mitigating this would mean other course activities would receive less effort, a boosting of the use of adjunct faculty, or increases in the regular faculty's workload—which would reduce their discretionary time. What mix of choices would produce the smallest impact on learning quality and research? Would this impact be acceptable, or does the university need to increase faculty numbers or radically change the teaching paradigm?[1] Similar issues would arise, but in reverse, if enrollments were to drop instead of increase.

The new AR models provide recurring data on class sizes for all courses in the curriculum and are extremely helpful in answering these questions. AR *historical* models, as described in this book, provide data on enrollment, credit hours, section counts, and teacher types—separately for lectures, breakouts, and labs if there are any—for every instance in which the course is taught. ("Instance" refers to a single teaching mode, location, and semester, as in "English 10 taught face-to-face on the main campus in the spring semester of 2019.") AR *predictive* models can forecast the values of these variables given the new enrollment figures. The models also estimate the teacher's in-class and out-of-class time requirements on a per-section and per-enrollment basis, the number of adjuncts needed to cover their share of sections, and the effects on workload and/or research time for regular faculty members. Members of the budget team could scan the model's dashboards to get a sense of the consequences of their proposed enrollment increases, or they could ask the budget staff to download the data and prepare additional tables, charts, and so forth—not a difficult task with the AR model in hand.

These data won't eliminate the need for judgments by the budget team. These judgments take the form of compound "what-ifs": "*What* will be the quantitative consequences for teaching operations *if* we make a certain choice, and then what will be the resulting qualitative consequences?" Quantitative consequences refer to "production arithmetic" (e.g., that average class size equals enrollment per teaching section), which I'll shorten to *operational detail*. Qualitative consequences refer to learning outcomes and the like. The model goes a long way toward answering the quantitative questions, but the qualitative part remains beyond the reach of modeling.

The qualitative judgments are mainly academic. However, they will be much improved when team members internalize the quantitative data on a recurring basis. In fact, it's hard to see how good judgments can be made when the quantitative consequences of actions are largely a matter of sporadic focus and guesswork.

The quantitative dataset can be expanded to include the revenue, cost, and margin to be expected from the new enrollments, with or without adding extra regular faculty to compensate for workload changes. This is another routine task for the model, which produces outputs for schools, departments, programs, and individual courses as well as for the university as a whole. Full-function AR models calculate the marginal direct and indirect cost for the incremental students, and also verify that classroom space would be available to teach them. The economic data may not turn out to be determinative for the budget team's decisions about enrollment targets, but it certainly produces rich and consequential conversations.

Narrative 2: Support Comprehensive Program Review

Many universities require faculty to review particular degree and other academic programs on a regular basis—say, every five or six years. The review processes may involve peer reviewers from outside the university, and there may be careful instructions about subjects to cover. These often include curriculum, enrollment trends, the quality and preparation of students, the capacity of assigned faculty to deliver the desired educational results, the sponsored research conducted by these faculty where relevant, and the quality of the teaching infrastructure and library support. Typically, these reviews provide the only real opportunity for strategically assessing a program's health and prospects. I use the term "comprehensive program review" to emphasize this fact. The comprehensive review process complements program portfolio management as discussed later, in that it dives deeply into particular programs as opposed to taking a broad but less detailed view of all programs.

Notably lacking are questions about the program's operational details, costs, and margins—the kinds of data obtainable from AR models. Program review would be much richer if these data were included. How big are the classes in various subjects, for instance, and what proportion of them are taught by adjuncts? What teaching methodologies are used? What are the estimates of faculty time utilization? How much effort is going into departmental research? Likewise, most program reviews have yet to incorporate the kind of modern market information described in the previous narrative. Program reviewers can gain great insight by comparing these data with the enrollment and operational trends generated by the AR models.

Program review also can benefit from the systematic consideration of market data. Using the second type of AR model discussed in this book (the marketplace model) alleviates this difficulty. Reviewers can evaluate variables such as student demand, employment prospects for graduates, competitive intensity, and strategic fit with the university's overall program offerings. These considerations add an important dimension to the academic thinking that is the hallmark of program review. Mission remains paramount, but conversations that include market-based evidence will be richer and more practical than those conducted in a vacuum.

The improvement and assurance of teaching quality is another subject that's notably absent from most program review conversations. For a long time, this could be justified by universities' inability to get good data on these matters. But this is no longer the case. Actionable data of interest and relevance to program reviewers can now be obtained with reasonable effort and cost. As with the market data, comparisons with the outputs from AR models are extremely valuable to program reviewers.

These lacunae reflect the current inattention to the economic, market research, and teaching quality data within universities. As noted, the inattention could be justified historically by the difficulty of getting meaningful data. Now, however, the inattention is purely voluntary. No good reason prevents the inclusion of these matters on the program review agenda or provision of the data needed for meaningful conversations about them.

Narrative 3: Manage Program Portfolios

Provosts and deans must consider the array of degree and other programs at their institutions or schools, a process that's called program portfolio management. A key question here is whether to expand or contract student admissions targets for the university's various programs. Sizing programs is a key element of university steering. The conversations focus on mission, but they also need to consider revenues, costs, margins, market performance, teaching methods, and delivered quality. Use of AR models and processes can transform one's approach to program portfolio management.

Many programs persist beyond what should have been their sell-by dates. In one dataset, for example, a daunting 48 percent of programs turned out ten or fewer graduates per year and collectively accounted for only 7 percent of all degrees. Bob Zemsky puts the matter succinctly: "We'll give students what they want. Most colleges can't afford to do so without understanding why they can't."[2] This doesn't mean all low-enrollment programs should go on trial, but campuses do need serious and well-informed conversations on the matter. These conversations are greatly enhanced by knowledge of each program's break-even point and how its margins can be expected to change as a function of enrollment.

Each program has a different cost and revenue structure, so some generate surpluses while others must be subsidized. As long as the campus generates sufficient surplus on some programs, it can afford to subsidize others that lose money. Suppose the university decides to add students in an expensive (money-losing) program. How many more students will be needed in the surplus-generating fields to pay for the added cost? Alternatively, how much would the tuition rate have to rise in order to absorb the losses?[3]

The costs, revenues, and margins for individual courses (discussed in the first narrative) are easily aggregated to the program level. One of the AR model's dashboards connects every course in the curriculum to the programs of its enrolled students and every program to the list of courses taken by its enrollees. This powerful linkage enables decision makers to rapidly gauge the consequences of program expansion or contraction. AR predictive models can quantify the effects of changes to the curriculum (in the sense of which courses will be required or recommended) and to enrollment. None of this should suggest that return on financial investment should be the dominating decision criterion, but knowledge of the economic facts is essential.

AR models also can quantify another kind of program change: adding new research capacity in particular fields. The most important decisions are whether to add new faculty or modify the research effort targets for some or all faculty members. Quantifying the cost of new faculty and the effects of changing research targets on faculty workloads (in light of teaching demands) will stimulate important and potentially fruitful conversations. At the very least, knowing the opportunity costs of such decisions will tend to temper unconstrained research aspirations.

The new market information systems provide detailed data on both primary and selective demand, broken down by student segment and geography, if desired. Forward-looking data on what's trending in the internet also are available, as are time-series trends for many of the important variables. The systems can tailor their reports to the particular programs being studied, which permits resource allocators to directly compare the data to the outputs of the AR models.

Narrative 4: Set Prices

Universities make two main kinds of pricing decisions: tuition rates and financial aid discounts, and what to charge for sponsored research projects. Both require accurate estimates of direct and indirect costs. Tuition pricing decisions must balance each program's expected student demand (at a given price) against its per-student contribution margin *and* recover the institution's full costs when all the programs are added together. The AR model calculates contribution margin for gross and net tuition and fee revenue. Some universities consider financial aid to be a pure institution-level expense and thus don't want to compare net tuitions across programs. Others want to at least see the comparisons. Still others want to target financial aid on a program-by-program basis in order to stimulate demand in particular areas or harvest hefty cash flows from others. It's hard to generalize, but my sense of things is that the more affluent and selective the institution, the less it wishes to identify financial aid with programs.

AR models are vitally important when negotiating with business firms and other sponsors that don't apply fixed pricing rules to research projects. (Pricing rules for government- and foundation-sponsored projects generally don't leave much room for negotiation.) One needs indirect cost estimates for the particular field and subfield of the project being proposed, which often vary markedly from one area to another. (The indirect cost rates referred to earlier apply to the whole university or to broad categories of projects.) I have heard high-level university officers emphasize the need for these data—a concern that's driven by the growing importance of university-industry research collaborations. The AR models described in this book can be configured to provide the needed cost data by field and subfield.

Narrative 5: Balance Faculty Workloads

Workloads are of increasing concern to faculty in many universities. For example, a recent book by Robert Zemsky, Gregory R. Wegner, and Ann J. Duffield, *Making Sense of the College Curriculum: Faculty Stories about Change, Conflict, and Accommodation*, describes the faculty angst that now swirls around this question. Enrollment increases without commensurate new faculty FTEs (full-time equivalents) often are cited as problematic, but so is the faculty's own tendency to add courses and programs while seldom subtracting any. Deans, chairs, and curriculum committees need to have serious conversations about stemming the tide or figuring out academically appropriate mitigations.

AR models can compare the teaching-related hours required for the department's courses to the faculty time notionally targeted for teaching. (This falls under the operational detail rubric discussed earlier.) Experience shows that situations where calculated demand exceeds nominal supply by 20 or 25 percent are quite common. Such a relation usually means that the faculty's actual workweek is longer than the one assumed in the model (usually forty or forty-eight hours a week). Small discrepancies generally aren't cause for alarm, but larger ones may indicate unsustainable workloads or a shortchanging of research and service. Conversely, figures significantly below the norm suggest that, in the aggregate, faculty may be spending more than the anticipated time on research and service, that the department has the capacity to handle more courses and/or students, or that reduced enrollments have generated slack.

Narrative 6: Manage Course Configurations

By "course configuration," I mean the things like whether a course will be offered in a particular semester; the types and numbers of sections and whether they are classroom based, online, or hybrid; whether there will be breakout discussion sections or labs, and if so how many; and so on. Faculty and staff have these data for their own departments, but few institutions are able to compare them across departments and over time. AR models are able to do these things. Identifying patterns in the data can be a great help when one is looking for ways to control costs or to make judgments about the effects of taking on additional enrollments. For example, a good AR model will help one identify situations where changing the course configuration can make a big difference. Some models also provide indications about whether a course is under- or over-resourced given the current number of enrollments.

The models also can identify courses that are good candidates for redesign. These tend to be ones with conventional face-to-face (F2F) configurations, fairly large enrollments, and large numbers of sections—all of which can be identified by using an AR model. Seeing the negative margins for these courses can help justify investments of time and money as needed to develop new approaches that save money while maintaining or enhancing learning quality.

Narrative 7: Manage Classroom Utilization

Classrooms have become a scarce resource in many universities, especially those that include special resources such as computer terminals and laboratory equipment. Decisions about program size and curricula need to consider classroom availability in these situations. AR models provide these data at the same levels of detail as for the other decision areas.

Some room types are scheduled much more densely than others. Certain facilities are both in short supply and "owned" by particular schools that are reluctant to open them up for other usage. Class sizes may be constrained by seating capacity, or small classes may meet in cavernous rooms that do not lend themselves to effective teaching. If this weren't enough, new teaching modalities are changing the relationships between course delivery and facilities. These situations can motivate a school to tap additional data sources, such as those available in learning management platforms, the IT department, and local academic department systems, so they can better understand the supply and demand for particular kinds of rooms.

Narrative 8: Inform Budget Makers about Costs, Revenues, and Margins

AR models contribute to budget-making in many different ways. Narrative 1 discussed the adjustment of faculty lines to compensate for enrollment changes. Narrative 3 worked through the expenditure implications of program buildup and cutback. The most general benefit for budgeting, however, is accurate reporting about course configurations, revenues, costs, and margins for schools and departments. These data help budget makers assess the pleas from deans and chairs that more money is needed to solve one problem or another. Without such information, decision makers will be unduly vulnerable to anecdotes, rhetoric, and other efforts to exert influence.

The configuration data enable close examination of course offerings, class sizes, faculty and adjunct usage, and other important details of teaching operations. This provides grist for constructive conversations about problem-solving actions other than simply the provision of more money. The case for additional funds becomes more compelling once all such possibilities have been explored.

The data on margins provide a very important context for budget decisions. Schools or departments that are making significant amounts of money would seem to have the capacity for funding their own problem-solving, whereas those that are losing money have less flexibility. One must be careful in upping support to money-losers, however, because the administration's willingness and ability to subsidize is not unlimited. As in the other narratives, conversations that are informed by good data about margins will produce better outcomes than those where such information is not available.

Narrative 9: Focus Budget-Making on Mission

Provosts and deans must deal with hundreds of funding requests in each year's budget process. Each request is buttressed by arguments and documentation that explain why funding it is important, and of course each one has its price—the amount of funding this option will require. Budget staffs analyze and vet these data, but in the end the choice boils down to judgments by senior AR officers and their immediate colleagues. These judgments can be excruciatingly difficult because not all the options can be funded.

"Chaotic" is not an inappropriate word to characterize the conversations that support the judgments. The options can be compared in a seemingly infinite number of ways, which makes it hard to proceed logically and coherently. There is no easy way to summarize the information, so decision makers will stress first one thing and then another. In the end, some selections may result more from exhaustion than from merit. At Stanford, we often spoke of the annual "lurch to a budget" despite our overall dedication to systematic thinking.

One of the AR models discussed in this book (the mission-market-margin model) helps budget groups organize their thinking and thus make their conversations as productive as possible. It cuts down on the number of options that must be compared at one time and allows the group to proceed iteratively toward a satisfactory result. Importantly, the process makes it easier to put the university's mission at the center of the budget process and also to bring in marketplace data where appropriate—all while staying within a predetermined spending limit.

Narrative 10: Support Scenario Planning

Sometimes a university envisions strategies that represent more than incremental changes to existing activities. These may be driven by shifts in the external environment: for example, in government policy, in student demand from a particular country or in a particular student major, or due to an especially disruptive technological change. They also may stem from internally generated ideas such as an exciting new teaching or research program, or the opening or closing of a campus. Whatever the cause, the needed plans will have many moving parts. The modern way of thinking about them is to construct "scenarios" that juxtapose assumptions about the environment with those about the university's own actions. AR predictive models enable one to quantify the operational and economic predictions envisioned by these scenarios.

Effective scenario analysis requires that one be able to model the environmental changes and the university's responses to them at a meaningful level of operational detail. Aggregate models that simply project revenue and expense lines don't provide the required planning information, and indeed they may prove dysfunctional by lulling planners into a false sense of security. AR models provide the needed planning discipline, arguably for the first time in higher education. They do this by providing a "terminal year" for anchoring a university's multiyear financial plan to detailed thinking about circumstances and responses three to five years in the future. Once again, conversations that are informed by this kind of thinking will be much better than ones that aren't.

These narratives provide a taste of how the new processes and models offer concrete assistance on what former American Council on Education president Stanley Ikenberry describes, in his foreword to Robert C. Dickeson's *Prioritizing Academic Programs and Services*, as a critical success factor for academic presidencies: "[engaging] the academic community in choosing among the ubiquitous and competing demands for financial and physical resources."[4] He goes on to say that "the relationship between academic quality and financial resources has always been apparent; an institution's financial health is crucial to its academic quality. The paradigm has shifted, however, or at least it has expanded, to recognize that academic quality also is linked to purposeful and efficient utilization of resources. Monies wasted or underutilized mean fewer dollars for the academic priorities of greatest urgency. Using financial resources in purposeful, efficient ways is precisely what one seeks to do in the prioritization of academic programs."[5]

I believe the truth of this statement to be self-evident. However, it goes against the conventional academic culture, which holds that teaching and other academic activities are the province of provosts, deans, and professors, and that economic questions should be relegated to the "bean counters"—that is, finance and accounting staff. One thesis of this book is that the newly available AR models can help breach this barrier. To see how, let us engage in one more thought experiment.

Suppose, as provost, you have decided to deploy an AR model at your institution. The first step, of course, is to acquire the model and verify that the data it produces are reasonably accurate and meaningful. That is mostly a technical task, which we shall see is affordable and relatively straightforward. But putting the model in play is only half the story. How do you overcome your faculty's reservations to the point where they are willing to accept and, indeed, begin to trust the model?

The first part of your strategy would be to consult with key faculty members early and often during the model-building process, and to provide information to other interested faculty on a periodic basis. Probably the best approach would include explaining why you need the model to inform your own decision-making (as in some of the examples given earlier), promising that the whole process will be transparent, and providing assurances that the data will not override your academic judgments. My experience is that few faculty will seriously question a provost's right to access data that he or she believes are needed for his or her own decision-making, provided the data have a reasonable claim to accuracy, are not too costly, and do not require substantial inputs from professors. The AR models described in this book meet these criteria.

Part two of the strategy is to use the completed model for your own purposes through at least one budgeting cycle, and to do so in a highly visible way. It's important, in other words, that you walk the walk as well as talk the talk. Part of this process will involve engaging the deans on issues that emerge during your deliberations. You will have given the deans and their staffs access to the model, with appropriate training, at the beginning of the budget cycle. They may not exhibit a lot of interest at first, but they will focus as soon as you start asking substantive questions. I have seen deans vigorously engage with the model to satisfy their own interest and to anticipate questions from the provost and his or her staff.

The final step in the strategy is to roll the model down from the decanal level to department chairs and program directors—hopefully during the second budget cycle after implementation. Ideally, this will be accomplished through questions from the deans to the chairs and directors, but you may wish to prime the pump by asking questions of your own. The important thing is to maintain transparency throughout the process, and to address challenges on their merits whenever they arise. Chapter 3 provides additional suggestions about how this process can work, and indeed about how trust in the model can grow across the institution.

Now it's time to dive into the details of how AR models and related processes can help transform your university in critically important ways.

Part One

Introduction to AR Modeling

Academic resourcing (AR) refers to the application of money, human resources, and physical resources such as facilities and equipment to the furtherance of a university's goals. By extension, AR modeling refers to the development of tools for use by academic leaders (e.g., provosts, deans, department chairs, and program heads) in furtherance of their academic resourcing tasks.

AR means more than budgeting. It includes all actions that fuel activities in colleges and universities. These actions provide impetus for movement in desired directions and inhibit movement in other directions. In other words, they provide a way to steer the institutions as well as simply enabling movement. It is for these reasons that I speak of academic resourcing rather than simply resource allocation. This section introduces AR modeling and how it can enhance teaching and research performance and drive broad-based institutional change.

Chapter 1 elaborates on the aforementioned and describes how AR models change important faculty and staff conversations about resource allocation. It starts by defining AR modeling in terms that are meaningful to decision makers, then goes on to describe how model usage changes the roles of academic and financial staff, as well as the conversations in which they participate, in subtle but important ways—which can leave active faculty participants with more influence and responsibility. Then the focus shifts to how evidence from the model can dislodge established modes of discourse, together with a related cautionary discussion about how these dislodgments can stimulate defensiveness and rigidity if they are not handled correctly. The chapter's final sections describe how the latter problems can be mitigated by focusing on "soft" as well as "hard" management and by bridging the so-called cultural divide between quantitative and qualitative decision styles.

Chapter 2 operationalizes AR modeling by illustrating one commercial platform that can be found in the marketplace: the Gray Associates Program Economics Model. We'll see how the model works and the kinds of results it produces. The next section classifies AR models into three levels depending on their complexity and power. (The Gray model falls into the middle level.) This is followed by advice about a college or university's model development process—including data readiness and various ways to get started.

Chapter 3 discusses the all-important matter of building trust in a new AR model. Trust is a critical factor because these models aim to support real decision makers in real settings. The first steps are to recognize the importance of prediction in decision-making, the key role played by evidence in making predictions, why it is that AR-type models do a better job of providing credible evidence than alternative analytical methods, and the precursors to AR models (called activity-based costing, or ABC, models) that suffered from problems of trust. The chapter ends by examining the well-established theory of innovation diffusion and its implications for the acceptance of AR models.

CHAPTER ONE

Changing the Conversation

America's colleges and universities could be better than they are. Schools spend large sums of money to achieve important goals, but there is growing evidence that the amount spent is too large and the achievement too small. Many voices now call for institutional transformation. The Bill and Melinda Gates Foundation puts it this way: "Colleges and universities should build their capacity to dramatically improve student outcomes and eliminate racial and income gaps, deliver on a student-centered mission, use data to make decisions, create a collaborative environment, set goals and be accountable for them, and make a commitment to continuous improvement."[1]

More and more people feel a sense of urgency about improving student outcomes. There's now evidence that universities fall short of their stated goals of broadening opportunity and achieving equity, that a significant number of students aren't sufficiently engaged with the university's educational processes, and that affordability problems produce unsustainable levels of student debt. The consequences are huge both in personal and societal terms. Fixing the problems will require universities to change systemically as well as to continue to encourage individual and small-group initiatives by faculty and staff members. The academic resourcing transformations to be discussed in this chapter facilitate such systemic change. University officers, faculty, and staff who engage with them report satisfaction and excitement, which bodes well for their eventual adoption.

All colleges and universities are governed by an "internal econ-omy," which I define as follows:

A university's internal economy is the network of decisions, processes, in-centives, and information that governs the scale and quality of what gets done, what it costs, and whether the resulting pattern of profits, losses, and cross-subsidies is sustainable.

Presidents, provosts, deans, and other academic leaders set the struc-tures and boundaries of their institutions' internal economies. They seek to steer behaviors in desired directions, but they do not and should not attempt to micromanage the individual actors. This is because the nature of expertise within universities requires decentral-ization of decision-making, particularly to faculty but also to key members of the nonacademic staff. Decisions about what to teach and how to teach it can only be made by faculty in their respective disciplines, for example, and the same is true for research.

This book demonstrates deep flaws in the internal economies of most colleges and universities—flaws that can and should be fixed as soon as possible. Most university decision makers tend to be highly competent and well meaning, but they lack essential information. To illustrate the problem, imagine what would happen if the entrepre-neurs and managers in a classic economy (outside the academy) didn't have good information about their actions in relation to those of others operating in the economy, or the costs, revenues, and margins resulting from these actions. However necessary, detailed knowledge about their own product or service would not compensate for lack of information about how their actions relate to the rest of the sys-tem. The same is true in universities, which leads to fundamental dif-ficulties at the very core of decision-making. The problem is serious, and it accounts for many of the current concerns about educational effectiveness and affordability.

The book's main theme is how academic resourcing models can be used to fix these problems and thus improve affordability and stu-dent success. (Research and scholarship is covered, too, but, as in most colleges and universities, the emphasis is on teaching.) Deployment of these models enables much more evidence to be used in academic decision-making, which is another subject we'll discuss at length. Nor will we forget the cultural challenges associated with such changes. The transformations take institutions into unfamiliar and potentially fraught terrain, which, though well aligned with their academic values, is likely to seem threatening on first exposure. Among other things, successful transformation requires that professors, who, as the saying goes, "are the university," broaden their role in academic resourcing. The same is true for deans and other senior academic officers.

Budget-making and related resource allocation processes set the boundaries for the university's internal economy. They provide levers for institutional steering and the stimulation of change.[2] Steering requires choices about whether to invest in new programs or activities or to disinvest in current ones—that is, to enable what higher education guru Robert Zemsky and I have called "growth by substitution."[3] More positive-sounding improvements are possible as well. Systems like responsibility center budgeting (RCB), which devolves responsibility from the central university to the deans, has been shown to stimulate the growth of operating revenue: for example, through academic program creation.[4] Some of the models and methods to be discussed allow institutions to gain such benefits on a recurring basis, without needing to implement full-scale RCB.

The innovations in this book can stimulate improvement at all levels of academic granularity. Sometimes the stimulation comes through explicit channels, as when the budget system provides incentives or rewards for particular kinds of activities. Most often, though, it arises from deep-seated academic desires to further student learning, research, and other worthy institutional objectives—desires that can be empowered by new data and more informed conversations. Higher education should treasure these desires, and care should be taken that no model or administrative process undermines them.

Academic Resourcing Defined

The broader view of budget-making espoused in this book stretches the traditional description of budgeting, which connotes a set of narrow and accountability-oriented processes. Therefore, I am proposing a new term: "academic resourcing," or "AR" for short. Its definition follows:

Academic resourcing (AR) decisions apply the university's human, physical, and financial resources to its portfolio of activities so as to maximize mission attainment in ways that are academically and financially sustainable given markets and the economy.

Academic resourcing decisions define the university's activities: what it does, how, and at what scale, down to the fine structure of teaching, research, and other elements of behavior. They refer to the processes by which decision makers navigate the university's internal economy in the interests of furthering its academic mission.

The sum total of activities in any school or department determines that unit's resource requirements. Deciding the mix of activities requires one to balance the quality and size of programs (among other mission-related options) with market forces and institutional capacities so that the activities can be sustained over time. For example, humans can only do so much, and there is only so much money. The "support of mission" may be direct or indirect. That is, it may involve work within academic departments or in the university's administrative and support services units.

Academic Resourcing Models

This book is about academic resourcing generally, and also about some particular models and methods that are important for supporting it. The main focus is on the new breed of academic resourcing models that inform the kinds of decisions described in the preface.

Academic resourcing models provide actionable descriptions of a university's teaching and research activities, together with their revenues, costs, contribution margins, and overheads. This information helps provosts, deans, and other university leaders develop strategic plans, manage academic program portfolios, set prices and discounting policies, and perform ongoing tasks like budgeting and balancing faculty workloads and facilities utilization. The models blend structured academic judgments with outputs from the university's data warehouse or transaction processing systems to support multiple levels of decision-making.

A full-scale academic resourcing model will include activity descriptions with enough granularity to inform decision-making about courses, programs, faculty workloads, and other topics of interest to academics. Good models link seamlessly with the new breed of market information systems and processes for ensuring that mission is front-of-mind when making academic choices—both of which are discussed in part III of the book. I also describe a "faculty-friendly" approach to academic quality assurance, which, in addition to being important in its own right, can add insights about academic quality to the interpretation of AR models.

Consideration of academic resourcing will be aided by the identification of three groups of decision makers. First come "academic officers": particularly provosts, deans, and their staffs, although presidents often play this role as well. Then come "finance officers," people on the business and finance side of the institution—from the chief financial officer down through all the financially oriented professionals in the central administration. Last but definitely not least come what I'll call "professors" or "faculty": for example, department chairs, course heads, and others who bear a measure of responsibility for academic resourcing. The three groups are defined purely for ease of referencing, and nothing more should be inferred from the classification.

A New Division of Labor

Professors "own" the fine structure of teaching and research. They are the only people who possess the knowledge and experience needed to make good resourcing decisions at the micro level—sometimes called the "coalface" of activity. Academic officers "own" the university's programmatic priorities, although they share the ultimate responsibility with presidents, boards, and others. Examples include the relative emphasis on teaching versus research and on different degree programs and disciplines. These officers also may care about the fine structure of activities, but they can never know enough to micromanage it effectively. That's why traditional universities generally delegate substantial responsibility for determining the "what" and "how" of teaching and research to academic departments. At the risk of oversimplification, academic officers determine the scale of activity, while most details of production are determined by departmental faculty. (These decisions are more centralized in for-profit universities, where teachers tend to be given less discretion than in traditional universities.) This division of labor is dictated by the nature of academic work, not because of tradition or overarching concepts like shared governance.

Herein lies the problem. Professors are trained in and dedicated to the substance of teaching and research. They say being productive means doing the best job they can for their students and their disciplines. They don't think about balancing quality with cost in the ways that businesses and some academic officers do, but instead seek to garner as many resources as they can for their programs.[5] The best professors are self-starters. They resist efforts by "bean counters" to intervene in the what and how of departmental activity—lest academic values be undermined by "crass" monetary considerations. Yet the fine structure of decisions within departments exerts a strong influence on academic outcomes and the direct costs of academic activity. Indeed, much of higher education's cost problem arises from the fact that people with the capacity, empowerment, and responsibility for making fine-structure decisions (the faculty) are neither trained in nor care greatly about cost, whereas cost-competent staff members have great difficulty with the academic side of the quality-cost trade-off—and thus are discouraged from active participation in fine-structure academic decision-making.

But cost is not the only problem. We will see that good AR decision-making requires full cognizance of the university's internal economy, as defined earlier. This includes, in addition to their costs, the various activities' revenues and margins. (As used here, an activity's "margin" equals its revenue minus cost.) One can describe the AR decision problem as "finding the set activities that produce the best possible academic outcomes subject to limits imposed by the internal economy." These limits are controlled to some extent by university policies, but mostly they must be accepted as givens. They do change over time, however, partly in response to shifts in the institution's "external economy": the markets for its programs and salaries, the prices it must pay for goods and services, and so on. At the end of the day, decisions about activities must be consistent with both the internal economy and external economy. Failure to maintain consistency means the activities are not academically or financial sustainable. In extreme cases, this will drive the institution to ill-health and eventually failure.

It is neither practical nor desirable for finance staff to learn enough to fulfill the academic officers' or faculty's roles, or even operate as coequals, in deciding the trade-offs between various activities' academic outcomes and financial consequences. (The same applies to second-guessing academic decisions.) This means academic officers and faculty must take ownership of the quality-cost balance.

But how? The answer lies in providing better access to data that are manifestly helpful for decisions they are making already, and that will lead them logically and inexorably in the direction of cost consciousness. That access must be hands-on and readily available. Requests for help from finance staff will happen only after the academic decision maker has become convinced about the information's usefulness. Importantly, close working relationships among academics and finance staff are commonplace on sponsored research projects. Faculty work closely with financial professionals, many of whom they hire on their own projects. However, faculty investigators retain ownership of how their precious research funds should be spent.

Such has not been the case for teaching. The reasons are complex, but one of them surely is that the requisite data have not been available. That is now changing, however. The information systems and models described in this book provide, for the first time, highly detailed data about teaching. This will enable informed consideration of activities at the granular level—which will illuminate needed trade-offs between academic consequences and economic limits. The trade-off decisions are and should remain the province of academic officers and faculty, who now can make them with full cognizance of the economic variables. Financial officers retain the responsibility for assessing and maintaining the institution's overall fiscal integrity, but the new data do not make them competent for trading off academic and financial consequences.

My tasks in this book include demonstrating beyond a reasonable doubt that academic officers and professors should concern themselves with economic issues, and to describe the methods and tools by which this can be accomplished. (That good academic resourcing decisions must involve professors is consistent with shared governance concepts but does not derive from them.) These tasks are less difficult than they might seem. For one thing, the deep involvement of academic officers, financial officers, and professors in AR decisions is in the best interest of all of them. Further, innovators from all three populations have found that evidence-based AR conversations are more meaningful and less frustrating than other approaches to decision-making. Failure of academic officers and faculty to step up to this challenge would mean that financial officers have to fill the void, which risks academic values taking a back seat to financial ones.

Well-Grounded Conversations

There are several reasons why conversations help leaders further academic resourcing in colleges and universities. First, conversation can unpack the inherent complexity of intellectual work and the needs and expectations of the faculty, staff, and students who perform it. Second, AR requires the integration of disciplinary, financial, and market-oriented knowledge and skills. This requires bridging the cultural gap that separates professors, academic administrators, enrollment managers, and financial specialists—a goal that is best achieved through conversational interactions. Finally, mission considerations are highly subjective and often controversial. At the end of the day, they are the province of senior academic leadership, subject to shared governance considerations, which again places a premium on frequent conversations.

But not just any conversations. The discussions need to be mindful, informed by evidence, and guided by a shared conceptual structure wherever possible. Uninformed and unstructured conversations tend toward dysfunctionality because they spawn chaos and controversy. The challenge, then, is to use appropriate concepts and data to build structure into the conversations without limiting their scope and independence. That's where the methods and tools discussed in this book come into play. Looked at the other way around, it is decision makers engaging in conversations (not analysts working in isolation) who represent the target audience for new AR insights. And it is the shared insights generated by conversation that allow people to work their way through the unfamiliar challenges presented by the new models and data.

Decision makers always have had conversations about resource allocation, of course. What's different is the depth of insight that can be brought to bear and the questions this elicits. The prologue provided many examples, and readers will see many others as they progress through the book. To quote a recent book on how to unleash an organization's potential, the goal of these model-driven conversations is to provide "routines and tools for exposing, exploring, and transcending people's limiting assumptions and mind-sets."[6]

Conversations also are important for facilitating model adoption in the first place. For most people, models conjure up images of small groups of analysts poring over screens or printouts of densely packed data and after thinking deeply producing reports about what they have found. The "decision support" models discussed in this book don't work that way. They must become an integral part of decision-making in order to be effective, and this cannot be done if their results are filtered through analysts. This may seem counterintuitive, but we will see many examples where direct engagement by decision makers is essential for digging through the data in search of insights and conclusions. Analysts certainly add value, but too many model results are "lost in translation" if decision makers eschew direct engagement with the models.

Yet the AR data are too complex for individual decision makers to assimilate, even in the somewhat unlikely event that they are trained in model-building and interpretation. Engagement must be a group effort, and this requires that the models be brought into the conversations that invariably precede decision-making and universities. The models discussed here have been designed for this purpose, and I hope readers will keep that in mind as we work through their descriptions and utilization examples.

Information as an Impetus for Change

In the fall of 2009, Embry-Riddle Aeronautical University was considering whether to close one of its campuses, which was losing money at an unsustainable rate. The president dispatched two of his vice presidents to the campus with instructions to assess the situation and, if appropriate, make plans for closure. One of them was the late Len Brazis, a skilled modeler as well as experienced administrator. Brazis looked at the data and constructed a simple academic resourcing model that calculated the revenues, direct costs, and overheads for each of the campus's programs. Discussing the results with campus administrators and faculty led to the identification of significant opportunities for improvement. A year of intensive effort to refine and begin implementation of the needed changes shifted the campus's 2010 budgeted margin projection to a positive $500,000, up from a loss of $3 million the previous year, without the need to close a single program. Summary before-and-after figures are shown in table 1.1.

Table 1.1. Program Operating Results at Embry-Riddle Aeronautical University

	Fiscal Year 2009			
	Net Revenue	Total Expenses	Overhead	Gain/(Loss)
Campus Operating Total	**$39,948,141**	**$25,681,290**	**$16,302,652**	**($3,035,801)**
Aviation Business Administration	$1,456,027	$614,842	$696,012	$145,173
Aeronautical Science	$1,456,027	$3,846,883	$4,756,023	$675,858
Aeronautics	$9,278,764	$860,854	$850,519	$372,020
Applied Meteorology	$2,083,393	$361,845	$346,725	($28,495)
Safety Science	$680,075	$451,606	$143,523	($177,763)
Aerospace Engineering	$417,366	$5,821,117	$5,484,621	($1,571,563)
Computer Engineering	$9,734,175	$231,267	$222,241	($83,051)
Electrical Engineering	$370,457	$487,390	$383,704	($199,899)
Mechanical Engineering	$576,273	$279,841	$319,631	($23,179)
	Fiscal Year 2010			
	Net Revenue	Total Expenses	Overhead	Gain/(Loss)
Campus Operating Total	**$38,491,004**	**$20,999,155**	**$16,979,531**	**$12,318**
Aviation Business Administration	$1,714,948	$639,897	$818,412	$256,639
Aeronautical Science	$8,583,774	$2,795,315	$4,510,538	$1,277,921
Aeronautics	$2,719,841	$777,824	$1,107,445	$834,572
Applied Meteorology	$775,461	$141,575	$411,911	$221,975
Safety Science	$697,271	$304,866	$263,917	$128,488
Aerospace Engineering	$9,332,370	$4,256,289	$5,391,934	($275,853)
Computer Engineering	$493,816	$282,348	$297,920	($86,452)
Electrical Engineering	$799,109	$454,777	$475,668	($131,336)
Mechanical Engineering	$750,993	$322,735	$409,592	$18,666

The Embry-Riddle model is the simplest of the three academic resourcing models that I discuss in this book. While uncomplicated, it meets the AR modeling definition presented earlier because it addresses both revenue and cost—and thus allows decision makers to focus on earned margin. Brazis used a spreadsheet to allocate these quantities directly to the programs listed in table 1.1. Spreadsheet models can go somewhat further than this (e.g., to calculate revenues and costs on a course-by-course basis and then roll them up as programs), but they are limited in size and complexity. The Gray Associates Program Economics Model to be discussed in chapter 2 uses database and display software to relax these constraints. The Pilbara Group's "full-function" AR model, to be described in chapters 4–6, which also operates at the course level and uses database and display software, provides a rich array of operating detail on activities as well as revenue, cost, and margin.

Brazis's subsequent descriptions of the turnaround emphasized three considerations: (1) identify the programs that produce the strongest operating margins, (2) understand best practices and work to replicate those across challenged programs, and (3) manage nonacademic functions across the campus more effectively. His successor, Adam Rabb, insists that the first of these could not have been accomplished without the model, which allowed the team to focus on high-priority programs and then compare one to another. This triggered conversations about best practice and investigations of the cost-effectiveness of various overhead functions. It was these conversations that made all the difference.

The state of the art in AR modeling has progressed enormously since 2009, but even the very simple Embry-Riddle model was sufficient to change the conversational focus from across-the-board cuts (including campus closure) to evidence-based discussions about targeted remedial activities. Notice, too, that the improvements did not require a tuition or fee increase. Nor was it necessary to cut an already-lean administrative infrastructure. Indeed, student services expenditures were increased to facilitate the various academic improvements.

Dislodging Experiences

The Embry-Riddle example demonstrates how an academic resourcing model can change the conversations about getting a university out of a financial jam. The model didn't identify the solution, but it focused people's attention in a new direction. It's fair to say this represented a "dislodging experience" for both the vice presidents and the people on the campus. It jolted them away from the "obvious" decision on campus closure and got them into more nuanced, and ultimately more powerful, conversations about the fine structure of academic activity.

Looked at more broadly, information's ability to trigger dislodging experiences can help resolve the tension between change and conservatism in traditional universities. There is a rough analogy with what goes on in economic and political life generally, where values favorable to innovation confront those aiming to preserve the comfortable and well proven. In Western economic systems, it is the price mechanism that regulates the pace and degree of change. New technologies and values affect supply and demand, and thus the relative prices of the new and the familiar. The "invisible hand" of the marketplace overcomes entrenched interests to an extent that's hard to accomplish through democratic governance. Economist Joseph Schumpeter called this idea capitalism's process of "creative destruction." It accounts for much of the dynamism of the United States and other Western economies.[7] Signals sent by a university's internal and external economies play the same role, even though we like to think in terms of progress rather than destruction. The models discussed in this book tap into and display information about both economies.

Prices and overt financial incentives can stimulate change within universities, but their effects are weak compared to other forces. Later chapters present examples of how granular data about the university's activities, costs, revenues, and margins can stimulate change where needed while inhibiting precipitous action when the status quo should be defended. The new data, and the evidence-driven conversations that derive from them, provide the "invisible hand" needed to effect change. (It is analogous to price data in this respect, but far broader.) Its provision helps decision makers adapt to continuous changes in the economics of teaching and other academic activities.

The importance of adaptation cannot be overstated. Professors Ronald Heifetz and Marty Linsky of Harvard's Kennedy School put it this way: "So if your community, at whatever scale you define it, needs to focus on one skill set, one capacity, one competency to help ensure going forward successfully, choose adaptability."[8] One can view data obtained from an AR model as a forcing function for adaptation. Academics are accustomed to taking evidence seriously, even when it contradicts previously held beliefs or self-interest. The process of model adoption can be viewed as building a culture that makes the evidence hard to ignore and encourages constructive problem-solving when change occurs.

The idea of adaptability is embodied in the "academic renewal cycle" depicted in figure 1.1. The process starts with receipt of revised AR data, as presented by the new models and tools. Processing this information (e.g., through conversations) triggers new and potentially dislodging experiences, which in turn can spawn valuable "out-of-the box" decision-making. Such creative decisions are what it takes to produce academic renewal—which can range from incremental growth by substitution instead of always relying on new resources, to highly innovative new ways of doing things.

The invisible hand of the marketplace drives Schumpeter's creative destruction in the general economy as users of resources plan their activities in light of changing prices and other economic variables. In universities, behavior is driven by the highly visible hands of provosts, deans, and others as they steer the institution's activities in response to new data and judgments about priorities. Yet the invisible hand of the university's internal and external economies always lurks close to the surface. It is a force that universities ignore at their peril.

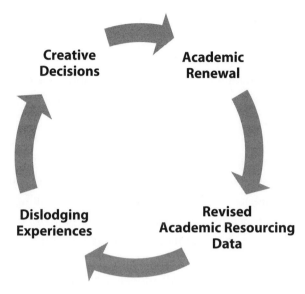

Figure 1.1. The Academic Renewal Cycle

Survive + Thrive

My years of experience as a change agent with universities and faculty have given me a healthy respect for the academy's capacity to maintain its traditional modes of operation in the face of potentially disruptive events. This is good in many ways but very bad when there is a need for academic renewal. The latter problem came home to me after I published my first account of AR modeling three years ago in *Reengineering the University*. Subsequent presentations, consultations, and interviews produced many enthusiastic responses, but they also triggered some unexpectedly high levels of resistance. At first, I attributed this to the "cultural divide," referred to later, as amplified by the academy's normal resistance to change. But analysis of my interview notes left me puzzled. Why does adoption proceed smoothly for some institutions whereas for others it starts off well but then falters badly?

Participation in a Gates Foundation convening on postsecondary student success exposed me to Professor John Kotter of the Harvard

Business School. Kotter's career has been in organizational behavior, and he is an expert on change agency, among other things. We had never met but have a number of mutually respected friends, and this led to a brief but highly substantive conversation after his presentation. I came away with an intense interest in his emergent "Survive + Thrive" theory of organizational change.

"Survive + Thrive" refers to fundamental attributes of human behavior that help explain why some organizations perform better than others regardless of country, industry, and corporate culture. Based on, as Kotter puts it, "straightforward Darwinian thinking and with help from researchers in brain science," it is a part of "brain/body hardwiring" that seems to explain how people respond to incoming stimuli at different times.[9] This idea sheds light on why some universities have been able to adopt AR models while others struggle.

Some stimuli activate our "survive channel," which detects threats in the environment and responds with emotions like "fear, anxiety, anger (directed at the source of the threat), perhaps even shame or guilt (that you have been inept enough to get yourself into the situation)." These emotions spike energy levels, overwhelm normal thought processes, and trigger an instinctive "fight or flight" response. This may involve active opposition, reversion to established routines, or, especially in truly new situations, denial that a problem even exists. It's not that problem-solving disappears in the face of fear, but that the focus is narrowed toward eliminating the immediate irritant rather than dealing with the underlying problem. The survive channel is ancient, and we humans share it with other conscious and evolutionarily successful beings.

Our "thrive channel" detects and acts on opportunities rather than threats. It evolved more recently than our survive channel and seems to explain why humans "have come to have grown so much, to invent so much—that we have gone on to literally dominate the earth." The emotions triggered by the thrive channel tend to be positive ones: "excitement, pride, the joy of winning, the wonderfulness of loving, the sorts of emotions which can win over our hearts [and] lift us off the ground." To this I would add the satisfaction of solving complex problems and creating new concepts. But these emotions are less powerful than the ones associated with fight or flight. Indeed, the fight or flight emotions can all too easily hijack and dominate those of the thrive channel.

I believe survive behavior is responsible for much of the resistance that AR models may encounter. I've described why these models seem to threaten the values of many academics, and also why the seeming threats do not need to materialize. But assurances have little effect once the survive channel has been activated. When fear has been triggered, it is difficult or impossible to see the opportunities the model opens up and the benefits that seizing them will deliver. And, alas, experience shows that fear is easy to trigger when talking about new models and processes—despite all good intentions to the contrary.

It is unfortunate that AR models frequently are introduced as "tools for cost analysis," which many academics interpret as code for "cost-cutting." The threat is amplified when first exposure is from finance and accounting staff. I speak of disruptions to higher education that force changes in the way institutional leaders and faculty conduct their business. Occasionally, as a speaker or consultant, I have deliberately invoked fear of serious disruption as a motivator for change. That may have sounded reasonable at the time, but it probably triggered the survive channel. There are a great many positive arguments for the use of AR models, and we should concentrate on making them.

The same is true for the academic quality improvement and assurance processes that are discussed in chapter 7. Administrations that introduce such processes may be viewed as doubting the faculty's commitment or ability to teach. The intent actually stems from desires to sustain best practices and to encourage faculty to do their best work despite distraction, disruption, and sometimes boring repetition. My colleagues and I always have spoken of quality *improvement* as well as assurance, and now I can recognize that as catering to the thrive channel.

The problem is not unique to higher education. In Kotter's words, "Organizational systems and processes, bosses, and even cultures can help activate the survive channels in ways that help enterprises cope well with serious immediate problems. Or they can set off Survive in ways that exhaust us, kill Thrive, and don't even guarantee that we will focus on and solve the critical short-term issues." So, what can one do? His answer is to "aggressively activate the Thrive Channel." This means emphasizing and proactively discussing opportunities and the satisfaction to be gained by seizing them, not just at the point of introducing change but also at every stage of its development. With AR models, the emphasis should be on support of the many academic resourcing decisions that people know they need to make rather than on measurement and metrics for their own sake. I have tried to do that throughout this book. My mantra has been that institutional leaders should take note of the new opportunities that are becoming available and reinforce them at every opportunity.

Kotter also speaks of using networks to elicit change.[10] Organizational hierarchies are essential for managing recurring activities and achieving routine goals, but they often stand in the way of innovation. Conversely, networks can cut across the hierarchies and get nonroutine goals accomplished speedily and well. One can achieve the best of both worlds by creating a "dual operating system" that consists of a hierarchy plus a network. The network is made up of volunteers who span the skill sets needed for innovation in addition to performing their day jobs. Led by a largely self-selected "guiding coalition" (rather than by an appointed team leader), they drive change for the joy of creativity and the satisfaction of doing something worthwhile. The conclusion describes how such a "volunteer army" can accelerate the adoption of AR models within a university.

"Hard" and "Soft" Resource Management

The AR models and related processes discussed in these pages address the core of what it means to be a university: what programs and courses should be offered, how they should be delivered, and where investments should be made in research capacity. They provide granular data about how resources have been deployed for the accomplishment of these goals, and this produces insights about possible improvement. Such information can contribute materially to academic administrators' and faculty members' thinking.

The Many Facets of Academic Resourcing

I've emphasized that academic resourcing decisions are tremendously important drivers of a college or university's direction and success. They enable investments in the human resources (especially faculty resources), operating support, and facilities that animate teaching and research. They steer the university by enabling or limiting what can be done in each area of activity. But they do more. How the decisions are made, who is involved in making them, and what conversations ensue during the process have a huge influence on how participants view the issues, and indeed on the university's overarching value system and culture.[11]

A decade or so ago, I characterized university resource allocation processes as involving much more than simply "divvying up the money."[12] I mentioned three of these outcomes earlier: to steer the institution, provide people and organizational units with incentives and rewards, and stimulate the growth of operating revenue and endowment. Other facets are technical: to ensure that inflation and other cost-rise drivers are predicted and taken into account as part of budgeting, that provision is made for capital spending and transfers to reserves, and that financial risks are understood and managed. A final task is to provide a framework for accountability, which is an essential element of the leverage that senior administrators exert on their far-flung areas of responsibility.

Many of these outcomes are achievable through combinations of "hard" and "soft" management techniques. For example, steering can be accomplished by the application of direct control, by formulas, or by persuasion. Operating revenue growth often depends on individual initiatives, which, in a university, often depend more on personal interest and values than on monetary rewards. Even accountability, which many be regarded as "hard" management, often is better achieved through conversation than attempts at direct control. The same is true for the provision of incentives and rewards.

People sometimes view academic resourcing models as harbingers of hard management, but nothing could be further from the truth. I have noted that the highest and best application of such models is to stimulate evidence-based conversations at multiple levels within the university. These conversations produce insights that can be acted upon by faculty in departments as well as by the central administration. In making sense of this, it may be helpful to review the classic "agency theory" of influence and management and its application to shared governance in universities.

Shared Governance and Agency

Universities are complex organizations. They have many organizational units that often are arrayed in a relatively flat hierarchy. Deans, department chairs, and other resource allocators enjoy considerable autonomy as they respond to academic needs and market forces. This is partly a matter of academic tradition, but, as noted, it also reflects the need for specialized local knowledge to deal with the great differences among academic disciplines and student subpopulations.

American colleges and universities generally operate on a system of shared governance that includes roles for the board of trustees, academic and financial leadership, and faculty. It is the faculty's role that distinguishes shared governance in universities. The reason is well summed up by two former college presidents, Brian C. Mitchell and W. Joseph King, in their recent book, *How to Run a College*:

> As a group, faculty are the only participants in shared governance who can legitimately lay claim to their pivotal role as the institution's historian/"keeper-of-the-flame." They live, re-create, and sustain the campus long after administrators and trustees move on.... [Faculty participants in shared governance] should have a deep campus-wide

support, sufficient gravitas, and an understanding of the world beyond the college gates. . . . They must rise above internal politics, "trust but verify" the policy and program direction proposed, be open to change, and educate and advocate for faculty interests.[13]

The authors go on to say that these shared governance roles should include strategic planning and elements of what I call academic resourcing. Furthermore, the faculty's role must be defined clearly and with due regard to the capacities and responsibilities of each of the groups involved. My often-repeated statements that at least some faculty leaders must take an active role in considering the economic aspects of academic resourcing rest on the same considerations.

But despite faculty autonomy and shared governance, essentially all central administrations want to steer their universities to a greater or lesser extent. Provosts and deans, with their institutional and school-wide perspectives, want to lead on strategic issues. They wish to fend off the threats that markets may pose for academic values while not ignoring the importance of the revenues that stem from market success. They consult with key faculty to gain insight and ensure that shared governance works as intended. Conversations along these lines take place now in most institutions, but they are less coherent and evidence driven than they might be.

To repeat a now-familiar theme, effective shared governance requires a deep and evidence-based understanding of both the university's current operations (e.g., enrollments, courses and other activities, and resourcing sufficiency) and its financial situation (e.g., market performance, revenue, cost, and margin). As noted earlier, this requires a shared information platform. The system should invite, indeed require, conversations about how to balance mission, market, and money. Financial considerations should not be allowed to dominate decision-making, but neither should they be shortchanged. Overreliance on markets, to the detriment of academic values, also should be avoided. A truly effective system will support the achievement of all these objectives.

Agency is defined as "an action or intervention designed to influence the behavior of another person, group, or process." That is precisely the situation faced by a provost or dean when he or she seeks to get something done, especially in the context of shared governance. Faculty often are described as "semi-autonomous intellectual entrepreneurs." Nonacademic staff are less autonomous, but many do exercise a good deal of decision-making discretion. Problems arise when the goals of the various groups are not fully aligned (e.g., professors often believe intrinsically in the paramount importance of their particular discipline). The agency model addresses these problems.

Agency theory defines the alignment problem in terms of "principals" and the "agents" they seek to influence. The classic case involves a manager who is responsible for a group of outside salesmen, but the ideas extend to the broader aspects of agency as defined earlier. (I have heard more than one dean liken the act of trying to influence faculty to herding cats.) The theory identifies three ways by which principals can influence agents:[14]

1. *Regulatory.* The principal restricts the agent's freedom of action (e.g., by requiring prior approval for decisions that involve resources). Tight control prevents resource diversion but at the cost of efficiency. The costs of regulation ("transaction costs" in the language of economists) become greater as tasks get more complex and the organizational distance between principal and agent increases. The so-called line-item system of university budgeting is rooted in the regulatory paradigm.[15]

2. *Formulaic.* The principal devises payment formulas that (hopefully) align the agent's objectives with those of the principal (i.e., so that, in pursuing his or her self-interest, the agent automatically furthers the principal's interest). Unfortunately, such formulas become less effective as tasks become more complex and the opportunities for misinterpretation multiply. They also can be "gamed," as when the agent exploits loopholes or omis-

sions in a cynical way. Devising good formulas and fine-tuning them as incentives for particular kinds of change can be a daunting task. RCB provides the quintessential example of formulaic systems in universities.

3. *Persuasive.* The principal uses persuasive discourse and the prospect of discretionary rewards to align incentives and motivate the agent to further the principal's goals. Discretionary rewards reinforce the message and supply tangible incentives. Persuasion even may convince the agent to change his or her goals to better align with those of the principal (e.g., by arguing that while resource diversion might be attractive in the short run, it eventually will prove dysfunctional). Persuasion-based systems work less quickly than well-functioning formulas, but they may be more effective over the long run. One-line or block-budgeting systems depend on the persuasive approach to agency.

At risk of some oversimplification, the regulatory and formulaic methods reflect "hard" approaches to management, whereas the persuasive method presents a "soft" approach. As noted, a commitment to quantitative AR modeling does not imply a predilection toward "hard" management. In fact, these models are indispensable for informing the effective implementation of "soft" approaches. They are necessary for truly effective shared governance, because without them faculty participation in academic resourcing decisions risks reflecting personal attitudes and beliefs more than evidence-based reality.

Academic resourcing models can be applied in all three of the budgeting systems used by colleges and universities. In line-item systems, the provost looks at detailed data down to the program and departmental level in order to determine what gets funded and what doesn't. These details are devolved mainly to the deans in RCB systems, where the provost uses AR modeling mainly to set mission-driven subventions that mitigate the more extreme effects of market action. Funding decisions also are made by the deans in block-budgeting, but only after sometimes-strenuous negotiations about goals with the provost. The bottom line here is that AR models can be game changers for all three types of budgeting.

Bridging Cultural Divides

Traditional universities are, at root, profoundly conservative organizations. Their basic structure dates back to the Renaissance and the early Enlightenment, and their fundamental goals change little from decade to decade. Yet a university's success depends on its ability to respond to changing conditions, technologies, and societal needs. This requires new ways of thinking that may seem to challenge traditional academic values. Effecting change requires one to upend the status quo in a process of creative disruption. The threatening overtones of creative disruption are sufficient, by themselves, to rally the forces of conservatism against those of dynamism and change. Yet a closer look shows this need not happen.

As noted, academics and their supporters tend to harbor deep-seated concerns about whether bringing economic analysis into academic resourcing decisions represents a step toward treating the university as just another profit-seeking business. Nowhere is this concern more focused than in discussions about margin, which features so centrally in AR models. Margin is the overriding concern in for-profit universities, so there is a prima facie case for why academics might be wary. For example, I have visited overseas universities where margin was elevated to be the institution's overarching goal by order of the government, the institution's governing board, or a well-meaning but misguided president or chief financial officer. "Programs that don't make money," it is said, "should be eliminated as soon as possible." But while this thinking may be appropriate in a for-profit university, such statements have no place in not-for-profit schools, where what is best for teaching, learning, and research should have primacy in decision-making.

Juxtaposing academic choices with their economic consequences can inflame the cultural barrier between professors and financial staff that I lamented in *Reengineering the University*.[16] Getting finance officers and staff interested in the new models and tools is not especially difficult, but these people are not empowered to address academic resourcing problems—where the need is greatest and to which the new tools contribute most directly. Provosts, deans, and faculty can be indifferent or even resentful of finance-initiated proposals. Indeed, provosts and deans may be wary of faculty reaction. I have heard statements like, "I see the need for the kind of thinking you're describing but am fearful of saying so publicly."

The problem can extend to university trustees and regents, who are justifiably wary of meddling in the university's internal affairs. I witnessed this comment from a trustee-participant at a recent meeting of the Association of Governing Boards of Universities and Colleges: "I don't know, and I don't want to know" (about the expenses and revenues of his college's majors). The *Chronicle of Higher Education*'s Scott Carlson described this as a "prevalent attitude up and down the ranks" and "the core of the financial problems in higher education."[17] It's true that academic officers and faculty have hands-on responsibility for delivering on the institution's mission, but they need oversight like everyone else. In this case, the oversight should include assuring that economic considerations get significant weight in academic resourcing decisions.

The justification for this assertion is provided by the so-called not-for-profit paradigm for guiding resourcing decisions in traditional colleges and universities. The paradigm and its implications are described in chapter 8, so I will provide only a brief introduction here. However, readers should keep the following ideas firmly in mind as they progress through the book.

Not-for-profit entities should *maximize mission attainment*, subject to the constraints imposed by markets, operating requirements, and financial sustainability. Maximizing mission attainment includes serving students, performing research and scholarship, and all the other things that academics value. It's up to provosts, deans, and faculty leaders to define these values in meaningful terms, but the working assumption is that "they know them when they see them."

Conversely, the constraints are not a matter of choice. They come from the exogenous factors I discussed in connection with the university's internal and external economies. As stated previously, to ignore these constraints is to risk a future that lacks academic and financial sustainability, or worse.

So how can a not-for-profit university pursue its mission while remaining cognizant of the constraints? Perhaps surprisingly, the answer is to do the following when making mission-driven academic resourcing decisions.

Compare the academic value created by each resourcing move with that move's estimated effect on margin. Acceptable moves require not just desirable academic payoffs but conditions on their margins as well: specifically, that the academic attractiveness relative to the effect on margin must be better than for other moves that might be taken. In addition, the university's or school's overall revenues must equal or exceed its overall costs after the margin effects have been taken into account.

Chapter 8 provides justification and a practical approach to implementation, but for now it is enough to remember that margin comes into AR decisions right along with mission-driven academic value, even though the university is maximizing mission attainment. Further, the existence of an overarching financial constraint means that comparisons among all pairs of resourcing options should be considered.

Reasoning by analogy with for-profit universities does not work in the context of not-for-profit academic resourcing. For-profits maximize margin (also known as profit), not mission attainment subject to a financial constraint. Positive margins drop to the bottom line for payment to shareholders in for-profit schools. They also drop to the bottom line in not-for-profits, but not for payments to shareholders. They must be used exclusively within the institution, quite possibly to cross-subsidize mission-critical programs that lose money. Without cross-subsidies, it would be the market, not academic values, that dominates decisions about programs—which means that mission has no agency in this case. This actually happens when universities teetering on the brink of failure exploit every available market opportunity in order to survive. While it may seem ironic or counterintuitive, paying strong attention to margin in academic resourcing decisions is the best way to preserve the primacy of mission and other university values.

Academic resourcing models that implement the non-for-profit paradigm are not like the "positive economic models" that Saul Morson and Morton Schapiro rightly criticize in their book *Cents and Sensibility: What Economics Can Learn from the Humanities*.[18] Without exception, the models discussed here "stop at the water's edge" when it comes to interpreting academic and humanistic values. What they do, instead, is to provide the empathetic and value-laden choices that universities must make with connection points to economic reality. I won't blame readers of the humanistic persuasion for being skeptical about this assertion. All I ask is for a suspension of disbelief while I present arguments and evidence that the models being discussed seek to inform academic resourcing conversations rather than to dominate them.

I'm reminded of C. P. Snow's "cultural divide" between the sciences and humanities, and the resulting adverse consequences for solving the world's problems.[19] Whatever one's view about Snow's particular assertions, there is reason to believe such a divide inhibits the adoption of economic thinking in academic resourcing. In addition to the issues noted earlier, the divide separates what might be called "quantitative or scientific" from "intuitive or empathetic" management, although those terms are inadequate for present purposes. Faculty in the humanities and social sciences (other than the disciplines of economics and business) generally feel the conflict most acutely— but the same feelings can be found all across the university. I think it's rooted in the belief that quantitative thinking ("science" in Snow's terms) cannot address all that's important in a university and a fear that, despite its manifest limitations, such thinking will come to dominate qualitative values in academic decision-making. I share those concerns.[20]

My position is that the stakeholders of every university should insist that academic officers and faculty give economic thinking its proper degree of attention in academic resourcing decisions. This includes the use of models for understanding the connections between academic activities and the university's internal and external economies. But to return to Snow's divide, the model-builders need the influence of humanists to ensure that their models don't overreach and thus undermine fundamental university values. The following chapters illustrate why I think this is possible.

CHAPTER TWO

Getting into AR Models

Chapter 1 described the internal economic type of AR model as extracting data elements from a college's or university's data systems, processing them, and presenting the results as information that decision makers can use to manage their institutions. At a minimum, such models require data from the financial, human resources, and student registration/timetabling systems. Full-function models also pull data from the facilities and research administration systems, and utilization of course management systems lies on the horizon. I describe the available AR model architectures and how a school should choose among them.

A Modern AR Model

Multiple vendors now offer academic resourcing models of the kind discussed in this book, and the number is growing. Among these are the Pilbara Group, whose model I discuss in part II, and Gray Associates, whose model is discussed in this chapter. I am enthusiastic about both models but note that other vendors' offerings may perform similar functions or will come to do so as the market matures. My decision to illustrate these two stems partly from their ability to illustrate the important AR modeling concepts and partly from the happenstance of my familiarity with them. As noted in the preface, I am deeply grateful to both companies for their transparency and active assistance.

The Gray Associates Program Economics Model

Gray Associates of Concord, Massachusetts, is best known for its higher education market information models, which I describe in chapter 7. About three years ago, the company recognized that while its market models capture the external economy of colleges and universities, they were silent on the internal economy. The Gray Associates Program Economics Model remedies that deficiency.

"What is a program?" was the first question that had to be answered during model development. From the institution's point of view, it's obvious that programs are collections of courses that lead to degrees, certificates, or other identifiable realizations of student attainment. Every institution maintains a list of programs as defined by academic awards. This drives the definition down two more levels: to the students who take the courses that lead to the given award and the course enrollments generated by the students as they move through their programs. For the moment, let us assume that each such enrollment can be tagged with the particular program in which the student currently is registered. Complications arising from delayed selection are addressed later.

Notice that the aforementioned definition includes all electives taken by students in the program. This is not the only possible definition, however. One alternative is to include only required courses as specified in the institution's catalog. Another is to include the required courses plus prespecified lists of popular electives or alternative ways of meeting requirements, with each option being weighted by its popularity. Still another is to eliminate the enrollments of students who drop out before graduation. I have studied this matter and believe the definition chosen by Gray, and all other models that I know about, does the best job of capturing what's important for institutional decision-making. It also has the advantage of self-weighting enrollments and, thus, simplicity.[1]

Revenues, costs, and margins also were identified as basic elements of the program economics model. In fact, getting data on these variables was the primary objective of the model-building exercise. After thinking about the options, the Gray team established a program's "direct variable economics," calculated from enrollment-driven revenues and costs, as the basic analytical level for comparing with market data. Shared and indirect costs would be added to the direct variable economics to get "fully loaded" metrics when needed.

The team recognized that the simplest approach for estimating a program's direct variable economics would be to allocate student revenues and departmental cost in proportion to enrolled credit hours. However, this would submerge one of the key elements of program portfolio management: namely, the course. While direct allocation to programs might be suitable for some purposes (including the Embry-Riddle situation described in chapter 1), that is not the way provosts, deans, and faculty usually approach their decision-making. Programs represent an institution's outward face to the marketplace, but decisions about departmental offerings, faculty loads, and other academic resourcing matters are made in terms of courses. Therefore, models that are intended to support decision makers need to include crosswalks between courses and programs.

University decision makers also care about how financial aid varies across groups of students. For example, athletes may generate more or less net revenue per credit hour than the average student, and the same is true for certain socioeconomic and/or racial and ethnic groups. A desire to support decision-making on these issues led the team to base the model's revenue calculations on individual students rather than on high-level averages. Gray's market analysis work enabled them to use powerful software techniques for the program economic model as opposed to relying on spreadsheet analyses that, among other things, would have precluded student-by-student revenue calculations.

These considerations led to three sets of overarching design specifications for the base version of the Gray model.

COURSE-LEVEL RESULTS

- Extract basic data on how the course is taught. For example, data on whether the course is "online" or "on-ground" (i.e., face-to-face), the number of sections offered, and in some cases the identity of the teacher can be obtained from the institution's timetabling and student registration system. Acquisition of other useful data about the course, including some items discussed in this book, is in the planning stage.
- Calculate tuition and fee revenue on a student-by-student basis, both gross and net of financial aid. Allocate tuition to courses in proportion to the student credit hours generated by the students enrolled in the courses. Allocate student fees so as to take account of fee type (e.g., lab fees go to lab courses) as well as credit hours.
- Allocate faculty and adjunct salaries and benefits to the courses the timetabling system shows them as teaching. (Any direct salary charges that appear in the accounting system, such as for adjuncts whose stipend is contracted for a particular course, would be applied before this step.) Pool the remaining salaries and allocate them across other courses in proportion to student credit hours. Salaries may be treated individually or averaged over faculty ranks (e.g., assistant vs. full professors).
- Apply any course-specific nonsalary charges that appear in the accounting system. Usually these are special fees or unusual cost items that are posted to the course when they are received or paid.

SHARED AND INDIRECT COSTS

- Shared costs are incurred at the level of the school and department (e.g., for the salaries of deans, chairs, and other administrators, and for nonpersonnel costs not associated with specific courses). Once again, these are allocated to courses in proportion to student credit hours.
- Indirect costs (also known as "overhead") are associated with higher-level administrative and support functions. Users can

specify whether allocations are based on credit hours, allocated
faculty full-time equivalents, or a blend thereof.

ROLLUPS TO PROGRAMS

- Apply the attributed revenues and costs for each enrolled
  student to the program, if any, in which that student is registered
  during the current semester. Revenue is the sum collected from
  that student (gross and net of financial aid), and cost is that
  student's prorated share of course expense based on credit hours.
- Prorate the revenues and costs for students who have not yet
  selected a program in proportion to the credit hour distribution
  for all programs. The formula can include particular student
  characteristics such as athletics or racial/ethnic factors, if desired.

These calculations produce data on revenues, gross and net costs, and
contribution margins (also called "loaded margins") for courses and
programs. The data can be displayed as totals or on a per-credit-
hour basis. Rollups to the departments that offer the course can be
calculated as well as those pertaining to programs, though these generally aren't relevant for program portfolio analysis—a subject to
which we will return in chapter 7.

The Gray Associates Program Economics Model runs in the cloud,
on a platform that is more flexible and powerful than any spreadsheet. The aforementioned procedures provide a basic picture of how
the calculations work, but many variations are possible. Indeed, anything that follows the general lines just described probably can be
accommodated. Gray works with users to find the best configuration
for their needs, consults with them on usage as needed, and then steps
back to allow free access to the model.

Sample Outputs and Usage

The Gray Associates Program Economics Model produces revenue, cost, and margin data for each program in which students are
registered. Many users start by comparing the direct margins of

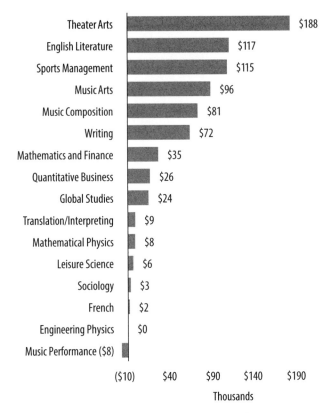

Figure 2.1. Direct Contribution Margin by Program

various programs, as presented for a hypothetical college in figure 2.1. The data have been adjusted to protect the institution.

Direct contribution margin is the excess of net revenue over direct expenditures generated by the program. The first thing to notice is the huge variation in this quantity: from almost $188,000 for theater arts to a negative of about $8,000 for music performance. (This is a small college, so none of the numbers are eye-popping in magnitude.) These data demonstrate no strong pattern, but it's likely that laboratory science and performance practice programs tend to have negative margins.

Table 2.1 shows the data that underlie the figure, presented this time in alphabetical order, on both a total and per-credit-hour basis.

Table 2.1. Sample Program-Level Data from the Gray Associates Model

Program	Student Credit Hours	Program Total			Per Student Credit Hour		
		Net Revenue	Direct Cost	Direct Margin	Direct Cost	Net Revenue	Direct Margin
Engineering Physics	275	$83,931	$83,713	$218	$305	$304	$0.79
English Literature	1,198	$397,745	$280,842	$116,902	$332	$235	$97.62
French	46	$8,036	$6,165	$1,871	$175	$134	$40.67
Global Studies	185	$57,245	$33,536	$23,709	$309	$181	$128.15
Leisure Science	131	$17,505	$11,281	$6,224	$134	$86	$47.51
Mathematical Finance	277	$75,213	$40,172	$35,040	$272	$145	$126.73
Mathematical Physics	102	$36,450	$28,068	$8,383	$357	$275	$82.18
Music Arts	817	$319,378	$223,848	$95,530	$391	$274	$116.93
Music Composition	873	$323,535	$242,636	$80,899	$371	$278	$92.67
Music Performance	568	$169,156	$176,666	($7,510)	$298	$311	($13.23)
Quantitative Business Admin	191	$53,774	$28,230	$25,544	$282	$148	$133.74
Sociology	97	$11,022	$7,881	$3,141	$114	$81	$32.38
Sports Management	6,943	$696,107	$581,282	$114,825	$100	$84	$16.54
Theater Arts	1,314	$442,193	$254,681	$187,513	$337	$194	$142.70
Translation/Interpreting	116	$24,534	$15,977	$8,557	$211	$138	$73.77
Writing	1,581	$485,714	$414,065	$71,649	$307	$262	$45.32

(Recall that "net revenue" refers to tuition and fees minus institutional financial aid.) As noted, the figures for programs are built up from course-level margins, apportioned by the fraction of each course's credit hours that is represented by students in the target program. Fortunately for the college, its largest program (sports management, with 6,943 credit hours) throws off a modestly positive margin per credit hour ($16.54). The programs in theater arts and English literature are much smaller but considerably more profitable ($142.70 and $97.62, respectively), so they rose to the top of the ranking in figure 2.1. In contrast, music performance loses $13.23 per credit hour, and engineering physics just about breaks even.

Figures 2.2 and 2.3 present the data in a more digestible form. These program comparison charts show direct cost on the horizontal axis and net revenue on the vertical one. The straight line represents breakeven, where revenue equals cost. Therefore, the contribution margin is the vertical distance between each point and the line. The first chart shows total revenues and costs, and the second one shows these on a per-credit-hour basis. The bubble's sizes are proportional to credit hours. The dashboards as seen by the model's users show negative contributions in red, but of course this cannot be rendered on the printed page. Hovering one's mouse over a bubble on the dashboard identifies the program.

Looking at the two figures provides an immediate picture of which programs are contributing strongly to the college's financial health and which are noncontributors or drags. A new version of the Gray model (for which data were not available at the time of this writing) allocates college overheads to courses and programs as described earlier. This allows the aforementioned data to be reported on a fully loaded basis. Gray reports that most direct program contribution margins it has observed are positive, but that many become negative when indirect costs are applied. The data also can be reported for segments of the student population: for example, comparing the margins for athletes enrolled in different programs. Both kinds of data can be important for program portfolio analysis and tuition setting.

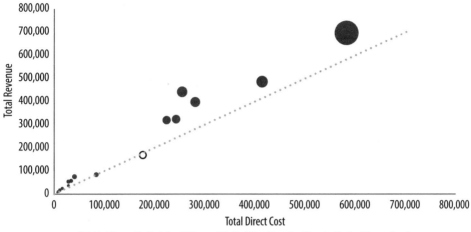

Bubble Size = Student Credit Hours; Fill: No Fill = Negative Margin; Dotted Line = Breakeven

Figure 2.2. Revenue and Student Credit Hours vs. Direct Instructional Cost Courtesy of Gray Associates

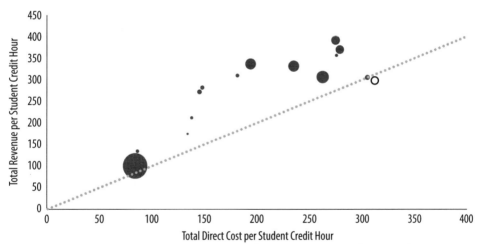

Bubble Size = Student Credit Hours; Fill: No Fill = Negative Margin; Dotted Line = Breakeven

Figure 2.3. Revenue and Student Credit Hours vs. Direct Instructional Cost, per Credit Hour. Courtesy of Gray Associates

Analyzing these data for programs and courses can provide insights about why margins are what they are, and what might be done about them. One such insight is that program margins don't only reflect the margins for the courses that students take in their major department. Most programs rely significantly on courses outside the major, which have a correspondingly significant effect on the program's margin. It's worth noting that this analysis requires costs and revenues to be estimated for individual courses, which then are rolled up to programs. Allocating directly to programs, as in the Embry-Riddle model discussed in chapter 1, cannot provide this information.

Table 2.2 shows the data for engineering physics. This program operates at breakeven overall, but that statement masks huge differences in the margins for courses taken by its students. Specifically, the physics and engineering courses lose about $631 per credit hour, but this is made up by courses in other fields—with those in theology and ministry, history/humanities/government, and English and modern languages having the largest surpluses. Faculty and administrators responsible for the engineering physics program would likely find this information very interesting.

Table 2.2. Distribution of Student Credit Hours and Margins by Broad Field for Engineering Physics

Broad Field	Student Credit Hours	Margin	Margin/Student Credit Hour
Biology and Chemistry	27	2,999	$111.07
Communication and Media	18	2,825	$156.95
Computing and Mathematics	61	11,490	$188.36
Physics and Engineering	65	(41,020)	($631.07)
English and Modern Languages	22	4,617	$209.88
Health, Leisure/Sport Sciences	17	2,672	$157.17
History/Humanities/Government	36	8,307	$230.76
Theology and Ministry (Undergraduate)	29	8,327	$287.12
Total	**275**	**218**	**$0.79**

Data of the kind presented here can help an institution identify which programs should be examined more closely, even though the Gray model does little to illuminate the causes of problems or opportunities for improvement. For example, revenue enhancement or cost reduction in large programs with modest margins per credit hour can pay off handsomely. Small programs with low margins per credit hour may be considered for consolidation or phaseout unless they are judged to be mission-critical academically. These observations apply especially to direct revenues, costs, and margins. Results that are loaded with overhead may require additional analysis because their elimination would cause the relocation of fixed overheads to other programs, even though the variable element of overhead will be saved. I'll have more to say about this in later chapters.

Levels of Academic Resourcing Modeling

Chapter 1 defined academic resourcing decisions as applying "the university's human, physical, and financial resources to its portfolio of activities, so as to further mission attainment in ways that are academically and financially sustainable given competitive and economic conditions." We now are in a position to amplify on the key elements of this definition as they apply to the models discussed in parts I and II of this book.

- *Activities* are represented by courses and programs. Key issues include the activities' configurations, scopes, and resourcing levels.
- *Market and other economic conditions* are represented by enrollments (often measured in terms of student credit hours), tuition and fee rates, and unit costs for the university's resource inputs.
- *Resources* are represented by faculty and other academic staff, nonprofessional and nonacademic professional staff, and facilities.

The model's objective is to combine the three elements in ways that provide decision makers with information that will help them further mission attainment while maintaining academic and financial sustainability.

As noted, the Gray Associates Program Economic Model calculates the revenues, costs, and margins associated with courses and programs, plus data on the types of teaching faculty utilized for each course. The model can cover all courses and programs offered by a college or university. It includes both direct and indirect expenditures, but as yet it doesn't address facilities, the fine structure of teaching activity configurations, or research. The included features do a good job of illustrating what can be done with AR models. However, they represent the middle range of what such models can do.

AR models can be divided into the three broad levels described in table 2.3. These are illustrated by the three models discussed in this book. The models are differentiated by scope of coverage and the detail with which revenue, direct cost, and indirect cost are modeled. The description provided earlier puts the Gray model into Level II. It covers all the institution's courses and teaching programs, assigns gross and net revenue as generated by individual students to the courses the students take, allows for reasonably complex allocations of faculty compensation and other departmental costs to courses, and

Table 2.3. Academic Resourcing Model Levels

Modeling Level	Example from This Book	Scope of Coverage	Modeling Detail for Key Variables		
			Revenue	Direct Cost	Indirect Cost
I	Embry-Riddle's campus model	Some or all teaching programs and departments	Student by student, to programs	Departmental average cost per student credit hour	Simple or no allocations
II	Gray Program Economics Model	All courses and teaching programs	Student by student, to courses	Complex student credit hour allocations	Simple allocations
III	Pilbara Full-Function Model	All courses, teaching programs, and research	Student by student, to courses	Structural descriptions	Complex allocations

can include indirect cost allocations based on credit hours and teacher assignments. Other providers are active in the market as well. For example, the Educational Advisory Group has offered what it calls its "Academic Performance Solutions." All but one of the commercially available models known to me share the aforementioned attributes and thus fall into Level II.

The Pilbara "full-function model," to be described in chapters 4–6, is currently the sole occupant of Level III. It covers departmental and sponsored research as well as all the institution's programs and courses, and it tracks revenue at the student level. The defining feature of Level III models is provision of detailed descriptions and analysis capacity for each course's sectioning and staffing structure, right down to individual instances as described in the institution's timetabling system. An example of an "instance" is the "lecture section of History 10 that meets Monday and Wednesday from 8 a.m. to 10 a.m. and its various discussion sections." (I provide further examples in chapter 4.) Staffing information is provided for each instance where it is available, which allows detailed representations of faculty workload—including time spent researching. Pilbara's indirect cost allocation procedures are quite granular as well, which enables detailed analyses of overhead for different programs.

Models like the Embry-Riddle example referenced in the previous chapter fall into Level I. Most, if not all, are constructed by the institutions themselves. Embry-Riddle estimates costs by allocating each department's average per-credit teaching cost to programs in proportion to the fraction of its credit hours that benefit the program, and the latest version of the model allocates students' revenues directly to the programs where they are enrolled. The model was built on a spreadsheet, which is a defining feature for Level I models. The original Embry-Riddle model was considered state-of-the-art at the time it was constructed, but now the art has moved to course-level modeling, as in Gray's and Pilbara's models. Spreadsheets can be used for course-level modeling, but the combined number of courses and programs must be of modest size. I elaborate on this point in the next section.

No one should be surprised that the cost of building and maintaining an AR model rises as one moves up the modeling hierarchy. But the benefits rise as well—and sharply. Table 2.4 gives a sense of the various models' applicability to different kinds of academic resourcing decisions. An institution's journey with AR modeling usually begins by exploring the possibilities in a preliminary way. This is represented by row 0 in the table. The remaining rows list areas of decision-making ("decision domains") as described in the prologue. A solid circle indicates that the modeling level is well adapted for the indicated purpose. Conversely, the slashed-circle "prohibited" symbol indicates that the model isn't really fit for this purpose. The doughnut symbol indicates the intermediate case, where the model will be helpful but to a lesser extent than a higher-level alternative.

The table shouldn't be taken as gospel, but here are some reasons why the entries are what they are. These thoughts are couched in terms of the Gray and Pilbara models, and what I think is a manageable spreadsheet model, but they apply to their levels generally.

Table 2.4. Applicability of AR Model Levels to Decision-Making Domains

Decision-Making Domain	Level I	Level II	Level III
0. Explore the Possibilities of AR Models	●	●	●
1. Adjust to Changed Enrollments	◐	◐	●
2. Support Comprehensive Program Review	◐	◐	●
3. Manage Program Portfolios	⊘	●	●
4. Set Prices	◐	●	●
5. Balance Faculty Workloads	⊘	⊘	●
6. Manage Teaching Operations	⊘	◐	●
7. Manage Classroom Utilization	⊘	⊘	●
8. Inform Budget Makers on Costs, Revenues and Margins	◐	◐	●
9. Focus Budget-Making on Mission	⊘	◐	◐
10. Support Scenario Planning	⊘	◐	●

Note: The table indicates which modeling levels are well adapted for an intended purpose (●), helpful to a lesser extent than a higher-level alternative (◐), or unsuited for the purpose (⊘).

- *Explore the Possibilities of AR Models.* Both the Pilbara and Gray models provide introductory tutorials for initial exploration, but institutions that are just starting to think about AR may wish to do some exploration of their own. Academic Impressions has offered seminars in this area for several years, and other entities are beginning to do so as well.
- *Adjust to Changed Enrollments.* All AR models allow users to vary enrollment to see what happens to cost, revenue, and margin, but only the Pilbara model gets to the capacity of individual class sections—which determines variable cost for small or intermediate enrollment changes.
- *Support Comprehensive Program Review.* Chapter 7 describes this as a deep dive into the academic quality, economics, and market factors for a particular program. All three models address program economics (providing the spreadsheet includes the program in question), but Pilbara provides more insight than Gray, and Gray more insight than spreadsheet models.
- *Manage Program Portfolios.* This requires one to model the institution's whole program portfolio, which is rarely practical with spreadsheets. The Gray model was designed with this in mind, and Pilbara does it, too.
- *Set Prices.* This requires the inclusion of indirect costs, which essentially rules out spreadsheets. Both Gray and Pilbara are fit for this purpose, though Pilbara is considerably more granular.
- *Balance Faculty Workloads.* Pilbara is the only model that describes workloads in enough detail to do this. Gray and other Level II models don't track workloads, and it would be difficult to build a spreadsheet model with the requisite level of detail.
- *Manage Teaching Operations.* This addresses the resourcing of individual courses, which in turn depends on things like enrollment, class size, teacher type, and section configuration. This is a sweet spot for Pilbara. Gray provides some but not all of the needed data, and spreadsheets usually provide very little.

- *Manage Classroom Utilization.* Pilbara's full-function model includes a detailed representation of facilities usage, which is something no other model does.
- *Inform Budget-Making on Costs and Revenues.* All the models can contribute to this purpose, but Pilbara provides better granularity.
- *Focus Budget-Making on Mission.* Both Gray and Pilbara do this to some extent, but neither address mission as directly as my new "budget choice" model—which is presented in chapter 8.
- *Support Scenario Planning.* This is another sweet spot for Pilbara because its detailed activity representation meshes with the needs of scenario planning (see chapter 6). The Gray Associates Program Economics Model can inform scenario planning in a general way.

In addition to describing the different AR modeling levels' fitness for purpose, the aforementioned list resolves confusion between AR models and activity-based costing (ABC) models. Both models are rooted in activities, but, according to its literal definition, ABC deals only with costs. Conversely, AR models include revenues and margins as well as costs. The term "ABC" has been applied to large-scale higher education models that have included revenues as well as costs, but this terminology proved unfortunate for several reasons. First, these models aren't as granular as the ones described here. Second, the term "ABC" has been confused with "cost accounting" as used in universities to determine overhead rates on sponsored research—which is an unpopular subject with many academics. Third, and most seriously, it leaves the impression that cost analysis is the primary objective.

A glance at the listed decision domains shows the error of the aforementioned views. Nearly all the decisions in the list require data on revenue as well as cost, only a few focus on overheads, and cost analysis is only one of many goals—and not the major one at that. One of my purposes in this book is to discourage further use of the "ABC" term.

Implementation Considerations

Let's assume your institution wishes to adopt some kind of AR model. The considerations discussed in the following sections are likely to loom large in such a decision. These observations are based on my own experience, and also on talking with representatives of institutions with successful implementations as well as people who install and maintain the Gray and Pilbara models.

Data Readiness

University leaders often ask whether their institution has the necessary data for building a serious AR model. The answer almost always is yes. Universities usually have more data than they think they have, but some critical pieces are buried deep inside their operations and financial systems. A commercial AR model developer will identify these data and embed them in its modeling platform. Some of the model's features depend on data that aren't available in all universities, but a good modeling platform will have been designed with enough flexibility that its key features turn out to be feasible anyway. The quick and inexpensive scoping study discussed shortly will let an institution know what to expect from its data before committing to a project.

IT professionals will debate about whether a data improvement project is necessary before starting a full-function AR project. The answer is yes if the data are bad enough, but for most universities a precursor data improvement project most likely will add unnecessary delays and costs. My belief, rooted in experience with systems development oversight at Stanford, is that iterative development works well in situations where the available IT tools make that possible. Full-scale IT planning may be a necessary precursor for data warehouses and other major system improvements, but efforts to be comprehensive in scope and definitive in process make such planning time-consuming and expensive. Smaller projects like building an AR model include their own data cleanup phase, and actual use of the data often provides a needed stimulus for data improvement.

AR modeling software has a good track record in starting from a university's existing data systems and then improving functionality and business rules over time as better data become available. For example, one university respondent told me that the experience of implementing and using his AR model actually informed IT planning by illuminating data needs that would not have been identified otherwise. Another observed that "everyone at [my institution] would have doubted our data readiness before we actually began considering the model. As it turned out, muddling through the bad data and fighting the territorial 'ownership' fights furthered the cause of good data as well as enabl[ed] us to get on with model building." Making significant IT data improvement work a prerequisite for AR model development (as consultants who sell such services often recommend) may well raise the cost of badly needed AR models to a prohibitive (and unnecessary) level. I generally prefer a "just in time" strategy, where the modeling process guides data improvement, to a "just in case" strategy, with its endless abstract debates about matters that may or may not turn out to be important.

The Development Process

What can a university leadership team expect when developing an academic resourcing model? I'll answer this for the Pilbara full-function (Level III) model because that has the most extensive development cycle. Level II models, including the one by Gray Associates, usually have somewhat simpler cycles. Pilbara's first step is to perform a scoping study. The study will determine which features and functions the institution's data can support and provide a cost estimate for the installation. The results are reviewed by university management, and if satisfactory, a formal project will be launched. Most such projects consist of five phases: organizing and cleaning the data, constructing the model, alpha or technical testing, beta or user testing, and initial rollout.

Development starts with constructing what might be called "data-facing modules." The first such module to be developed usually organizes data from the general ledger and human resources systems. Examples include financial transactions, faculty and staff FTEs, and average salaries and benefits. (Individual salaries are not necessary.) A second module is concerned with facilities: including, for example, what rooms are used for teaching, research, faculty and staff offices, and so forth. A "student module" collects data on program and course enrollments, tuition and fees paid, and financial aid received. An important attribute of this module is that revenues and financial aid "follow the student" right down to the course level. Still other modules elaborate the activity configurations for teaching, research, service, and various administrative and support services. All these modules collect data from disparate university sources and put them into canonical forms suitable for the main modeling effort.

This first phase will expose many questions pertaining to data definitions and the compatibility of one source system with another. This requires hands-on involvement with the actual data (teamed with an institutional person who knows the school's systems). The work is painstaking and requires deep knowledge of what will and will not work in the model—including experience with the creation of workarounds. Much of it is done off-site with frequent email and phone communication between the developers and various university representatives. The result is a relatively clean dataset from which the actual AR model can be constructed.

Model construction connects the data-facing models together to form the actual AR structure. This is done by using formal modeling logic and user-specified "business rules" that describe the institution's policies, ways of operating, and preferences for reporting. A good modeling platform will allow the business rules to be revised with relatively little effort, which is important because their development is an iterative process. Some of the rules will deal with matters the school has never consciously confronted: for example, how to treat unused classroom hours and the cost associated with them. (The process of thinking these matters through turns out to be valuable in its own right.) This phase of development also identifies important quantities that don't currently reside within the university's data systems: for example, how faculty divide their time among teaching, research, and service, and the time they spend on teaching activities over and above their measured contact hours. Once again, experience counts when defining these variables and finding unobtrusive ways to tap local reports or obtain judgments to get their values—matters that I discuss extensively in chapter 4.

The rule of thumb in AR modeling is to build from the data you have, but in a way that allows a development path into the future. Often this involves making assumptions that can be confirmed or amended later. The identification of important variables may serve as a "stone in the shoe for better data." The management of instructor assignments in the timetabling system is a good case in point. These systems almost always include a field for instructor name, but many institutions don't make serious efforts to post the names correctly. However, departments are less likely to use shortcuts like "staff" when they rely on an AR model for tracking faculty workload. The same thing happens when models are used in conversations about out-of-class workloads for high-enrollment courses, where improvements benefit both the decision maker and the model.

The next two steps involve what's called "alpha" and "beta" testing. Alpha tests are performed by the model-builders themselves. For example, all the cost and revenue flows must balance within the model because the underlying data come from the general ledger—which is itself balanced. Failure to balance means there are errors somewhere, which is unacceptable. In beta testing, university finance, accounting, and institutional research staff members exercise the balanced model in search of anomalies that can be tracked down and corrected or at least explained in terms of the real-world situation. (Usually the problems turn out to be matters of data definition or interpretation, which can be hard to identify but are not difficult to correct.) This step should not be shortchanged, since anomalies that arise unexpectedly during use can undermine the model's credibility.

The rollout phase asks key academic resource managers to begin using the model for actual decision-making. This provides a final reality check and begins the process of building credibility. University leadership should have discussed AR models in general, and the institution's model in particular, with these people early and often during the development process. However, this will be the first time they have been exposed to actual results. A typical approach is to begin with personal staff to the deans and provost and then move on to their principals. The objective is to develop understanding and search for anomalies. Often the conversations begin with questions like, "Do these results reflect your school as you know it, or, if not, where do they violate your sense of reality?" In a well-constructed model, drill-downs in response to questions are likely to resolve the issue. Hopefully they generate learning by all parties and enhance the model's credibility and usefulness. The next best thing is to identify an understandable and fixable anomaly, which has the effect of improving the model and boosting its credibility. The worst-case scenario is that the modelers must go back to the drawing board and then relaunch the process after significant changes have been made—a result that is undesirable but which does produce useful learning.

The model should be launched to broader groups of academic resourcing managers only after it has demonstrated its usefulness to the key players. Acceptance by department chairs is more likely to occur after a dean has decided to use the tool in his or her decision-making, for example. As in all such matters, it's important that the senior managers "walk the walk" as well as "talk the talk." Actual usage is important both as a matter of role modeling and, importantly, because people on the receiving end of a model-based decision will be strongly motivated to engage with the model to further their own self-interest. (It's sometimes said that "it takes a model to stand against another model.") One must expect criticism as chairs and faculty begin picking at the model's structure. However, it will be easier to deal with such criticisms when one has a well-constructed

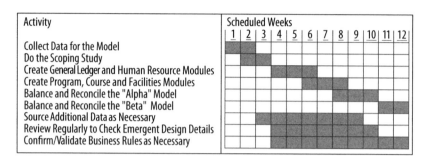

Figure 2.4. Typical Timeline for a Full-Function AR Project

structural model with a good forward development path than if the model relies on many unintuitive and dead-end approximations.

Project Duration and Cost

The time required for development will vary from institution to institution, depending on the model's desired features, readiness of the data, and the in-house staff time that can be assigned to the project. Figure 2.4 shows a typical development schedule as estimated by Grant Thornton LLC for installation of Pilbara's Level III model. Notice that the tasks' durations are measured in weeks, not months. The company is quick to add that achieving these timings depends on prompt responses from the university at the conclusion of each task. Staff unavailability, unexpected data problems, and a variety of other factors can make this difficult to achieve, so actual times almost always are somewhat longer. Even so, most institutions can reasonably expect to get through the beta testing phase in six months or less.

It's harder to generalize about project cost than it is about duration. Still, it's worth noting that a full-function AR model usually can be installed in a large research university with an outlay in the lower part of the six-figure range, not including the time of internal staff, with less cost for smaller and less complex institutions or slimmed-down versions of the model. Costs for implementing the Gray Associates and other Level II models will be lower as well. Notice that the durations and costs do not involve a preliminary project to enhance data readiness. Data cleaning and improvement is included as part of model development except in the rare cases where the scoping study indicates otherwise. It's also worth noting that the scoping study can be done in a few weeks at modest cost (included in the aforementioned estimates), and that a school can walk away at that point with useful insights about its data.

All AR models need to be updated annually as data for a new fiscal year become available. This may be done by the original vendor or in-house, depending on the model's complexity and the availability and skills of local staff. There also is an annual license fee. But while the costs of licensing, installing, and updating a full-function AR model are not inconsequential, they are small in relation to the amount of money on the table in academic resourcing. It's hard to calculate the return on investment for the models, but effectiveness improvements in the order of a small fraction of 1 percent will more than offset the cost of modeling.

Choosing the Right Development Path

I have participated in lively discussions about whether an institution should "start simple," with a Level I AR model, or proceed directly to a Level II or III model. The case for starting simple may seem obvious, but it becomes less so on close examination. First comes the matter of cost. It might seem that institutions should start with what can be done using in-house resources, just as Embry-Riddle did. Simple Level I models can be built in Excel, but the task usually is more complicated than it looks at first. The models tend to become more complex as users demand more detailed representations. It's not long before the models require complicated lookups and/or the replication of formulas over multiple linked worksheets. Soon the model becomes opaque, unwieldy, and prone to obscure errors that materially affect results. These problems are compounded if the person who designed the model leaves the institution or is promoted.

Elapsed time to delivering results is another consideration. The original Embry-Riddle model is said to have been built in a week, but this is exceptional. Internal AR projects get sidetracked as their developers are called to fight fires elsewhere and data anomalies raise unexpected barriers. Internal developers usually have little experience with these anomalies, nor with the workarounds needed to overcome them. Using database and specialized modeling technologies can get around the spreadsheet difficulties but not the problem of inexperience. Even highly skilled database people will have trouble building any but the simplest AR model without climbing a steep learning curve. In short, homegrown AR models are likely to take much longer and cost a lot more than expected.

Then there is the matter of simplicity itself. It's easy to think one's institution cannot cope with the complexity of Level II or III models, and that one should "walk before running" wherever possible. However, there are good reasons for not letting these concerns dominate the development decision. Users readily assimilate the Gray Associates Program Economics Model, and I believe the same is true for the other Level II offerings. For Level III, much of the full-function model's complexity need not be experienced except when answering questions about why the model produces what may appear to be questionable results—at which point a structural model will be easier to explain, and if necessary improve, than the rough approximations of Level I models. I also suspect that some Level II model users eventually will wish to migrate to the full functionality of a Level III model in order to extend the scope of model-supported decision-making.

Another problem of starting simple is that academics' support for AR modeling may erode due to oversimplifications in the initial model. First, the approximations themselves may seem counterintuitive to faculty and other academic resource managers. Second, an inability to answer "why" questions limits interest in the model, as it prevents drilling down to resolve anomalies. Accounting professionals have become comfortable with rough allocations of costs and revenues for purposes of analysis, but provosts, deans, and faculty tend to view things differently. They find it difficult to trust a model that consists entirely of rough approximations, and their requests for more refined representations founder because such models lack the necessary development path. (This wasn't an issue for Embry-Riddle because the remedial decisions were imposed from the top due to overriding financial imperatives.) In contrast, Level II and III models often can be changed in ways that satisfy their users' objections.

CHAPTER THREE

Building Trust in Your AR Model

I now address the all-important question of how a college or university can build trust in its new AR model. Chapters 1 and 2 demonstrate the importance of such trust, especially by academic users. AR models must contribute meaningfully to academic resourcing conversations in order to be effective, but, as important as these conversations are, they also provide ample opportunity for participants to criticize the model as providing data that are wrong, irrelevant, or inimical to core values. Faculty are very good critics and may relish the process (as I discuss shortly), which means the model must be introduced carefully and be capable of delivering on what has been promised.

So, what is it that really is being promised with AR models? Certainly not "accuracy" in some absolute sense. No model can deliver that. Nor is there a clear recommendation about what should be done. That may be a possibility in some decision situations (e.g., for optimizing product mix in an oil refinery) but not for anything remotely as subjective as academic resourcing. I argue throughout this book that AR models are intended to support human decision makers, and the truth of this can be demonstrated only through real examples. Some broad generalizations are useful, however, starting with the notions that prediction lies at the core of decision-making and that AR models are in essence "prediction machines."

AR Models as "Prediction Machines"

The division of labor between models and human decision makers is of particular importance in decision support situations. Getting this right is an important milestone in the process of adopting decision support models generally and for university AR models in particular.

Prediction as an Essential Element of Decision-Making

The two essential elements of any decision are the *prediction* of its outcomes and the *evaluation* of their consequences. In the Embry-Riddle case (chapter 1), for example, the two vice presidents predicted that changing the expenditure patterns in key programs would solve the campus's financial problem, and they used their new AR model to decide which programs would be worth looking at. When they evaluated the consequences of these changes in comparison to those of closing the campus, it became obvious that the turnaround strategy was superior. This example reflects the division of labor between the things that can be done with an AR model and those that require human judgment.

Economists Ajay Agrawal, Joshua Gans, and Avi Goldfarb describe this division of labor in their recent book, *Prediction Machines: The Simple Economics of Artificial Intelligence*.[1] They argue convincingly that humans tend to be poor at prediction and much better at evaluation. That the human brain is not well adapted to deriving predictions from complex information has been demonstrated in both experimental and real-world settings—the latter including the reading of radiology films, identification of baseball talent, and judging the flight risk of bail applicants. Some experiments demonstrate that humans make poor predictions in uncertain situations even after they correctly identify the relevant probabilities. And, in the author's words, "These biases don't just show up in medicine, baseball, and law, they are a constant feature of professional work."[2] *Prediction Machines* argues that, under the right conditions, artificial intelligence

(AI) can do a significantly better job of prediction than humans can. This conclusion extends to the use of models in general, and to many academic resource managers' predictions about the effects of decisions on their institution's operating environment, costs, and revenues. The models described in this book are intended to help these managers make the difficult predictions that confront them every day.

The tables are turned when it comes to evaluating the consequences of predictions. Humans generally do better on this task, probably for at least two reasons. First, the evaluation criteria often involve human values rather than the effects of changing complex systems. This puts people in the driver's seat, whether their own values are at stake or whether they are interpreting the values of others. Second, the evaluations are highly subjective. They involve many factors that have not and may never be quantified. Models and AI don't do well in this kind of environment unless real people have carefully encoded specific value-defining algorithms.

Decision support models respond to exactly this distinction. They pull data together and process information that either results directly in predictions or assists humans in making them. The matter of evaluating the consequences of prediction is left to the decision maker, which is as it must be given the inherent limitations of models. The case of university AR models is particularly interesting in this regard. Even the most advanced Level III model can't predict the effect of academic resourcing on the *quality* of teaching, learning, and research—which, at least at this point in time, cannot be measured well. What they *can* do is predict enough operating detail (e.g., class sizes and teaching loads) to allow human decision makers to make their own inferences about quality. The provision of such operating detail is one factor that can distinguish an AR model from accounting and similar information systems.

Lessons from Artificial Intelligence

A good AR model can be viewed as a "prediction machine" that provides deep and evidence-based forecasts about both the university's current operations (e.g., enrollments, courses, resource utilization) and its financial situation (e.g., revenue, cost, and margin). But it is not an "artificial intelligence" model. Even so, AI has been much in the headlines recently, and readers should not be blamed for wondering whether some of the commentary it has attracted also applies to AR models.

The short answer is that AR models aren't the same as AI. Both rely on computation, but the way they work is entirely different. Modern AI depends on so-called deep learning procedures. Data are fed into the machine, which then teaches itself to recognize patterns—which in turn can be used to make predictions. These procedures are quintessential "black boxes" in the sense that not even their developers can figure out how the predictions are made. But predict they do, and often at levels that exceed human competence. For example, IBM's Deep Blue chess-playing system famously defeated Grandmaster Garry Kasparov, and a Google algorithm recently mastered the ancient and exceedingly complex game of Go. Agrawal and his colleagues describe countless applications of AI in business and other applied fields, and the number grows every month.

What AI applications have in common is the availability of huge quantities of data that can be used for training the deep learning algorithms. Such data may be generated from business transactions, from individuals' use of social media, or, as in the case of chess and Go, from the behavior of experts as they solve the target problem and, after a certain point, play against themselves. Chapter 5 of *Prediction Machines* calls data the "new oil" because it has become a hugely important strategic asset.[3] Data are strategically important for universities, too, but the kind of data needed to use AI in the development of AR models does not exist.

AI models make predictions for what are essentially homogeneous processes. For example, it's usually inappropriate to train a medical diagnostic procedure on data from geriatric patients and then use it on children. Yet that is the situation when it comes to modeling the economics of teaching over periods of years and disparate academic disciplines. One can pool cognate disciplines and collect data for multiple years, but even so the number of data points will fall far short of the number needed for AI training. The power of AI comes from its ability to detect complex interactions among variables, interactions that wouldn't be imagined by human analysts. Yet that very power becomes fatal when working with small datasets, in which case the "detected" interactions will probably be spurious.

AR and similar models use human judgment to prespecify the causal structure of the system being modeled, after which the structure is used as a framing mechanism for analyzing the data. (AI models use no such mechanism.) Judgments about the structure are informed by logic, previous research, and the ability of human beings to infer causality from experience. These judgments are not infallible, but they do inject critical information into the model-billing process. It is this information that makes the use of small datasets practical.

Agrawal and his colleagues reflect the aforementioned in their description of how AI-based predictions falter.[4] They cite former Secretary of Defense Donald Rumsfeld's distinction between "known knowns, known unknowns, and unknown unknowns," and add their own "unknown knowns." Rich datasets allow good AI predictions that can be demonstrated to work well in situations where we "know" and "know that we know." Small or heterogeneous datasets like those encountered in AR modeling represent "known unknowns" (so far as AI training is concerned) because we know the data are sparse. The sparse data problem sometimes can be circumvented by prespecifying the model's structure, however, because the structure adds a priori information to the analysis. Rumsfeld's "unknown unknowns" are events that aren't reflected in past experience (and thus won't appear in any dataset) but will affect the current result. They cannot be captured in a structural specification because nobody imagines they will be important. Good predictions are bound to be elusive in this case, but evidence-based insights from AR models may be of some help anyway.

Finally comes the very important case of "unknown knowns": associations that appear strong based on past experience but are, in fact, spurious. Often these apparent associations are little more than anecdote-derived myths enabled by an information-poor environment and reinforced by uncritical repetition. Academic resourcing abounds in such unanalyzed associations. One of the biggest benefits of AR modeling is that it confronts these associations with evidence, which stimulates conversations about what might be the real truth and its consequences. AI procedures can do this, as noted, but they cannot be constructed from the small datasets that must be used in academic resourcing.

Thinking about the economics of AI reveals yet another benefit of the AR models discussed in this book. What has made AI a game changer in its domain is that it has dramatically lowered the cost of making predictions. This means many more predictions get made. Put another way, "cheap changes everything."[5] The same is true for AR models, which enable more and better predictions about the consequences of one's actions. Implicit and often myth-based views of what's likely to happen are replaced by explicit and evidence-based judgments. Academics still must evaluate the consequences of their actions, but the availability of better predictions significantly improves the performance of their universities.

Evolution of AR Modeling

The vision of academic resourcing models dates from the 1960s, when the first comprehensive models of university operations, costs, revenues, and margins began to make their appearance. This was a time of great optimism about how data collection and model building could lead to better decisions. World War II had spawned the new field of operations research (also known as management science), and the ideas had been vigorously applied across business and government. So why not universities, which had grown rapidly due to the GI Bill and postwar research funding, and which many commentators had come to view as alarmingly inefficient.

Few readers will remember the first two model-building efforts: CAMPUS (Comprehensive Analytical Methods for Planning and University Systems), and RRPM (Resource Requirements Prediction Model), which were developed by researchers at the University of Toronto and the University of California, Berkeley, respectively. Both were competently implemented but foundered due to inflexibility, opaque yet oversimplified core assumptions, and the "black box" problem to be discussed later. They enjoyed a short-lived interest by some financial administrators and higher education oversight bodies but never came close to acceptance by academic resourcing managers. Less ambitious modeling did achieve success, but it was not possible to connect the dots to get the single, integrated picture needed for academic resourcing.[6]

The next big push for comprehensive modeling of universities came in the 1990s, with the advent of activity-based costing. Originally developed for industry, the models were sold to universities by large accounting firms. Adopters aspired to what CAMPUS and RRPM had failed to achieve: a comprehensive picture of university operations, costs, revenues, and margins. Alas, these "classic ABC" models also fell short due to inflexibility, opaque but oversimplified core assumptions, and the black box problem. Some of the implementations also were time-consuming to run. For example, a model I encountered at the National University of Singapore in the early 2000s required many hours on the university's mainframe computer to process each change in data or assumptions.

That brings us to the present era, where the ABC-related concepts built into academic resourcing models seek once again to connect the dots. Chapter 4 of *Reengineering the University* described how AR models differ from classic ABC models.[7] The differences are crucial. As noted, they include a more granular focus on activities, especially those associated with teaching, and on revenues and margins, than the word "costing" might seem to imply. There are reasons to believe that these modeling techniques, together with today's database, computational, and networking infrastructures, have made it possible to produce genuinely useful and trustworthy decision support tools for academic resourcing.

Benefits Achievable from AR Models

The prologue showed how academic resourcing decisions can be improved by using detailed data as provided by AR models. This information is not available in conventional accounting and financial reports. For example, Maria Anguiano, a former vice chancellor of the University of California, Riverside, and now with Arizona State University and a University of California Regent, cites the "almost complete lack of visibility on how much it actually costs to deliver post-secondary education." It would seem axiomatic that the academics responsible for allocating scarce resources to activities should understand what the activities cost, but the fact is that they don't.

Anguiano goes on to describe how these information shortfalls make it hard to predict the effects of academic resourcing decisions.

> So, when needing to reduce costs, many institutions have turned to simplistic actions such as across-the-board cuts. These types of non-strategic cuts generally achieve only marginal savings and can often lead to higher local costs and poor delivery of services. Moreover, effective and efficient departments can go unrewarded or are forced to cut muscle while inefficient departments have little incentives to improve. The flip side of this issue is that institutions also cannot calculate the effect of innovations on their cost structure, such as implementation of new learning technologies. Thus, they end up treating spend on new learning methodologies as one-off initiative costs, not as part of the change in the operating model of the institution, and thus cannot effectively scale these innovations.[8]

Anguiano was calling for information at the level of individual courses and programs: not only what they cost but also operational details like mode of instruction, section counts, class sizes, usage of adjunct faculty and teaching assistants, and the kinds of facilities utilized. Courses represent the fundamental building blocks of every institution's teaching program, no matter what the mission and mode of instruction. I have described how data on programs (e.g., undergraduate majors) are obtained by aggregating course data for students registered in the given program. The same is true for revenues earned by courses and programs, and thus for the margins calculated by subtracting cost from revenue. These features can be found in some Level I and all Level II and III AR models, as introduced in chapter 2.

Beyond Benchmarking

A good cost study will speak to two kinds of questions: *what something costs* and *why it costs what it does*. Yet the typical benchmarking study asks only the "what" question. The "why" question is addressed by other means, if it is addressed at all. When academic resource managers compare costs, they usually want to benchmark against other institutions. At least two models currently provide such data in the United States: the Delta Cost Project and the Delaware Cost Study. Both are worthwhile, but they don't dig deeply enough to help with the "why" questions that are critical for effective academic resourcing.

Delta Cost Project data focus on what are called "functional" categories of activity as used in the Integrated Postsecondary Education Data System (IPEDS), the federal government's information system. The most important ones for our purposes are instruction, research, public service, student services, academic support, institutional support, and operations and maintenance. An institution can perform the calculations using its own data and then compare the results with national data for its IPEDS-defined institutional segment. This kind of macro information is useful for research and government policy purposes as well as high-level institutional benchmarking, but for decision-making it's like looking at terrain from above ten thousand feet. You can see the broad outlines but not enough detail to land the plane.

The Delaware Cost Study data provide more detail but still not what one would really like for academic resourcing. The study's website lists the following outputs in its "descriptive summary."

- How do the teaching loads of tenured faculty in your academic programs compare with national benchmarks?
- What proportion of undergraduate teaching at your institution is done by regular faculty, and how does that compare with other colleges and universities?
- Does it cost more to deliver a student credit hour of instruction at your institution than it does at your peers?
- How do externally funded research and service within your academic departments measure up against your competitors?[9]

One gets a broader selection of variables than with the Delta Project, but the lowest level of aggregation remains above the individual course. The emphasis of these models is still, and in my opinion must be, on benchmarking rather than directly supporting the kinds of academic resourcing problems discussed in the prologue.

Such data certainly are helpful for benchmarking. However, they don't support the drill-downs needed to answer "why" questions: for example, the details of course instances and the nexus between courses are revenues for particular student groups. AR systems do offer these advantages, and the more so as one moves from Level I to Level II to Level III models. These models invite, even demand if one possesses a degree of intellectual curiosity, a deeper exploration of the all-important "why" questions than is possible with simple "what" models. Perhaps more importantly, models that provide satisfying insights about "why" questions will generate more trust than those able only to address the "whats."

Complementing Academic Judgment

Good AR models will complement rather than challenge their users' academic judgments. I have presented many examples of complementarity already and will present more in subsequent chapters. An example of challenge rather than complementarity is provided by the following passage from *Cents and Sensibility*, cited in chapter 1: "Government officials, trustees, and the public at large have implored colleges and universities to 'act more like businesses,' presumably in an attempt to become more 'efficient.' But 'efficient at what?' is a question they do not ask, as if it were unproblematic."[10] The passage goes on to point out that universities value "love of learning, curiosity, and appreciation of diverse points of view,"[11] even if these cost more than simply ramming home job-related skills and abilities. Smaller and less "efficient" classes often produce more learning overall, not to mention the liberal perspectives mentioned earlier. Does considering these values make the university wasteful and inefficient? Definitely not, but that's the implication of the "efficiency models" the authors have in mind. But how can one build these intangible factors into a decision support model?

The answer is, "One can't!" An AR model should include only those constructs that can be modeled credibly with the kinds of data that are available—and, for example, we do not currently have good data about the quality of student learning. But the use of disaggregate course, student, and timetabling data comes to the rescue. We can model the operational and economic variables of teaching while leaving learning performance to academic judgment. For example, Level III AR models display operating details like class size and faculty assignments as well as economic data on cost, revenue, and margin information. Data on the operating details invite, or even demand, academic users to use them for making inferences about relative learning efficacy. But those inferences belong to the academics, not the model.

This dichotomy anticipates the not-for-profit paradigm described in chapter 8. Its basic tenet is to maximize mission attainment subject to production, market, and financial constraints. (In contrast, business firms maximize profits subject to production and market constraints.) Mission attainment incorporates learning quality as well as the intrinsic discipline-based values one associates with various academic fields, degrees, research initiatives, and so forth. These things can't be modeled. What can be modeled are the financial constraints and the quantitative details of production and the marketplace. Universities track revenues and expenditures to the penny and are held accountable for doing so. This book demonstrates that quantitative data also are available for operations and markets. The goal of AR models is to summarize these data in ways that trigger actionable insights on the part of academic resourcing managers. I hope that dispelling the confusion between university and business goals will remove a barrier to trusting AR models.

Trust and the Adoption of Innovations

Users of decision support models must learn to trust the information the models generate before they will be willing to use it. I hope the previous section has dispelled one potential element of mistrust: that AR models threaten academic values. As noted, however, one still must understand something about how the model converts raw data into information and what can be done with the information. Explanations by experts are necessary but not sufficient. Trust does not arise solely through knowledge acquisition and logical reasoning but also through interactions with peers and the model over a period of time—as, working with colleagues, one tests seeming anomalies against potentially corroborating data and common sense. But how do individuals and institutions get to that point?

Generating Trust

We professors have been conditioned since our graduate student days to offer critical commentary about data and the conclusions drawn from them. The conversations that swirl around AR models generate many opportunities for such criticism. That said, I learned early in my administrative career about how creating faculty understanding can indeed lead to acceptance. The time was the fall of 1974 while, as Stanford's vice provost for research, I was serving as a member of the university budget group. Federal research support and the stock market had dropped sharply, and it had become clear that our effective endowment spending rate (which was approaching double digits) could not be sustained. Huge budget deficits loomed on the near horizon, and no "business-as-usual" solutions could solve the problem. Hence my colleague David Hopkins and I developed what came to be called the Stanford Budget Equilibrium Model, which estimated the budget adjustments (a combination of budget cuts and income improvements) that would be needed to restore financial viability. The result came to 17 percent of the current budget base—which was more than sufficient to get the attention of both the administration and the faculty.

President Richard Lyman and Provost William Miller convened a commission of well-respected faculty to look at the model and its underlying concepts, as well as the proposed Budget Equilibrium Program for deciding the budget adjustments. A contemporaneous description of the group's findings provides a sense of how the commission approached its assignment: "The forecasts and analyses were basically reasonable as far as [the commission] could tell, and in particular that the [model] was just what it was intended to be, namely, an aid to understanding the university's financial difficulties and not the cause of them or the administration's perceptions of them. Some commission members expressed concern about the plan to reduce the endowment payout rate but in the end that, too, was accepted."[12]

The model had passed an important test: its logic was judged to be understandable and sensible, its results not too surprising, and its main conclusions reasonable (e.g., no plausible increase in stock price or other revenue assumptions would make the needed difference). A more sophisticated but arcane model probably would have failed, if indeed it would have been seriously considered in the first place. Perhaps the model's greatest impact was as an organizational catalyst: to rally people across the university around the proposed Budget Equilibrium Program target of $10.2 million. This is not unlike what happened in the Embry-Riddle situation.

It's worth ruminating on the conditions that led to this early modeling success at Stanford. Our professors certainly were not less prone to criticize than those at other universities (indeed, the contrary could very well have been true), although our shared governance arrangements did provide rank-and-file professors with assurance that the judgment of senior colleagues was independent of the administration. Second, Stanford's administration believed in transparency with respect to academic resourcing, even though it was understood that final decisions rested with the university officers and trustees. This transparency made it possible to open the model to scrutiny. Third, the model simply clarified the problem: it left the priorities for solution to the judgment of academic resource managers. Finally, its structure and assumptions made common as well as technical sense, and the reasons for its conclusions were reasonably understandable.

The Budget Equilibrium Model was no black box. Instead, it enabled anyone willing to exert a little effort to develop his or her own conclusions based on the evidence. The art of modeling in universities has developed dramatically since 1974, and complexity certainly has increased. However, the importance of a model's understandability, in tandem with its technical applicability, has not diminished. For more insight about this point, we turn to the decades of research on the adoption of innovations.

Stages of Innovative Behavior by Individuals

Everett Rogers (who pioneered the field) described the diffusion of innovations among potential adopters in his landmark book *Diffusion of Innovations* (last updated in 2003). Early research included the adoption of hybrid corn by farmers, new drugs by doctors, diesel engines by railroads, and my own master's and doctoral theses on modeling the adoption of monochrome and color television by American consumers.[13] I'll briefly describe the stages of innovative behavior for individuals acting as sole decision makers (as with the farmers and doctors just mentioned) or as decision makers within organizations, and the diffusion of adoptions in the overall user population. I believe that trust plays an important role in both processes, even though it isn't always identified as such.[14]

Rogers views the innovation process for individuals as consisting of five stages.[15] In our case, they refer to everyone who is in a position to support or inhibit AR model adoption in a college or university. It's important to approach each stage in a planful way, because failure anywhere can doom an AR modeling project.

1. *Knowledge.* When the decision maker is exposed to an innovation's existence and gains an understanding of how it functions. The knowledge relevant for adoption comes in three distinct flavors: awareness knowledge (e.g., that the innovation exists, who is using it, and how well it works), how-to knowledge (what it takes to use the innovation and what problems this may present), and principles knowledge (the functioning principles that underlie usage, which may allow potential adopters to judge the innovation's efficacy). This book presents examples of all three information types as they apply to AR models.

2. *Persuasion.* When the decision maker forms a favorable or an unfavorable attitude toward the innovation. This involves attitude formation and change, which may or may not be caused by the activities of a purposeful change agent. In Roger's words, "At the persuasion stage the individual becomes more psychologically involved with the innovation. He or she actively seeks information about the new idea, decides what messages he or she regards as credible, and decides how he or she interprets the information that is received."[16] According to this view, becoming persuaded is an active process that may (or may not) follow knowledge acquisition. Like so many processes discussed in this book, a favorable outcome depends heavily on whether one trusts the information received.

3. *Decision.* When the decision maker engages in activities that lead to a choice to adopt or reject the innovation. Favorable outcomes at this stage are characterized by active steps toward commitment and implementation. This is where the process tips from a "neutral" evaluation of information to a commitment to move forward (or not), accompanied by various manifestations of the same by, for example, public statements, garnering orga-

nizational support, and seeking implementation bids. Rejection can be active in the sense of taking an overt public decision, or it may be passive by slow-walking or never seriously considering adoption in the first place. The adoption decision can be reversed in light of new information or changes in attitude, but one's basic position has changed from "I'm still up in the air" to "yes" or "no."

4. *Implementation.* When the decision maker first puts the new idea into use. It is one thing for an individual to decide to adopt a new idea but quite a different thing to put the innovation to use—at which point the reality becomes clear and unexpected negative information may emerge. These problems can be more difficult in settings where implementation brings in large numbers of people who must be brought and kept on board. The lesson here is that a decision to implement is simply a starting point: what's actually required is successful follow-through.

5. *Confirmation.* When the decision maker seeks reinforcement of an innovation decision already made, but where conflicting messages may lead to abandonment of the idea. This may reflect efforts to fend off "buyer's remorse" (called "cognitive dissonance" by psychologists), or to overcome negatives encountered during the implementation stage. In organizations, this can reflect leaders' efforts to maintain the support of associates. University implementations of AR models sometimes founder because the confirmation step is omitted or performed badly, in which case the press of normal business may crowd out model usage once the initial novelty has worn off.

Two more useful topics that come out of adoption research relate to "champions" and "change agents," and the role of "reinventions" during the adoption process. Champions draw attention to the innovation and its benefits, and become the go-to people for making adoption happen. They usually come from within the college or university itself, because internal people have the credibility and staying power to persist in supporting the innovation over time. Champions may be leaders in a formal sense: for example, provosts and deans are especially well positioned for this task. Or they may be influential senior staff or perhaps even faculty members. The bottom line here is that people don't usually go through the aforementioned stages easily and on their own. Some well-positioned person or small team needs to inspire and manage the process on a continuing basis. This is why the change processes described in John Kotter's thrive channel (see chapter 1) usually are driven from high up in the organizational hierarchy.

Change agents facilitate movement through the stages of decision-making. These are people who assist would-be innovators with the details of adoption. Their work needs to be "hands-on," so it is not easily performed by the champions just described. Universities that adopt AR models generally use a combination of internal and external facilitators: the former to provide most of the direct interaction with the adopters (perhaps as members of Kotter's "volunteer army") and the latter for secondary and tertiary consultation. Change agents must mesh well with the innovators' needs, and they must be trusted by them. Research shows that the adoption of unfamiliar innovations is fraught with uncertainty, and that the choice can be hard even when the expected benefits are large. I argue in the conclusion that the current shortage of qualified and trusted change agents for AR models in the United States threatens to significantly slow the rate of adoption here.

Reinvention appears in the adoption literature as the redesign of a product or process partway through the diffusion process. Researchers debate whether such redesign represents an adoption success or a failure in the sense of "going back to the drawing board." I'd say it represents a success if the new version is close enough to the original that the previous adopters will recognize it as improving rather than superseding what they have already struggled to assimilate. A tenet of this book is that the design and usage of academic resourcing models will evolve during their adoption process and that this is a necessary and healthy thing. Would-be innovators should understand that all the details of usage cannot be anticipated in advance, and that active learning will be an essential part of the adoption process.

Stages of Adoption

It also is useful to consider organizations as entities in their own right for analyzing the adoption process. Most innovations do not launch and then "go viral" in the sense that large numbers of organizations clamor to adopt them as soon as possible. This certainly is true for AR models, where vendor concerns about long sales cycles for such models are not at all uncommon. The now is ample evidence that organizations (and also individuals, for that matter) that adopt the innovation at an early stage can exert disproportionate influence on potential later-stage doctors. This, in turn, leads to the idea of a "critical mass" for the adoption of an AR model. Adoption becomes much easier once a certain number of institutions have selectively used the model, whereas, before this point, every part of the process may be seen as difficult and fraught with risk of failure.

Rogers divides adopters into the five groups shown in the following table, whose names have come to be characterized as the "stages of adoption."[17]

Adoption Stage	% of Population
Innovators	2.5
Early adopters	13.5
Early majority	34.0
Late majority	34.0
Laggards	16.0

His characterizations of the groups are more applicable to individual farmers and doctors than to the complex organizations presented by railroads and universities, but, nevertheless, they provide insights that are relevant for AR model adoption.

- *Innovators*. Venturesome. The innovators' interest in new ideas leads them into more cosmopolitan social relationships and peer networks than is usual for the local social system. Communication patterns and friendships among a clique of innovators are common, as is the ability to understand and apply complex technical knowledge. The innovator must be able to cope with a high degree of uncertainty about an innovation at the time he or she adopts, and have a certain amount of staying power in the face of setbacks.
- *Early Adopters*. Respect. Early adopters are a more integrated part of the local social system than are the innovators. This adopter category, more than any other, has the highest degree of opinion leadership because they are viewed as not being too far ahead in innovativeness. Early adopters represent a critical group for the adoption of AR models because they are the ones who will figure out how to use the models and make the information available to other institutions.
- *Early Majority*. Deliberate. Adopting the new ideas just before the average members of the system, the early majority interact frequently with peers but seldom hold positions of opinion leadership. The early majority deliberates carefully. Their mantra is "Be not the first by which the new is tried, nor the last to leave the old aside,"[18] which gives them special credibility with more conservative potential adopters. They constitute an important link in the diffusion process by vastly expanding the positive communication networks associated with the innovation.
- *Late Majority*. Skeptical. The late majority adopts new ideas only after the average member has already done so. Adoption may come from economic necessity, or peer or outside pressures. The innovation is approached with a skeptical and cautious air and not adopted until the weight of systems norms definitely favor it. Many in the late majority have few discretionary resources, which means that most of the uncertainty about new ideas had to be removed by earlier groups before they could be deemed safe to adopt.

- *Laggards*. Traditional. They are the last in the system to adopt if they adopt at all, and they possess almost no opinion leadership. Their point of reference is the past and they tend to be suspicious of change in general. Laggards often make decisions consistent with what has been done previously, and they interact primarily with others who also have traditional values. Their innovation-decision process is likely to be lengthy, with positive attitudes, adoption, and use lagging far behind awareness and knowledge.

It would appear that the Pilbara Group's Level III academic resourcing model has penetrated well into the early majority group in Australia, where after more than a decade of availability it has been adopted by nearly twenty of their fifty or so universities and become quite familiar to many individuals and groups within the sector. The situation is vastly different in the United States, where AR models have been available for only a few years and most adopters fall into the "innovator" category. Thinking ahead to part III, I'd say that market information models like the Gray Associates Program Evaluation System probably are penetrating the early adopter category. The Constrained Choice Budget Model of chapter 8, which attempts to reduce the not-for-profit paradigm to practice, has not yet been made available for general use.

The categorization embodies the idea of risk in a number of ways. Briefly, these include a behavioral tolerance for risk on the part of innovators and early adopters (and the converse for late majority and laggards); the degree of risk presented by new methods as opposed to the older, "tried and true" ones; the role of peers and opinion leaders in providing reassurance about workability; and the existence of "staying power" to overcome setbacks, should they occur. The descriptions also allude to the tendency for people to operate within social groups that are similar to themselves, which inhibits information transfer and slows the innovative process.

Adoption research has identified certain attributes that tend to characterize individual innovators, but efforts to find those for corporate innovators have been less successful. It appears that corporations (and, by extension, universities) are too complex to permit development of statistical associations from the available numbers of instances. This certainly seems to be the case for adoption of academic resourcing models by universities. Innovators in both Australia and the United States have run the gamut from research universities to modestly sized colleges and community colleges. Hence virtually any institution can be considered a candidate for adoption at this point in time.

One thing that does come through strongly, regardless of innovation or innovator type, is the importance of diffusion networks for transmitting peer-generated information about the innovation to potential adopters. Members of these networks generally are called "opinion leaders." As the name implies, they are viewed as credible sources that can be relied upon by innovators and early adopters before information about the innovation has become generally available. Research shows that information usually flows through a two-step process: first from supplier or championing organizations to opinion leaders and then from the opinion leaders to the larger population of would-be adopters. The relatively fast penetration of AR models into the Australian university population may be due in part to that country's compact higher education sector—where most people of consequence know many if not most of the others. This book describes many examples of influential communications within organizations: for example, "volunteer networks" cited in chapter 1's discussion of Survive + Thrive. Unfortunately, however, the networks can carry negative as well as positive information, as witnessed by the self-reinforcing concerns of some academic senates, unions, and departmental councils.

The phenomenon of "critical mass," which I believe Australia has achieved with the Pilbara full-function model, reflects the relationship between individual innovators and the larger system of which they are a part. Research shows that innovation moves faster when innovators are able to communicate with one another and have occasion to do so. One reason cell phone adoption moved so quickly was that the phones could connect with landlines from day one, whereas the early landlines allowed communication among only a few people. One can expect the adoption of academic resourcing models to accelerate when there are enough users to permit effective benchmarking. In Australia, this is being accelerated by the government's recent decision to require more detailed reporting on costs. No such requirement exists in the United States, and institutions have been slow to carry benchmarking data at the course and program levels.

Part Two
Full-Function AR Models

Full-function AR models (also known as Level III models) provide detailed representations of important academic activities, especially those associated with teaching. The representation of activity data is what differentiates these models from their activity-based costing predecessors. Today's full-function AR models describe teaching activities in "structural" terms: that is, with respect to variables that make sense to operational and strategic decision makers as well as to financial analysts. This makes them interesting to department chairs and faculty in their management of day-to-day operations, as well as to provosts, deans, and others concerned mainly with budget-making and strategy development. The Level I and Level II models introduced in part I describe the activity structures in only enough detail to provide a good basis for cost and revenue estimation.

Part II begins by describing, in chapter 4, how the full-function models work. The first section, "Activity Analysis of Academic Operations," looks at faculty effort profiles, course instances, course profiles, classroom utilization, and research (including departmental research). Next comes a deep dive into the estimation and use of data on costs, revenues, and margins—which, in a full-function model, is firmly grounded in the structure of activity. The last section of the chapter illustrates the kinds of user interfaces offered by full-function models. The availability of interactive dashboards is particularly important, because free-form, real-time searches are necessary for driving the decision-making conversation.

Chapter 5 discusses the use of "historical" full-function AR models to aid academic resourcing decisions. (Historical models enable judgments based on records of what actually happened, as opposed to making what-if predictions, as described in chapter 6.) This discussion is organized around the kinds of decisions that provosts, deans, and other AR managers need to make, rather than the internal workings of the models themselves. The four categories of decisions deal with school and departmental margins, faculty effort, the organization of courses and course instances, and the sizing of degree and other teaching programs. In addition to describing the utilization of full-function (Level III) models, the chapter also provides additional insight about the Level I and II models.

Chapter 6 deals with predictive Level III AR models and their use in scenario planning. It begins with how decision makers use scenarios to envision their university's future and to define and evaluate actionable alternatives for dealing with it. How a full-function AR predictive works, and how it can contribute to the envisioning and evaluation process is described next. The chapter's final section shows how the modeling- and scenario-planning results inform the university's legacy financial planning and budgeting processes—including responsibility center budgeting, where that is being used.

"God is in the details" when looking at the full-function AR models, but I have tried to limit the presentation to those details that are necessary for general understanding. Even so, some readers may wish to focus on the overarching narratives rather than on sweating the details. Certain details from the three chapters are elaborated in appendix A. They are important for understanding how and why the models work the way they do, but they can be skipped without losing touch with the essential narrative.

CHAPTER FOUR

Pilbara's Full-Function AR Model

Full-function AR models capture the *structure* of teaching, research, and support activities rather than simply allocating cost and revenue on the basis of drivers like student credit hours. They represent the state of the art. The models to be described are built on a platform developed by the Pilbara Group of Brisbane, Australia, with whom I have been working these past several years. The company has built the core concepts presented in chapter 4 of my *Reengineering the University* into its model, and I work with them on further development. Theirs also happens to be the only full-function AR model in the marketplace at this time, though other offerings surely will be forthcoming.[1]

Structural models provide important insights for decision makers, ones that are not available from allocation models. This is important in its own right and also because it makes the model easier to accept. I have emphasized that acceptance is a multistep process. Briefly, users must understand the model well enough to enable informed judgment, and that judgment must be favorable. The inner workings of Level I and II AR models (chapter 2) are accessible to lay users as well as to experts. Understanding a full-function AR model requires greater effort, but experience shows the results to be worthwhile. In particular, the elaborated structure of Level III models helps assure informed skeptics that the model really does produce meaningful results.

But why should the provosts, deans, department chairs, and the other academic resourcing managers I hope will read this book bother to internalize these ideas? Can't they leave that to experts inside and outside their institutions? The next section describes why the answer is "no," but it all boils down to this: you, the responsible decision maker, are almost sure to be surprised by some of the model's results— at which point you will need to decide whether to accept, modify, or reject the conclusions. Experts can be helpful, but in the end it's your decision and you'll need to know enough to make it wisely. President John F. Kennedy illustrated this principle in his handling of the Cuban Missile Crisis. The best experts in the country were advising him on how to interpret the aerial photos, yet he felt the need to learn enough about that art to see the Russian missile deployment for himself. He could rely on experts' assessment for the details, but the central, existential judgment had to be his alone.

A school's decision to adopt a full-function AR model also has deeply strategic implications, though, of course, without the apocalyptic overtones of the Cuban crisis. The AR applications described in the prologue penetrate to the core of what it means to be a university: what programs and courses should be offered, how big should they be, how the teaching should be delivered, and where the university should invest in research capacity. No one who is responsible for academic resourcing can or should rely on model-based information without gut-level comfort that the model makes sense. That, in turn, requires a threshold understanding of how the model works. Reaching this threshold is important if one wants to harness the power of full-function AR models.

I understand why gaining the needed understanding might seem problematic. When, as Stanford's vice provost for research, I asked about our models for overhead recovery, the answers from the university's finance and accounting staff often were mind-numbing in jargon and irrelevant detail. I'll do my best to avoid that here, though a certain amount of special terminology and detail does turn out to be necessary. I do hope, however, that readers will keep the purpose of AR modeling firmly in mind as they evaluate these details. The models should be intuitively reasonable, but they need not be precise. The ultimate test is whether their use will lead to better decisions than judgments made without the aid of models.

Activity Analysis of Academic Operations

How do full-function AR models handle the various kinds of activities that take place inside universities? This material falls under the rubric of what I call the AR Activity Model. (The AR Economic Model is discussed in the next section.) I'll concentrate mainly on teaching, because that's the "business of the business" for universities and also where the models have been advanced the furthest. Then comes research, where significant progress has recently been achieved. Detailed models for administrative and support processes, and public service processes, have yet to be developed, but this will change over time as resource managers ask modelers to give these functions more attention. The Stage II AR model described in chapter 2 includes some of the teaching-related logic to be discussed here, but not at the level of detail included in the full-function models.

This also is the time to introduce the vehicle I'll use to describe the full-function AR model: "USA University," or USAU for short. It's a full-scale AR model implementation, rooted in real-world data that have been disguised to maintain confidentiality. (Examples for "Australia University," a similar demonstration platform, also will appear from time to time.) The remainder of this chapter mostly describes the model's core engine, which provides the highly detailed information needed by finance and accounting staff. User institutions have full access to and can make certain modifications in their core engines. The engine bridges the gap between a university's understandable desire to maintain control of its model and the extreme difficulty of building a full-function AR system, from scratch, for a single campus.

Academic resource managers usually prefer to focus on the interactive dashboards and other reports that sit on top of the core engine. Built in Microsoft's PowerBI, the dashboards provide a dynamic reporting system that university staff can adapt rapidly to their changing needs. (Both the engine and the dashboards connect seamlessly to Excel.) I describe representative dashboard displays at the end of the chapter and present more in chapters 5 and 6.

Faculty Effort Profiles

A university's ability to track the fine detail of faculty effort hasn't changed much over the decades. Asking faculty to quantify their effort distribution will likely conjure up visions of lawyers who charge in six-minute intervals and consultants who worry about billable hours. "Faculty don't punch time clocks," they say. "That is not how things are done in academe"—nor, in my opinion, should they be done that way. This view stems from the nature of faculty work, not from some self-serving cultural mandate.

Faculty efforts in support of teaching, research, and service often overlap and merge into one another to the point where even the individuals doing the job can't parse their activities at particular moments in time. Lecturing on basic material may well be considered "pure" teaching and pursuing an arcane scholarly question as "pure" research, but what about the seminar that spontaneously spins off research ideas or insights from research that change the teaching paradigm? And what about students studying for research degrees? Faculty involvement with them often meets the economists' definition of "joint production," where the process cannot be teased apart, even in principle.

But this doesn't mean faculty effort distribution is beyond the reach of analytics. Both institutions and faculty maintain expectations about such effort in order to function, and the two parties' expectations need to be reasonably well aligned. As with so many things in academe, there should be regular conversations about faculty effort regarding these expectations, both as a matter of broad policy and with respect to what specific individuals will do during particular time periods. Some institutions hire faculty with the expectation that, absent sponsored research or other "buyouts," they will spend, say, 40 percent of their time on teaching, 40 percent on research, and 20 percent on institutional service.[2] Other schools may have significantly different norms. In many such schools, a particular professor may agree with his or her chair or dean that, for example, a 30-60-10 or 60-30-10 distribution will hold for the next year or two—with teaching loads being adjusted accordingly. I engaged in many such conversations during my time as an associate dean of the Stanford Business School. Of course, institutions that don't consider research to be a key part of their missions will have higher teaching percentages.

Like their classic activity-based costing predecessors, full-function AR models use these expectations as the basis for assigning faculty effort to the teaching, research, and service functions. (It is what's done within these three "buckets" that varies between the classic and AR models.) The models described here rely on user judgments about the splitting fractions—a task that, perhaps surprisingly, is not usually problematic. Results are stored in a hierarchy of "faculty profiles." The top level in a typical hierarchy refers to the institution as a whole, the second to individual schools, the third to divisions within departments, and so on down to the lowest-level unit where faculty are employed. The teaching, research, and service fractions for the overall university (e.g., the 40-40-20 split) are the only required inputs. However, deans can provide different data for their schools and often do so. The same goes for department chairs, perhaps subject to approval by the dean. The system is one of "inheritance." Information automatically propagates from higher to lower levels, and from semester to semester and year to year, unless modified by the user.

This scheme works satisfactorily in every university where my colleagues and I have conducted interviews. However, recent developments suggest that improvements may be possible. These involve the development of faculty workload models that refine the effort expectations for individual professors based on their planned assignments—while steering well clear of the dreaded "time clock" concept. In effect, the models capture and refine the policies and conversations referred to earlier. They stem from an institution's desire to better understand what's actually expected of its faculty and more accurately align expectations. These developments are occurring independently of any desire for AR modeling. Once such a model is in hand, however, the resulting data can be tapped into easily.

Modeling faculty workloads requires codification of certain policies and practices, which are collectively known as "business rules." The treatment of sponsored research provides one example. Should the notional 40 percent for research be applied to effort net of buyouts, or should buyouts be part of the 40 percent? How should one adjust a professor's teaching percentage when she serves as principal investigator on a large sponsored project that, while not funding any buyouts, requires significant work during the academic year? Similar issues arise on the teaching side. Should the percentages be revised when a professor teaches a very large or complex course, for example? How should the percentages be changed when professors teach an "overload" of small courses, as in the example presented in chapter 1?

These questions can be difficult to answer on an ad hoc basis, but developers of business rules can take them in stride. The resulting rules are neither as rigorous as accounting policies nor as difficult to change, but they do provide useful guidance for people who make operating decisions. Clarifying them is important whether or not an AR model is to be constructed.

Course Instances

Course instances are defined as the propagation of content according to a particular mode of delivery, in a specific semester, and on (where applicable) a particular campus. They are the most detailed level of activity represented in the typical university's timetabling system. Therefore, it should not be surprising that they represent the building blocks of activity for full-function AR models. This usage of "instance" should not be confused with "class sections," which in the model's terminology represent various meetings within the same instance.

In table 4.1, for example, the "instance" of Biology 230 in the spring semester consists of two lecture sections and four laboratory sections, and "produces" 992 credit hours of teaching. (A face-to-face "lecture" as defined by USAU includes all teaching modes that bring students together in a single room.) The 248 students are assigned to one or the other of the two lecture sections, and each group is further subdivided into lab sections for each lecture section. Each section type is characterized by average class size, contact minutes per week, and the number of regular faculty members utilized for teaching. The average lecture size for the referenced biology course is 248/2, and the average lab size is 248/6. The lecture meets for 110 minutes a week and the lab for two hours—the number of meetings need not be specified because only the total durations matter for resource utilization. One of the two lecture sections is taught by a regular faculty member, the other presumably being taught by an adjunct, and all the lab sections presumably are taught by teaching assistants.

Two instances of Accounting 10 are presented: one taught by conventional means in the fall semester and one by distance learning (DL) in the spring. This course has no lab, but otherwise the layout is the same as Biology 230. Distance learning is accommodated using the same structure as F2F. However, some business rules had to be employed to translate DL nomenclature for duration. Basically, the idea was to define "sections" in terms of scheduled group sessions (e.g., instructor presentations and chat rooms). Other modes of DL teaching might require different rules, but none of the model's users reported any difficulties with doing that.

The data in table 4.1 represent what I call the "physical descriptors" of teaching activity. The data come from the university's timetabling and student registration systems, not its accounting system. These systems are the province of academic support people rather than financial people, so they are familiar to academics. It is the use of such physical descriptors that distinguishes AR models from their predecessors. More elaborate representations of teaching activity

Table 4.1. Illustrations of Course Instances at USA University

	BIOL 230	ACCT 10	
Course Instance	Spring (Face-to-Face)	Fall (Face-to-Face)	Spring (Distance Learning)
Credit Hours	992	168	30
Student Head Count	248	56	10
"Lecture" Sections			
Number	2	3	1
Reg. Faculty	1	2	1
Avg. Size	124	19	10
Duration (min.)	120	180	180
Lab Sections			
Number	6	–	–
Reg. Faculty	0	–	–
Avg. Size	41	–	–
Duration (min.)	120	–	–

configurations are possible, but the ones shown are sufficient to support the current state of AR modeling.

The physical descriptors are connected by a so-called structural teaching model, which shows how the different variables relate to one another. Appendix A describes the structure used in the Pilbara full-function AR model. It highlights the trade-offs between quantities such as class size, duration, frequency, and replication, on the one hand, and faculty teaching loads, on the other. These quantities lie at the core of academic resourcing as seen by provosts, deans, and so forth. Models that start at the level of costs don't provide insight about these trade-offs. Structural models of physical quantities always can be extended to provide estimates of costs and revenues, but the converse is not true. This is why academic resourcing models are relevant for both academic and financial decision makers, whereas cost-based models such as ABC are of interest primarily to financial staff.

Course Profiles

Most of the data needed by the full-function AR model come from the university's timetabling, student registration, facilities, and other transaction systems. But not all. Certain important data must be obtained by judgment or from ancillary sources like departmental spreadsheet models. The core engine provides input screens for these data and then stores them in so-called course profiles. As with the faculty profiles discussed earlier, profiles for particular section types are subject to inheritance rules that propagate a given data element down to instances within the hierarchy unless it is explicitly overridden.

Table 4.2 illustrates the course profile data for noncontact teaching effort. The first two rows estimate the *class preparation* time needed for a given section type: for example, two preparation hours per contact hour ("hrs/hr") for the first section in a semester taught by full professors and one hour for subsequent sections of the same course in the same semester. Academics argue that the varying roles and experience levels of different faculty ranks, and of adjunct faculty, cause them to spend different amounts of time in class preparation. Hence the model includes the possibility of such distinctions.

Table 4.2. Sample Course Profile for Out-of-Class Effort

	Full Prof.	Assoc. Prof.	Asst. Prof.	Adjunct
Class Preparation	2 hrs/hr	3 hrs/hr	2 hrs/hr	2 hrs/hr
Repeat Preparation	1	2	1	1
Lab Preparation	2	2	3	2
Repeat Preparation	1	1	1	1
Fieldwork Preparation	0.5 hrs/hr	0.5 hrs/hr	0.5 hrs/hr	0.5 hrs/hr
Repeat Preparation	0.5 hrs/hr	0.5 hrs/hr	0.5 hrs/hr	0.5 hrs/hr
Advising	1 hrs/stu/sem	1 hrs/stu/sem	1 hrs/stu/sem	1 hrs/stu/sem
Assessment and Grading	1.5 hrs/stu/sem	1.5 hrs/stu/sem	1.5 hrs/stu/sem	1.5 hrs/stu/sem
Course Development	20 hrs/yr	20 hrs/yr	30 hrs/yr	–

The figures are likely to differ by class type (lecture, lab, fieldwork), so these differentials are included as well.

The next two rows, for "advising" and "assessment and grading," estimate the hours required for each student in the course, for the semester as a whole ("hrs/stu/sem"). The last row, "course development," refers to the amount of time that regular faculty members spend on that task, on average over the whole calendar year ("hrs/yr"). This is not associated with any individual course but instead is allocated over all the department's courses in proportion to total teacher effort. The varying dimensionalities illustrated in the table demonstrate the model's inherent flexibility, which makes it possible to accommodate many different institutional modes of thinking about teaching.

The figures in table 4.2 come from judgments by deans and their staffs, often in consultation with representatives of the provost and/or chief financial officer. I observed such meetings at the university on which USAU is based and can report that participants showed a willingness to engage that sometimes bordered on enthusiasm. Participants welcomed the idea that the profile data would be included in the university's new AR model. Many interview respondents at other institutions echoed this sentiment. Instead of being an onerous and meaningless exercise, they tended to view the judgmental process as a way of codifying "what we believe to be true, generally." When dissent occurred, it usually stemmed from the mistaken notion that (unattainably) precise measurements are necessary. While such measurements have their place in research, a "quest for perfection often is the enemy of the good" in decision support modeling.

Classroom Utilization

Course teaching draws on yet another important kind of resource: classrooms, laboratory space, and other kinds of facilities. The space inventories maintained nowadays by most universities supply the data needed to model these resources. Timetables provide room numbers and class durations because they must inform students about where to show up and how long they will have to stay. Room numbers can be referenced back to the facilities inventory, at which point conventional cost accounting can be used to estimate the course's room average utilization cost. Other results such as the amount and cost of unused capacity for different kinds of facilities also can be calculated.

The full-function model tracks each course's classroom utilization down to the level of individual room and even the building in which the teaching occurs.[3] While this detail may sometimes be helpful to users, high-level summaries are better for routine use. The following shows one kind of summary for two of USAU's schools:

	Utilized Area as Timetabled	Unutilized Area as Allocated
College of Arts and Sciences	29,187	69,956
School of Architecture and Design	16,172	49,072

The figures for utilized area sum the square footage of the rooms assigned to the schools' courses, weighted by the courses' duration. Unutilized area is obtained by subtracting the utilized space from the total space theoretically available if all the rooms were occupied during all possible teaching times and then allocating the result in proportion to the utilized space. Similar figures can be obtained at the level of a department, course, course instance, or room type. (Some rooms are specified as computer classrooms, laboratories, studios, or study areas, for example.) They also can be broken out by campus or specific building. Institutions that would prefer a different method of summarization can specify what they want, either when the model is being constructed or later.

There is no reason why classroom inventories cannot reflect seating capacity in addition to square footage. More ambitious datasets might even include the enrollment capacities (numbers of seats) for different kinds of rooms, and the reported information for course instances could include these data where they are available. This would allow calculation of the percentage of seating capacity used by each course, which would be valuable for calculating marginal cost per student as well as tracking classroom utilization.

Research

Research activity is too complex and varied for its structure to be described in canonical form, as in the case of teaching's course instances. Hence the model's research structure defines "activity" in a more implicit way. The "organized research project" is the most detailed activity level for which most universities maintain centralized research data. Most such projects are funded by outside sponsors (e.g., government agencies, foundations, or corporations), but university funds may be used as well. Much research takes place outside organized projects, however, so such projects cannot serve as the model's only measure of activity. Conversely, modern universities do obtain regular reports from faculty about publications and perhaps citations, collaborations, conferences and other events attended, and other indirect indicators of research activity. The challenge is to summarize this in a meaningful way.

The resources going into research are easier to ascertain. The main one, faculty effort, is either recorded as time spent on organized projects or subsumed in the unfunded research percentage stored in the faculty profiles. Significant nonacademic staff effort almost always is assigned to projects or at least coded as "research" in the accounting system. The same is true for most other direct expenses. Modern facilities inventories code laboratory and similar space as research or teaching depending on actual usage. General faculty support such as office space, IT support, and travel are treated as indirect and allocated among instruction, research, and teaching, as described later.

As with all other decision support systems, the design of Pilbara's research model was guided by user needs. On-campus discussions and consultations with experts revealed the most central need to be improved strategic resource allocation. "How can my university build research prowess?" is the question academic resource managers most often raise. Success brings higher rankings and a stronger reputation generally, which are intrinsically important and also confer benefits in areas from student recruiting to institutional advancement—and, of course, to the winning of grants and contracts that further fuel the research process. It's universally understood that the fine structure of research activity, and the information needed to support decision-making, should be left to faculty principal investigators. But what kinds of data will facilitate the strategic decisions that university administrators need to make?

The key strategic research decision for most universities is how much of their discretionary funds to invest and where to invest them. The biggest research-related discretionary investments go into infrastructure like laboratories, specialized equipment, and research administration capacity. Next come investments in new faculty, who, it is hoped, will open new areas for research or sustain and advance existing ones. (Recall that the time percentages for unsponsored research are maintained in the faculty effort profiles, which allows unfunded effort to be estimated as a function of faculty full-time enrollments.) A third category represents funding pools that can be used to support research teams during "down periods" between sponsored projects, and to provide seed money for the development of new project proposals. Knowing the existing patterns of spending and revenue generation by academic area and subarea, and their trends, is of great help in making these investment decisions.

Universities generally collect these data to the level of schools, departments, and organized laboratories and institutes, but only rarely at a more refined level. They also track research initiatives and grant and contract outlays by potential funders—which, of course, represent the market for sponsored projects. The great difficulty in research strategy development is that market information tends to be organized in terms of research fields and subfields rather than the organizational structures of universities—which, though at least loosely based on academic discipline, vary greatly from institution to institution. It's hard to match one's sponsored research performance against the potential market and even harder to compare unsponsored research effort with external data. What's needed are fine-grained expenditure and revenue data that can be compared against externally available information organized around research fields and subfields.

Full-function AR models can do just that. They have been implemented in Australia, where national research data are organized in a taxonomic hierarchy that defines fields and subfields down to a "six-digit level." I'm not aware of a similar hierarchy in the United States but believe the National Science Foundation and perhaps other entities have hierarchies that could serve the same purpose here. The way forward is to apply the methodology described in appendix A to whatever classification scheme the institution thinks will prove useful. It's also worth noting that classification schemes need not have the same level of detail in all research areas: one may wish to concentrate only in those areas where the analytics will be important for the strategy questions being considered.

The basic strategy is to map faculty research outputs into the fields and subfields that the institution judges to be important for developing its strategy. Suppose the school wants to develop capacity in a particular branch of engineering, for example. It might start by assessing the capacities of its current faculty as demonstrated by publications, involvement with conferences, and so forth. To be useful, these assessments must penetrate down to the fine structure of activity in the field. Members of the faculty research community as well as agencies such as the National Science Foundation can help design the taxonomy and also assist with the assignments of individual publications, and so on, to particular subfields. Similar assignments can be performed for significant sponsored research projects in the university's portfolio.

With the assignments in hand, it is possible to allocate faculty effort and research revenue to fields and subfields. The result is a comprehensive picture of the resource usage and revenue associated with the identified fields and subfields. Knowing one's current capacity is the essential starting point for deciding the strategy for new investments. The same methodology is used to track progress against the particular research improvement goals.

The Full-Function Economic Model

What remains is to determine the activity analysis's financial implications: in other words, the costs of the various activities, the revenues earned by them, and the resulting margins. (This is the AR Economic Model referred to earlier.) The Pilbara Group's system uses a flexible and robust methodology to derive the direct cost and revenue of teaching and research based on the activity data described in the previous section. This enables the calculation of gross margin (also called contribution margin) for courses, degree programs, research fields and subfields, and so forth. Then the models apply highly detailed cost accounting methods to allocate indirect (overhead) costs to teaching, research, and service, and thus calculate "locally burdened" (e.g., with departmental overhead) and "fully burdened" net margins.

Cost Pools and Drivers

All institutional costs (and revenues, for that matter) are recorded in the university's general ledger, the comprehensive transactions record that lies at the core of every accounting system. The first step in processing these costs is to organize them into summary categories called "cost pools." The most important pools are listed in the sidebar. Each pool is further divided according to the organizational unit incurring the charge: for example, "faculty salaries and benefits charged to the chemistry department." The scheme accounts for every dollar of cost that appears in the general ledger. This allows crosschecking between model and general ledger, which is important for data integrity and also to prevent important costs from "falling between the cracks" in the university's complicated transactional structures. Faculty and other users are assured that no shell game is being played with hidden funds and allocations.

Structurally based drivers are used to allocate teaching costs to courses and research costs to fields and subfields. The definitions of

Illustrative Cost Pool Definitions
- Faculty salaries and benefits
- Adjunct faculty salaries
- Nonacademic staff salaries and benefits (often broken down by job classification)
- Other operating expenses by type (e.g., travel and office supplies)
- Facilities operation and maintenance

these drivers are anything but arbitrary. They reflect the best available thinking about how the activities actually are performed and what demands they make on resources. In the case of teaching, for example, the allocation scheme is mathematically equivalent to the commonsense structure based on section counts, class sizes, and so on, that I described earlier. Such equivalence allows faculty and other academic resource managers to relate teaching cost to the particular teaching tasks rather than viewing them as abstract black box constructs. The methodology is transparent, and suggestions for improvement usually can be accommodated provided the needed data or judgments can be made available. The result of using these drivers is to distribute appropriate shares of the cost pools to teaching at the course level and to research fields and subfields.

Indirect cost allocations use drivers similar to those employed in standard cost accounting, though generally at a more detailed level. The USAU model separates indirect costs into almost sixty separate categories, ranging from simple to complex and large to small, with some randomly selected examples being shown in the sidebar. (Institutions have considerable discretion in choosing the categories.) Each category has its own driver or drivers. Many of these involve student and staff FTEs, but variables specific to given situations also can enter the picture. The indirect cost drivers don't reflect the fine structures of their associated activities, so, as noted earlier, it may prove desirable to build fine-structure models in some cases.

Illustrative Indirect Cost Categories

- Academic computing
- Admissions
- Student affairs
- Residential life
- Alumni relations
- Human resources
- Controller's group
- Counseling and wellness
- Security
- Chief financial officer

The cost pool and driver definitions are known collectively as "business rules." Designers have great flexibility to build rules that match the institution's practices and culture. Construction and testing of the business rules, and resolving any circular references that may arise, are important technical tasks when applying the model at a particular university, but these are accomplished by experts during model development.

Revenue Pools and Drivers

The model extracts institutional revenues from the general ledger using a scheme similar to the one described earlier for costs. (One of the model's strengths is that the same basic methodology can be customized and used for a variety of purposes.) There are two broad categories of revenue: money earned by the modeled activities and money acquired from other sources. Earned revenue consists mainly of tuition, student fees, direct and indirect cost payments for sponsored projects, and fees for dormitories, food service, public service programs, and athletic events. Direct government subsidies for student enrollments and degrees also are considered as sources of earned revenue because they depend directly on the level of teaching activity.

Other (unearned) revenue includes things like general government subsidies, gifts, and payouts from endowment.

Business rules can assign unrestricted revenue streams to organizational levels in ways that are consistent with the institution's budgeting system. Responsibility center budgeting systems assign tuition and fees to schools, for example, whereas line item systems assign them to the central administration. Restricted gifts are assigned as determined by the donor's instructions. Payments for the direct cost of research go to the project's principal investigator, and indirect cost recovery (which comes in as unrestricted money) goes to the central administration. The result is a set of revenue pools defined by category, organizational unit, and restriction, if applicable. As in the case of costs, the pools account for all revenue coming into the institution.

The final step is to distribute revenues to their appropriate places in the model. Drivers again play the dominant role: for example, tuition is distributed to courses based on the students enrolled in them. However, there is an added twist as compared to most revenue allocations. It's important to differentiate certain revenue streams according to their source (or perhaps other attributes): for example, tuition income from in-state versus out-of-state students or sponsored research income from federal or private sources. The model "tags" students and their associated revenues with relevant descriptor(s) and then tracks these tags through the model's distribution and reporting processes. The tagging technique enables tuition to be reported by type of student, and many other breakdowns as well, without slowing execution of the model by ballooning the number of revenue and cost pools. Tagging is less frequent on the cost side, though it does arise occasionally: for example, in the differentiation of faculty salaries by professorial rank.

Students also are tagged with the programs in which they are enrolled. Hence the model can report course-taking, enrollments, credit hours, costs, revenues, and margins by program as well as by the departments that own the courses. Users can toggle back and forth between these views with a single click, which enables them to map courses to programs and programs back to courses in a seamless way. This powerful feature looms large in the application of AR models to course and program planning.

Margins

Calculation of margin is an easy task once the revenues and costs are in hand. The model does this for individual courses and for research fields and subfields, and then rolls the results up to departments, schools, and the central administration. It calculates three different kinds of margins at each level, each of which is important for certain purposes.

- *Gross contribution margins* consider only the direct costs of the activity: for example, the cost of teaching a course or performing research in a particular subfield. ("Contribution" means the money helps fund overhead costs, cross-subsidy pools, and the like.) Direct costs are useful for comparing the effects of alternative teaching methods and similar variations that won't materially change the load on administrative and support activities. Recall that facilities charges are treated as direct costs for purposes of the model (i.e., class sections are assigned to rooms), so facilities costs may well change as teaching methods are modified.
- *Locally burdened contribution margins* include allocations of departmental or laboratory overheads along with direct costs. They are useful for analyzing shifts of enrollment among courses and programs, as well as in other situations where the local costs may change but calls on central administrative and support services are not materially affected.
- *Fully burdened margins* include central overhead allocations along with local overheads and direct costs. These figures are essential for deciding on prices, which in the aggregate must recover all the institution's costs, including overheads. Tuition

certainly falls into this category. So do decisions about what to charge for sponsored research, a subject that is particularly important when contracting with industry and other sponsors that are willing to negotiate full-recovery indirect cost rates.

Questions about what to include for different analyses also arise on the revenue side of the margin calculation. The main one pertains to student financial aid. Opinions differ about whether aid should be considered a deduction from tuition revenue or as a cost of acquiring students. The AR model for USAU identifies financial aid as a deduction from each course's tuition revenue. However, universities can set their own business rules for the treatment of financial aid.

Full-Function AR Interfaces

Whether the model can support effective academic resourcing conversations depends on the flexibility and intuitiveness of its interfaces. Full-function AR models offer two types of interfaces. The first type follows the model's data structure in a strictly hierarchical way. Analysts use it to trace out particular data threads and connections: for example, when they are tracking down and correcting apparent data anomalies. The hierarchical structure also is used for entering data into the course and faculty profiles. The second type of interface caters to the decisions that people make when using the model. It consists of interactive dashboards, which can be understood and utilized by decision makers without any necessity for staff intermediaries.

The Core Engine's Data Hierarchy

The core engine arranges its data in the form of hierarchies like the one illustrated in table 4.3 for a hypothetical Australian university that, like USAU, was created for demonstration purposes. The table displays margin and effective full-time student load, the Australian equivalent of credit hours), but it could show any of the model's variables. Users can customize the variables to be displayed using simple "build and select" tools.

Table 4.3. Illustration of an Academic Resourcing Data Hierarchy

	Margin	Equivalent Full-Time Student Load
Overall University	$35,933,373	16,490.98
Teaching	$64,831,727	16,490.98
School of Science	$27,027,861	6,419.93
Computer Science Department	$6,236,038	1,024.33
Undergraduate Fourth Year and Honors	$422,781	108.84
Database Theory and Design	$285,221	43.38
CS 436: Systems and Database Design	$43,481	4.88
Sydney (Face-to-Face, Fall)	$14,285	2.5
Sydney (Face-to-Face, Spring)	$13,297	2.25
Sydney (Face-to-Face, Summer)	($2,298)	0.13

The hierarchy's structure is determined when a model is configured for a particular institution. University-wide figures appear at the top, followed by activity type (e.g., teaching), school or other organizational unit (e.g., science), department (e.g., computer science), course level (e.g., undergraduate fourth year), content specialty (e.g., database design), and, finally, the course itself (e.g., CS 436). The last lines list the course's three instances in the current academic year (fall, spring, and summer, all F2F). Navigation up and down the hierarchy is easy. The Pilbara platform uses Microsoft's standard data management scheme, but other arrangements are possible. For example, clicking on "Teaching" displays the teaching data for all the university's faculties, clicking on a "Faculty" displays its departments, and so on.

Notice how the margin and effective full-time student load figures roll upward through the hierarchy, from individual course instances to the overall university. A glance at the margin rollup shows that the aggregate positive margin for teaching is offset by losses elsewhere—presumably in research. Even this simple table provides insight into the economics of teaching, and the simple step of displaying columns for revenue and cost would add even more. The core engine can support many analyses by calling up more complex combinations of variables and then downloading the results to Excel, if necessary.

Interactive Dashboards

The Pilbara model constructs its dashboards in Microsoft's PowerBI business intelligence and visualization system. I illustrate two such dashboards here and more in chapters 5 and 6. Keep in mind, though, that an institution's dashboards will be designed in close collaboration with the decision makers they seek to support—a task that is greatly facilitated by the power and flexibility of the PowerBI tool. Other vendors offer tools that can accomplish much the same thing. However, the effective use of any such tool depends on having an appropriate modeling platform.

Typical dashboards contain more information than can be accommodated on a printed page, especially when the rendering is in black and white rather than full color. Further, the static nature of such exhibits makes it impossible to demonstrate the dashboards' interactive capability. My narrative tries to overcome these limitations, but it can only go part of the way. Some data are presented in tables, which are easier to read and less expensive to reproduce than the dashboards, but in every case the data came or could have come from dynamically navigable dashboards. The data pertain to USAU's College of Arts and Sciences (introduced earlier in this chapter) unless otherwise noted. The dashboards to be illustrated pertain the university's overall expenditures and revenue.

Figure 4.1 illustrates some of the expenditure data that academic decision makers find helpful. The top panel shows the model's expense estimates for teaching, research, public service, and other functions, broken down by the major departments of the College of Arts and Sciences. USAU takes pride in its research program, but the college does not spend a great deal on it compared to teaching. (The figures are different for other colleges, especially engineering.) Public

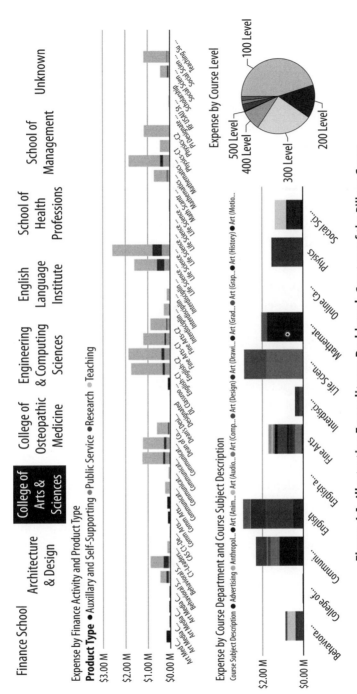

Figure 4.1. Illustrative Expenditures Dashboard. Courtesy of the Pilbara Group

service expenditures also are negligible. The pie chart in the figure's bottom panel breaks out the teaching expenditures by course level, which allows one to gauge the college's distribution of effort among different levels of students. The stacked bars at the left of the bottom panel distribute the departments' expenditures according to the subject descriptions associated with their departments. The key to this chart is too long to display here, but the categories are listed in appendix A. (As with all of the interactive dashboards, the category and numerical data can be viewed by hovering one's mouse over the desired spot on the bar.) Among other things, this view can be helpful in gauging the breadth and depth of the university's offerings.

Drill-downs are achieved by clicking on various parts of the dashboard. Clicking on a slice of the pie chart converts the other images to data for that course level, for example, whereas clicking on a bar segment in the upper panel displays data for that department and function, and clicking on one in the lower panel displays data for just that department. This seamless movement from display to display is critical for gaining insight and stimulating conversation, especially when people are not accustomed to analyzing the details of datasets. To change schools, one simply clicks on the list to the right of the top panel. Ratios such as cost per credit hour and per faculty FTE also can be accessed easily.

Figure 4.2 provides similar kinds of information for the revenues associated with departmental activities. The total length of the bars in the upper panel shows the gross revenue associated with teaching, research, and so forth in the college's departments. The position of the bars allows one to break out student aid expenditures. For example, student aid for students taking English courses amounts to about $4 million (the amount by which the bar protrudes below zero axis), which leaves $14 million of net revenue. The bottom panel breaks out revenue according to the categories used in the university's accounting system: tuition, student fees, student aid, grants and contracts, and so on. The pie chart divides the teaching-associated revenue according to course levels. As with the expenditures dashboard,

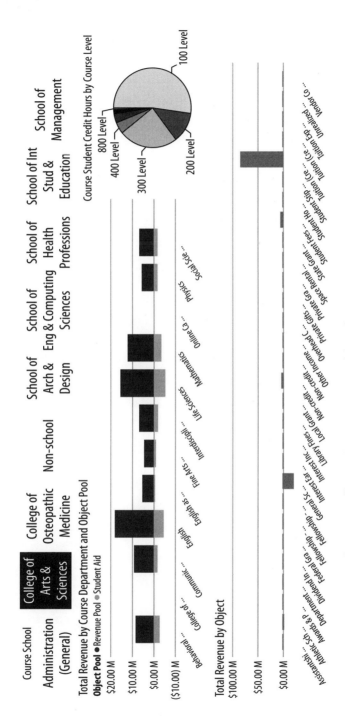

Figure 4.2. Illustrative Revenues Dashboard. Courtesy of the Pilbara Group

clicking on any part of the exhibit brings up data relevant to that descriptor.

The dashboards put a great deal of information onto each screen and then allow users to drill down to get more detail. This strategy is designed to make digesting the data and following up on ideas as easy as possible. This will mean different things in different contexts and for different kinds of institutions. Happily, because the PowerBI is very flexible, there is no need to settle for dashboards that don't meet your needs. University support staff can make changes on their own, or they can learn to develop reports de novo without a great deal of effort.

Users report little difficulty in learning to navigate within and among the dashboards. The approach reflects the kind of experience I had in mind when envisioning resource allocation displays in chapter 5 of *Reengineering the University*. The design and use of the dashboards are still in fairly early days, but it's already clear that they do, in fact, stimulate the desired kinds of conversations.

CHAPTER FIVE

Historical Models and Operating Decisions

Schools and departments make countless decisions about how to allocate their scarce resources. Some of these occur during the annual budget process, as when a dean or provost decides to add a faculty line or some other resource to a particular department. Others occur within the budget year itself, as when a department chair decides whether or not to offer a particular course in a particular semester. This chapter addresses such decisions one at a time. It describes how data obtainable from a full-function academic resourcing model can be used to improve the effectiveness of decision-making. Knitting the individual decisions together into an overall budget and financial plan is considered in chapter 6.

School and Department Margins

Margin is arguably the most sensitive single indicator of a school's, department's, or program's financial health. This section elaborates on the importance of being "margin conscious" and the kinds of things one can do with this information. Being margin conscious doesn't mean managing the university like a business, but it does reflect a businesslike approach to money where that is appropriate. I justify this assertion in chapter 7, if indeed justification is necessary. For now, readers should keep in mind that what follows aims to improve the university's ability to fulfill its academic mission, not to undermine that mission with imported ideas from business.

An institution's investment in programs depends on its overall margin, after deductions for necessary operating and financial reserves. Margin is also a litmus test for good financial management because unintended but persistent deficits signal a lack of fiscal prowess. I return to these issues in chapter 6. However, much of the action for academic resourcing managers occurs at the level of schools and departments. This is where one can identify, diagnose, and act to mitigate difficulties and take advantage of opportunities.

Summary Information

Summary information about margins in USA University's College of Arts and Sciences is given in figure 5.1. Figures for the college's overall revenue, cost, and margin are shown in the right-hand top panel along with data on total credit hours and full-time equivalent faculty and staff. The pie chart breaks down the data by expense type (direct, various overheads). The bottom panel breaks the total down by department.

As with the illustrative dashboards described in chapter 4, clicking on any display element changes the whole dashboard to show data for that element. Clicking on "Behavioral Sciences" gets data for that department, for example. Clicking on "Direct Cost" in the pie chart changes the departmental total costs and margins to direct costs and margins. This dashboard also includes a bar chart that breaks

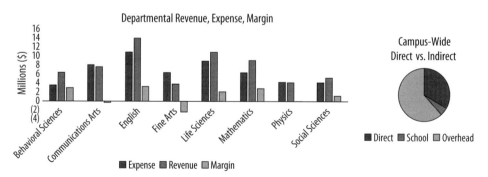

Figure 5.1. Economic Data for the USAU College of Arts and Sciences

down the cost and margin according to teaching, research, and public service. Once again, clicking on one of those bars causes the rest of the dashboard to show figures for the chosen function. Other dashboards provide similar detail at the course and program levels.

Short-Term Interpretations

Margin data contain signals that are relevant for both short- and long-term academic resourcing decisions. The signals are never unambiguous, but the informed conversations stimulated by the AR model can cut through the noise and point toward meaningful actions. There are plenty of places to start this discussion, but I found it instructive to watch the deans at a client institution engage with time-series charts like the one shown in figure 5.2. Such time-series data can be very instructive—though, of course, data must be available for a sufficient number of years to make this worthwhile.

Convened by the university's vice president for planning, the meetings engaged the senior staff of each school in separate two-hour

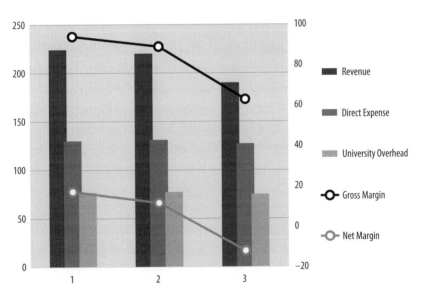

**Figure 5.2. School, Department, Program, or Campus
Financial Performance**

sessions to discuss the implications of the AR model's results for the upcoming budget cycle. The discussions focused mainly on short-term issues, which was not surprising given that the deans were concerned about the next year's budget. They generally proceeded along the following lines.

- The group would consider several different issues before focusing on the school-level time series for revenue, cost, and margin. When it did, the discussion became more coherent. (This was the first time the schools had seen the third year of data, which had only recently been loaded into the model.) Whether the trend was up or down didn't affect the energy in the room very much, though, of course, the specifics of the discussion did depend critically on the trend.

- Next would come drill-downs to departments, programs, and campuses (the university has several). The process was seamless because the lower-level data, including the charts, are obtainable with a single click. Usually drill-downs would narrow causality to the point where participants could begin to generate hypotheses about what was happening.

- The hypotheses would be probed by looking at appropriate details from other model elements. This was followed in many cases by agreements about follow-up analysis using the AR model or the schools' internal spreadsheets. (The schools had direct access to the model and could use it in their own analyses.) Occasionally, the issue would revolve around an emergent data problem, in which case the follow-up would be to fix the model. Mostly, though, the issues were substantive and amenable to deeper probing.

- Ideas for action would emerge organically from the consideration of causal hypotheses. These, too, would be explored and notes made for follow-up. Participants would leave the meeting with a sense of satisfaction that, although many problems remained unsolved, something had indeed been accomplished.

It's worth knowing that, although the meetings were held separately, all participants were given access to the data for all the schools. The deans were unanimous in believing that this was a good policy, that it would put the data for their schools in context and be a significant source of mutual understanding and collegiality.

The action ideas fell under the familiar rubrics of revenue enhancement and cost reduction. This is consistent with the general proposition that margin data provide signals about market factors and operating efficiency. For USAU, revenue enhancement boils down to getting more tuition dollars or spending less on financial aid. (Other institutions will include fund-raising and sponsored research as major priorities.) More tuition would require boosting the rate and/or increasing student numbers, and both occasionally entered into problem-solving conversations. Tuition-setting and most financial aid distributions are central functions at USAU, but ones that evidence-based, school-level analysis can influence to some extent. Methods for analyzing enrollment effects are addressed later, in the section on programs. Marketplace data like those discussed in chapter 7 also enter the picture for both price-setting and enrollment management, as does the university's marketing and communications strategy.

Price-setting is aided by the AR model's ability to estimate fully burdened costs and net margins down to the course level, especially when the overhead allocations vary significantly by field. These costs don't fully determine prices, but knowing them is essential for informed consideration of pricing decisions. As in other areas of academic resourcing, regular work with the model breeds familiarity with both the concepts and the data, and this can prove invaluable when pricing decisions need to be made.

Approaches to cost reduction are considered later, in the discussion of courses and programs. For now, it's enough to note that one needs to be cautious about burdening margins with overhead when thinking about cost reduction. Table 5.1, taken from the pie chart back in figure 5.1, shows three kinds of cost figures that go into the margin calculation. They are the direct cost of the teaching activity,

Table 5.1. Different Kinds of Costs

Type of Cost	Percent
Direct	36%
School Overhead	1%
Global Direct	5%
University Overhead	58%
Total	100%

overhead at the school level, and overhead at the university level. In the present context, most cost calculations should include school and departmental overheads because the deans and chairs can control them, but not the university-wide overheads. Deep dives into specific departmental activities should exclude the school overheads. Evaluation of alternative teaching delivery methods would consider only the direct and local costs, for example, because adding the higher-level overheads makes it harder to see relationships among the direct inputs.

Long-Term Interpretations

The long-term signals provided by margin data relate more to the university's value system than to year-to-year budgeting. I explain in chapter 8 how this proposition is deduced from the not-for-profit model of university decision-making, but an intuitive explanation will suffice for now. A well-run university that sustains deficits for a school, department, program, or course over a period of years must be looking for something other than profitability. The "something" is academic value—by which I mean intrinsic contribution to mission. In other words, the value derived from the program is worth the cost of its negative margin.

The long-term signals can best be seen by smoothing out the year-to-year changes in margin. Table 5.2 illustrates what ideally would be a moving average of net margin for each of USAU's six schools.[1] (Use of five years is a judgment call, but the idea is to allow time for

Table 5.2. Smoothed Estimates of Margin by School, USA University

	Arts and Sciences	Osteopathic Medicine	Architecture and Design
Revenue	$69,978	$63,608	$14,591
Expense	$56,926	$33,968	$15,685
Net Margin	$11,051	$29,640	($1,094)
Credit Hours	91,927	48,953	17,356
Margin/Credit Hour	$120	$605	($63)
	Engineering and Computer Science	Health Professions	Management
Revenue	$40,860	$17,500	$20,022
Expense	$29,274	$10,826	$22,876
Net Margin	$11,586	$6,673	($2,857)
Credit Hours	52,503	17,745	26,560
Margin/Credit Hour	$223	$376	($108)

adjustment to short-term variations.) Net margins are used because allocated university overhead should be viewed as a real cost when evaluating a school's resource consumption. The table also includes student credit hours and margin per credit hour. Credit hours don't measure research output, but they still can be used to scale margin to the school's resource base because departmental research tends to vary in rough proportion to the size of the teaching program.

The table provides an example of how data obtained from an AR model can be used in contexts not envisioned as part of the model's original development. Such displays can be added to the model, but for infrequently used relationships it's better to simply download the relevant data to Excel and construct the desired spreadsheet model. The data suggest that USAU (which is assumed to be well run) has made a considered decision to cross-subsidize the Art and Architecture and Management Schools from surpluses generated elsewhere.[2] This kind of result becomes even more meaningful when one looks at the data for individual departments or academic programs.

This decision can be expected to persist over time, absent significant shifts in the university's markets, cost structure, or sense of mission. The not-for-profit model tells us that the cross-subsidies are ethically as well as legally acceptable. In fact, it's the way universities assert their not-for-profit missions in opposition to short-term market forces. This is an essential characteristic of a traditional university—the same one that justifies the favorable tax treatment of gifts, real estate, and endowment returns that are used to further the university's academic purposes. Universities should not hesitate to disclose these data. They should be prepared to defend their decisions or change them if there is sufficient reason to do so. At the very least, knowledge about relative margins will generate lively and perhaps eventually constructive conversations among deans and faculty.

Faculty Effort

In chapter 1, I mentioned the concern that successive curricular redesigns can result in unsustainable faculty workloads, and in chapter 4 of *Reengineering the University* I described how successive budget cuts can do the same thing. The common thread in these examples is that the effort required from faculty can drift up, slowly but steadily, as the result of small operational and policy adjustments that aren't focused on workload at all. It's like the frog in the pail of water on a hot stove. The frog isn't impaired at the beginning but doesn't jump out because the changes are imperceptibly small. It simply hunkers down and adapts to change after change—until eventually it loses its ability to function. Equipping the frog with a thermometer and the ability to use it would allow problem-solving before the situation becomes debilitating. One of the important tasks in budget-making is to get the right-sized faculty and allocate or reallocate positions so that workloads remain reasonably balanced across departments in light of their respective missions.

How Much Faculty Effort is Required and for What Purposes?

The amount of effort required can be estimated from the data described in chapter 4: specifically, information on teaching assignments, class durations, out-of-class teaching profiles, and expectations for effort distributions. The dashboard in figure 5.3 unpacks the estimated amount of work required for teaching in the USAU College of Arts and Sciences. The bars in the left-hand panel show the total hours required for each task in the course profile, together with the number of hours supplied by each type of faculty. Preparation requires twice as much time as actual teaching, with the other tasks requiring smaller amounts. These results depend on judgmental information supplied to the model, which is summed over the mix of courses actually being taught. What may be more surprising is the heavy dependence on adjunct faculty for everything except course development. This may be something the university will wish to watch closely over time.

The three pie charts at the bottom of the figure partition total hours according to department, course level, and faculty type. Clicking on a pie slice changes the bar graph to reflect that particular pop-

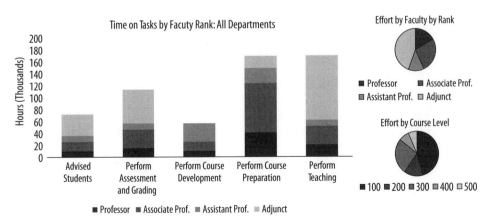

Figure 5.3. Faculty Effort for Teaching-Related Tasks

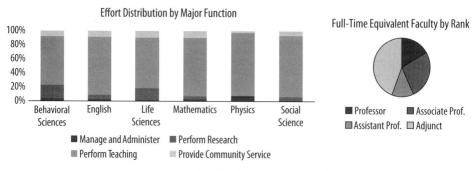

Figure 5.4. Distribution of Faculty Effort

ulation. This allows the user to drill down on interesting results without losing his or her train of thought. The model also can produce data for two- and three-way combinations (e.g., by department, course level, and teacher type), but this cannot be displayed on the USAU dashboard.

Figure 5.4 extends the analysis to include research, administration, and public service. The bars in the upper panel show the percentage effort, in total and for a few select departments. (The actual dashboard includes all departments.) USAU doesn't do a lot of research, but it is important for a few departments. The pie chart at the left shows the breakdown of FTE faculty. Clicking on one of those slices shifts the upper bars to reflect that particular population. The two figures give decision makers a big leg up on understanding how much faculty effort is required and for what purposes.

Comparing the Supply and Demand for Faculty Time

Having estimated the demand for faculty time, a logical next step is to compare it with the supply. That calculation is relatively simple: multiply the number of faculty FTEs by one's chosen standard workweek figure multiplied by the number of weeks in the academic year. (See chapter 4 for a discussion of this estimate.) The result for the College of Arts and Sciences is a deficit of about 19,000 hours, which is about 6 percent of the supply.

Demand (hours required)	331,000
Supply (hours available)	292,000
Imbalance (excess or deficit)	−19,000
Percent of supply	6%

Figure 5.5 shows these results for a few selected departments. Clicking on the right-hand chart displays data for the selected semester.

Deficits up to, say, 25 percent of supply may simply reflect a normal professorial workweek of more than forty hours, so they won't be cause for alarm in most situations. Significantly larger percentages should trigger on-the-ground investigation. The same is true for significant surpluses. The comparisons are available for each department or other faculty-employing unit, and for rollups to higher levels.

Workload metrics based on a full-function AR model provide more information than the student credit hours per faculty full-time equivalent (SCH/FFTE) measure currently used at many institutions. For example, it includes all the effort that goes into teaching: contact hours, the noncontact hours associated with assigned sections, and noncontact hours that vary directly with student head counts. It takes account of charge-outs to sponsored research and expectations for service and departmental research. And, because the underlying data and linkages are transparent, department chairs, faculty, and others can satisfy themselves that the measure is indeed meaningful—or present an informed case that the assumptions should be changed. Typically, the earliest stages of model usage are characterized more by the challenge and correction of assumptions than by substantive conclusions, but the emphasis shifts over time as the assumptions are honed and confidence in the model grows.

Academic resourcing decision makers should deal with workload imbalances, but that's not the whole story. Zemsky and Shaman's *Making Sense of the College Curriculum* suggests that faculty themselves should become more aware of the effects of curricular and enrollment changes on their workloads.[3] They should help solve such problems on their own rather than (or more likely in addition to)

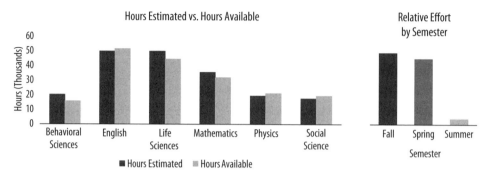

Figure 5.5. Supply and Demand for Faculty Effort

asking deans and provosts for more money. (To be realistic, professors will be sensitive to overloads, whereas potential slack will be interesting mainly to deans and provosts.) Workload creep applies particularly to the design of curricula, so the AR model's workload supply-and-demand data should be of interest to curriculum committees as well as department chairs and individual faculty.

Departmental Research

Departmental research comprises a significant portion of faculty effort in many universities. Accounting systems consider this time to be part of teaching, if for no other reason than they don't contain the data needed to separate it out. Whether this unfunded effort is a necessary element of teaching (a pure "joint product" in economic terms) is subject to debate. AR models take no position on this question, but the faculty profiles described in chapter 4 do allow estimation of the unfunded research effort in each department. For example, figure 5.4 includes data on the percentage of time that faculty of each rank and each department are estimated to spend on departmental research. These data can be reported externally as part of either teaching or research, but there are strong reasons to treat it as research for purposes of institutional decision-making. Failure to do so fundamentally compromises one's ability to understand faculty effort and thus to develop coherent research strategies.

The data on unfunded research and scholarship aid academic re-sourcing managers in three ways. As noted, the first refers to the distribution of faculty effort. Astute deans and chairs will think hard about what faculty are expected to do. This is important for morale, recruiting, and retention because professors care a great deal about how they spend their time. The AR model displays estimates for all the elements of faculty time utilization: teaching contact and out-of-class effort as well as sponsored and unsponsored research. To lump unsponsored research with teaching fundamentally distorts the real situation.

I've noted that these percentages are based on policies or estimates, but that's sufficient for estimating the supply-demand imbalance. Research is one of the things that may be shortchanged if the imbalances are large. (The other is class preparation time.) This provides another reason for paying attention to the departmental faculty effort deficits if the university maintains significant research expectations.

Gauging the institution's research footprint in a given discipline provides a second reason for unbundling departmental research. One cannot have meaningful conversations about research strategy without doing so. Financial reports on sponsored research projects do not provide a full picture of an institution's research activity. Few such projects occur in the humanities and softer social sciences, yet it is wrong to say that most universities do nothing by way of research and scholarship in those fields. The problem, of course, is that such reports don't include departmental research. Chapter 4 described how identifying departmental research as a separate activity category contributes to the development of a university's research strategy. That subject is of great importance, but I won't revisit it here.

The third reason for unbundling departmental research is to determine whether teaching subsidizes research or vice versa. This is a politically fraught question for many public universities. They know that research is important both intrinsically and as a means of acquiring and retaining good faculty, but they find it difficult to convince governors and legislators of this fact. Sometimes they try to duck the problem by refusing to collect data that might bear on the cross subsidy. This is shortsighted. Without sustained and evidence-based conversations with political stakeholders, research universities will face increasing pressure based on the body politics' worst-case fears. One may doubt the viability of such conversations in a charged political environment where facts too often are denied or weaponized in support of preconceived ideas, but taking a know-nothing attitude exposes the sector to existential problems over the long run.

AR models can estimate the cross-subsidies to or from research with reasonable accuracy, but they don't answer the question, essential for the political discourse mentioned earlier, about whether research should be viewed as a separate activity or a necessary adjunct to teaching. Doubtless the answer will vary by field and circumstance. Higher education needs to accumulate a body of experience and analysis in this area, and then communicate it effectively outside the institution. Looking at the relevant data is necessary for doing these things.

Courses and Course Instances

What can be done if there is a supply-demand imbalance for faculty effort, or if one is anticipated due to impending enrollment changes or budget resizing? Rethinking tuition rates, fund-raising, and so forth is always an option, but it is becoming increasingly clear that universities also need to address their own "teaching production" processes. Once again, the full-function AR model provides the data needed to begin this process. These data pertain mainly to courses and course instances.

Such analyses represent mostly uncharted territory. Academics have become accustomed to working with summary information at the department level or higher and commissioning special studies in response to specific problems. They rarely see data at the course level, let alone data for particular course instances. But course-by-course data have great value. Many of the levers for achieving change in teaching are attached to courses. Treating courses as black boxes excludes such changes from consideration. Academic resourcing managers have not been actively calling for course-level data, but, as occurred with Steve Jobs and the iPhone, it seems likely that their newfound availability will create its own demand.

Alternative Delivery Options

One lever for intervention relates to the ways course material is delivered to students and their implications for costs and margins. To address this, we must distinguish among three different dimensions of the delivery process.

- *When*: semester or quarter/academic year
- *How*: face-to-face, online, blended, or contracted to external parties
- *Where*: campus/city, state, or country

Department chairs and other decision makers must work across these dimensions in a kind of three-dimensional chess game. I illustrate data pertaining to each dimension.

WHEN A COURSE INSTANCE IS OFFERED

Decisions about when to offer a course arise frequently in departmental planning. Suppose a course has good enrollments in the fall and spring semesters but loses money due to small enrollments in the summer. One question one might ask is whether most of the summer enrollments are by students who need the course to complete their degrees, or whether they are electives taken by students in other programs or institutions. The financial consequences of closing the course will be different depending on the answer, and one also should consider the effect of closure on the degree students' progress toward their awards.

Appendix A analyzes the financial implications under the heading of "Cost Savings from Eliminating a Course Instance." The illustration has been simplified, but it points the way to the kind of analysis that can be performed using data from a full-function AR model. To summarize briefly, closure of an instance with one student changes the course's margin from negative \$2,298 to positive \$781 if the student reenrolls in the fall or spring, or \$738 if he or she does not reenroll at all. (These figures may seem small, but they become more significant when the number of students is larger.) The result depends on the availability of capacity in the fall or spring semesters, which is another datum provided by the model. One can do these analyses by using Excel on a one-off basis. AR models provide the means to do them on a routine basis, to the point where the trade-offs become second nature to the people who schedule courses.

HOW THE MATERIAL IS DELIVERED

Another familiar question pertains to whether the material is delivered face-to-face, online, or in some kind of blended format. Decisions about mode are driven by academic considerations, costs, and the numbers and locations of interested students. I will mention only one of these now: the cost of delivery.

Table 5.3 shows the cost per credit hour for in-person, blended, and online delivery at USAU's College of Arts and Sciences. These data cover all courses in the college, but they are easily stratified according to teaching department, course level, and other attributes. The costs are interesting in and of themselves, and comparing them across schools and over time will produce even better conversations.

As in all analyses of the cost of online versus in-person teaching, the matter of learning quality should be considered carefully. It may be desirable, for example, to get data on group or class sizes, teacher types, and other detailed course attributes. This is something the AR model can usually accommodate. In the end, of course, there is no substitute for ground-level analysis of learning—including the measurement of relative value added, where possible.[4]

Table 5.3. Cost per Credit Hour by Delivery Method

Delivery Method	Cost per Credit Hour
In-Person	\$663
Blended	\$514
Online	\$190

My original illustration of course instances, back in table 4.2, showed the "where" effect clearly, even though I didn't comment on it at the time. USAU is challenged by the fact that it teaches courses at an urban and a suburban campus (as well as at some foreign locations). Perhaps there are important reasons for maintaining the two domestic venues, but there's no doubt that this boosts teaching cost. For example, the data show that ACCT 12 is taught in the spring and fall semesters on both campuses. There may be good reasons for this, but the separation by campus has brought the average fall class size down to only four students. Combining the two instances would have produced a more respectable eight students. The situation in the spring was a little better, but still the two campuses enrolled a total of only nineteen students.

What seems unusual in this case is that, while separate, the campuses are within commuting distance of each other, and, further, that the delivery has been coded as distance learning. One of the objectives of distance learning is to reduce the friction of space, so it's not clear why the courses are taught separately. Perhaps the course has some DL and some F2F components and should have been coded as "blended," but even if this is true, combining the F2F sessions would not have been impossible. Or, depending on the course design, offering just the F2F sessions on the two campuses might save money without compromising learning. The model had not been in use very long when the illustrative data were extracted, so it's possible that one of these options has been implemented by now.

Differences by Course Level

Everyone knows that upper-level courses tend to cost more than lower-level ones, and that science courses tend to cost more than, say, humanities courses. But few institutions understand the particular patterns or effects on margin associated with these differences. Having data for all courses across the institution allows one to become

familiar with these patterns and effects. Among other things, this will
prove valuable when predicting the financial effects of boosting student persistence rates and deciding whether to enroll more or fewer
transfer students.

Table 5.4 presents cost per credit hour at different course levels
for the departments within USAU's College of Arts and Sciences.
(Blanks mean the department offered no courses at the indicated
level.) These are total costs, but the figures exclusive of overheads
also could be used. As might be expected, cost tends to rise for the
more advanced courses—probably because of smaller average class
sizes and use of more senior faculty. Some departments are systematically costlier than others: for example, fine arts, which is taught
mostly in a studio setting. The very high costs for 400-level communication arts and English courses are something of an anomaly. The
arts and sciences dean may know why this is true, but it might well
be worth drilling down to the individual courses in these and other
interesting categories. Breaking courses down by course level will be
especially helpful for universities that benchmark their costs against
other institutions.

Course-level reports on margin per credit hour, and on cost and
margin per FTE faculty member, also can be obtained on a routine
basis. Margin per credit hour reflects revenue and financial aid differentials, which may well drive, or be driven by, cost differences.
Cost per FTE faculty member is one of the metrics often cited by pro-
ponents of benchmarking, and though it can be misleading if used
by itself, it certainly is worth tracking.

Enrollment Slack and Marginal Cost

The AR model for teaching activity reports the number of sections,
by type, on an instance-by-instance basis. Accommodating a few new
students in a section with unused capacity incurs only the per-student
costs (e.g., grading). At some point, however, adding more students
will require extra sections and incur the extra cost that entails. Determining section capacity is more of an art than a science, but it is

Table 5.4. Average Cost per Credit Hour by Course Level and Department

Course Level	School Overall	Behavioral Sciences	Communications Arts	English	Fine Arts	Life Sciences	Mathematics	Physics	Social Sciences
All Levels	$637	$421	$803	$536	$1,136	$591	$545	$608	$554
100	$547	$401	$774	$541	$1,283	$500	$541	$620	$523
200	$628	$445	$759	$427	$1,216	$589	$521	$508	$649
300	$576	$415	$891	$529	$1,265	$617	$592		$525
400	$868	$433	$1,171	$1,192	$1,510	$686	$768		
500	$590								
600	$738		$749		$709				
700	$669		$636		$787				
800	$109				$169				

important for understanding marginal cost at the course instance level. (Sometimes analysts use the term "incremental cost" instead of "marginal cost," but the two mean the same thing.) This is especially true when, as may well be the case, policy or professorial preferences trump classroom seating capacity as the limiting factor. This means that faculty conversations about capacity are well worth having: for example, to better understand the effect of class size on learning quality for different modes of teaching. Conclusions from these conversations can be entered as "capacities" in the relevant course profiles.

Unused capacity represents "enrollment slack," defined as the number of empty classroom seats or online slots that could be filled without materially changing the nature or quality of instruction. The relation between slack and the marginal cost of enrollment is not difficult to understand. Adding to enrollment eventually will require the addition of new sections, which adds a step function to cost. Hence a course's calculated marginal cost will depend both on its initial enrollment and the amount of slack given the number of sections currently offered. Having some slack confers desirable flexibility, but too much represents waste and inefficiency.[5] Academic resourcing managers need to consider enrollment slack as well as educational content and quality.

New class sections are added when new enrollments strain the capacity of existing ones. Very large enrollment increases require so many new sections that the initial level of slack becomes unimportant. In this case, the marginal cost per enrollment will approach the course's average variable cost (~direct cost divided by enrollment). As a general rule, one should look at enrollment slack when considering the elimination of particular course instances, but it's safe to ignore it when considering whether to upsize or downsize whole programs. The full-function AR predictive models discussed in chapter 6 can be configured to handle this housekeeping automatically, without the need for supplementary analytics.

It's conventional to assume that all overhead costs are fixed, but this can be misleading. First, overheads obviously will tend to increase or decrease with significant changes in the university's scale of operations. Adding many students will require the addition of student services personnel, for example, even though a few extra students probably won't overload the existing staff. The general situation is complicated, however. There's only one president no matter how many students are enrolled, but the president's staff may increase somewhat. Ferreting out these relationships requires special analysis. This analysis is not included in most historical AR models, but, as noted in chapter 6, it can be incorporated in predictive models.

Candidates for Course Reconfiguration, Redesign, or Elimination

Reconfiguration, redesign, and elimination of courses involve more radical change than narrow decisions about a few low-enrollment instances as described earlier. By reconfiguration I mean rethinking the arrangement of when, where, and how the course instances are offered, whereas redesign requires a deep dive into how content is delivered within each instance. Eliminating a whole course means excising all its instances from the department's list of offerings. All these options have implications for the curriculum, so any changes must be made with knowledge about all programs that rely on the course—a subject that's taken up in the next section.

These decisions usually are made on a comparative basis. This means one should scan the department's whole list of offerings before focusing on a single course. "Waterfall charts" like the one illustrated in figure 5.6 for USAU's physics department can be used to one's advantage here. The courses' margins are sorted in descending order and arrayed cumulatively across the chart, above their course numbers. (A color rendering would show the positive margins of the left-hand courses as green and the right-hand ones as red.) The last bar, zero in this case, shows the department's overall margin. The chart allows one to see at a glance where a given course fits into the departmental profile. As with the other charts, hovering one's mouse over a bar gives the margin's exact value.

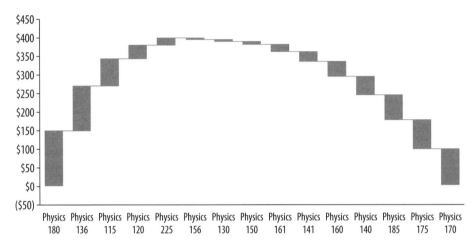

Figure 5.6. Waterfall Chart for Physics Teaching Margins at USAU

Course Instances as Scaffolds for Organizing Ancillary Data

Relating the fine structure of teaching activity to variables other than revenue, cost, and margin is largely uncharted territory. Specialists have made progress at the micro level (e.g., relating data on computer-mediated teaching methods to particular learning outcomes). These analyses are more granular than the course instances used in AR models. But there also are opportunities for analyses at the course instance level.[6] Most universities have more data available than meets the eye but don't organize it in an effective way. Better ways of organizing and using the information might well stimulate the creation of more and better data.

Some AR models already track the fraction of students who withdraw from courses before the end of the semester, and a few also track student grades. Some institutions use the "WFD" metric (the fraction of students withdrawing or getting an F or a D) in describing certain courses, and there is no reason why WFD can't be tracked at the instance level. This metric may reflect course design and/or teacher effectiveness (as well as student characteristics of course), and thus is worth watching for that reason. Another application is to post faculty-developed learning quality measures to their respective course instance records as discussed under chapter 7's learning quality rubric. Fine-structure data at the course instance level would allow one to correlate variables such as class type and size, adjunct usage, distance learning, and blended learning with performance variables.

Expanding the course instance record to include more data on student characteristics and performance need not be long in coming. What's required is the ability to release student data for this kind of analysis. Examples include admissions information on academic and nonacademic preparation, race or ethnicity, year in program, and location of residence prior to matriculation (perhaps down to the zip code). Today's models tag students' current residence for purposes of tuition determination, but that is limited in scope. What's needed for general application are more flexible and efficient systems for multidimensional dataset management.[7] Technical progress is rapid in this space, and AR modelers will be quick to adopt the new approaches—to speed up and simplify calculations as well as for the reasons given earlier. The new models also will permit the calculation of revenue and margin, both gross and net of financial aid, by program for any subset of the student population.

Solving the dimensionality problem also will allow academic resourcing decisions to relate teaching activities in one course to student performance in subsequent courses, again at the level of individual instances. Imagine being able to click on a course instance and see the WFD performance distribution of its students in downstream courses, for example. Couple this with the availability of student characteristics, and one could explore the performance of any student subgroup. As noted, these capabilities are not practical now, but they will come in the not-too-distant future.

Degree and Other Teaching Programs

Programs present the institution's face to the educational marketplace. Items 2 and 3 in the prologue point out that provosts and deans must repeatedly examine the size of programs in relation to changes in market demand. It notes that "a daunting 48 percent of [programs] turn out ten or fewer graduates per year and collectively account for only 7 percent of all degrees." While this certainly does not mean that all low-enrollment programs should go on the chopping block, it can't be denied that the health of a university's internal economy depends on a reasonable balancing of program capacities with student demand.

Such balancing may involve the adjustment of admissions targets and financial aid policies, but it also requires a deep dive into why the programs cost what they do. For example, money-losing programs can sometimes be returned to viability by eliminating unnecessary costs. Finally, decision makers need estimates of what costs will (or will not) be saved if a program is downsized or, conversely, the extra costs that will be incurred if enrollments increase. Answering these questions requires visibility into the courses that students take as they work toward the degree in question.

It is an unfortunate fact that data available in a typical university don't support the kind of thinking just described. Accounting systems do not collect data on a program-by-program basis. While special studies can be performed, this does not make the data available on the regular basis needed to keep an institution's degree programs operating efficiently and in balance with demand.

But AR models do. Full-function AR models provide excellent windows for examining the courses associated with particular degrees and then aggregating the results to gain insight about the degrees themselves. The models I discuss consider every course taken by a student in a given program as being "associated" with that degree, whether it is a specific requirement, part of the distribution requirement, or an elective. Other definitions are, of course, possible. For instance, any full-function AR model can be modified to accept a list of required courses for each program and report separately for that subset. It also may be desirable to report on courses that, though not strictly required, are closely associated with the program—as, for example, when they are listed as recommended options.[8]

Any analysis that can be done for a particular course, department, school, and so on also can be done for a program. The next section describes how the process works and how provosts and deans (and also, effectively, program directors) can use it for planning, budget-making, and other kinds of decisions. We also will see how the course-level analysis abscesses described in earlier sections become more focused when approached in the context of particular programs rather than through the lens of the departments that teach them.

Cross-Walking between Programs and Their Associated Courses

The first requirement is to provide a flexible interface for working back and forth between the data for programs and courses. The USAU model includes a dashboard that enables seamless transfers from programs to courses and vice versa. I can't demonstrate that interaction on a printed page, but table 5.5 gives a taste of how this works.

Imagine you work for USAU's dean of arts and sciences and have been asked to dig into the BS program in biology. (We shall see in chapter 7 that periodic reviews of this kind are desirable even if there is no clear and present problem.) The first thing you see on opening the dashboard is a list of all the college's degree programs. A portion of that list is shown in the top panel of the table. Note that the "Total for all programs," in the top panel, shows that the college teaches 48,043 credit hours at an average cost of $684 per credit hour, and that this teaching generates a positive margin of almost $1.9 million.

The table's middle panel initially shows six of the many courses offered by the college, but clicking on "BS Biology" narrows the list to courses associated with that degree. "Associated with" means enrolling at least one of the program's students, regardless of whether the enrollment fulfills a requirement or is an elective. The data include overall student head counts as well as credit hours, plus the margins generated overall (for the instance) and for just the students enrolled in BS biology. (The head counts and credit hours for those students are not shown in this particular table, but they could easily be included on the dashboard.) The bottom line for this panel (after narrowing the list) shows that biology generates 686 enrollments and

Table 5.5. Illustrative Programs and Course Instances

Program (for CAS)	Credit Hours	Cost/ Credit	Net Margin
...	...	...	...
BS Behavioral Sciences	582	$490	$104,459
BS Biology	**2,374**	**$566**	**$117,894**
BS Chemistry	204	$628	$89,913
...	...	...	...
Total for All Programs	48,043	$684	$1,886,335

Course Instances for BS Biology	Campus/ Semester	Head Count	Credit Hours	Cost/ Credit	Net Margin Overall	Net Margin BS Biology
...						
Biology 110	(2-Spring)	63	252	$542	$22,801	$5,889
Biology 150	**(1-Fall)**	**18**	**72**	**$1,107**	**($24,699)**	**($2,233)**
Biology 150	**(1-Spring)**	**21**	**84**	**$812**	**($7,541)**	**($3,294)**
Biology 150	(2-Fall)	67	268	$507	$24,907	
Biology 150	(2-Spring)	139	556	$479	$73,552	$5,212
Biology 210	(1-Spring)	21	84	$778	$2,612	$2,247
...			...			...
Total for BS Biology		686	2,374	$566		$117,894

Program (for the two shaded instances of Biology 150)	Credit Hours	Cost/ Credit	Net Margin
BS Biology (CAS): Fall	4	$1,107	($2,233)
BS Life Sciences (CAS): Fall	64	$1,107	($20,996)
BS Computer Science (SECS): Fall	4	$1,107	($1,500)
BS Biology (CAS): Spring	24	$812	($3,294)
BS Life Sciences (CAS): Spring	48	$812	($1,705)
BS Computer Science (SECS): Spring	4	$812	($29)
BS Psychology (CAS): Spring	8	$812	($2,513)

2,374 credit hours. The average cost is $566 per credit hour, and the total margin is $117,894. Biology seems to be doing all right financially, but could it do better?

Analysis at the course instance level is a big help here. Take a look at the four instances of Biology 150 shown in the middle panel. Their cost per credit hour ranges from $479 to $1,107. These two instances cost the college $32,400, of which $5,527 is attributable to the BS in biology. Perhaps unsurprisingly, the money-losers both have low enrollments, and both occur on Campus 1. This particular table doesn't get to the level of course configuration or teacher type, but it's a simple matter to change dashboards and compare these instances' details with the rest of Biology 150. What we *can* do with the present dashboard, however, is examine the programs associated with the two high-cost course instances with an eye to merging the two instances.

The new program data, displayed in the bottom portion of table 5.5, were obtained by clicking successively on the two instances and recording the results. We see that both instances cater mainly to the BS in life sciences, another College of Arts and Sciences program, and that the BS in biology also has a strong representation in the spring semester. We'll need to consider the effect of merging the two sections on these students' ability to progress toward their programs, but one shouldn't automatically rule out the possibility of eliminating one of the two instances. The enrollments from the School of Engineering and Computer Science and the College of Arts and Sciences' BS in psychology probably represent electives, and thus shouldn't raise student progression issues. I've worked with many deans during my career who would be interested in a $30,000 recurring savings, at least to the point of asking a staff member to test the merger possibility with the involved faculty members.

One doesn't need a powerful model to do the analysis described earlier if, and this is a big if, one knows where to look for the possibility of savings. My point, as with so many illustrations in this book, is that having a model vastly facilitates the search for such possibilities. One is looking for needles in haystacks, but, while one might rely on serendipity or luck, it's better to have a powerful magnet—or in this case a model. My experience suggests that there are many such needles. Finding them reduces the need for common but ill-informed and potentially disruptive actions like "eliminate all course instances with fewer than X enrollments."

A Note on Benchmarking and Research

Questions about the relative cost of various degree programs have interested decision makers and researchers for decades, and many approaches have been advanced and implemented. For example, state higher education boards sometimes fund universities based on courses offered or degrees produced, with relative cost coefficients obtained by some process of empirical estimation. The governments of England, Hong Kong, and other countries have been doing the same since at least the 1970s. Growing interest in productivity within colleges and universities is giving the issue new life, yet controversy remains about how best to do the needed research.

To my knowledge, a 2018 working paper by Steven W. Hemelt and colleagues for the National Bureau of Economic Research represents the current state of the art.[9] This paper uses what the authors correctly describe as "novel department-level data" from the Delaware Cost Study to construct an econometric model for explaining differences across field in cost per credit hour. The abstract states that "costs vary widely across fields, ranging from electrical engineering (109% higher costs than English) to math (22% lower)." The paper is pathbreaking because it is the first to use such data and also due to the rigor and care of the econometric analysis. Hopefully the work will stimulate more analyses using the Delaware department-level data, which is much better suited to program-level analysis than to anything available in the Integrated Postsecondary Education Data System (IPEDS). The potential for using these data to assist in benchmarking is clear, and I hope schools will avail themselves of this opportunity.

Nevertheless, department-level data has some distinct limitations when it comes to program analysis. There are two reasons. The first, the one cited often in this book, is that a deep understanding of costs depends on getting to the fine structure of activity: that is, on descriptions of what's actually happening at the coalface of teaching. Econometrics based on departmental aggregations give us clues about differences but don't get very far toward explaining them. They also may be vulnerable to variations in the departments' research intensity and thus raise the issue of whether departmental research should be considered as a "cost of teaching" or not. I've covered these points elsewhere and will not repeat those arguments here.

The other issue concerns the nature of courses and programs. Most but not all departments have undergraduate majors, and some have graduate programs as well. Many also do service teaching. For example, most English departments spend the lion's share of their energy teaching English and writing for majors elsewhere in the university. The Hemelt et al. paper sidesteps this problem by characterizing itself as measuring the cost of *teaching courses* in different departments rather than the cost of *programs* such as math and English. Program cost is more relevant for many purposes, however, and it's worth noting that the costs for programs include the costs of courses taken outside the major.

AR models provide good estimates of program cost. They can differentiate between the cost of courses within the major and those outside the major. This often produces surprises, as illustrated with the nursing example in chapter 2. Full-function AR models also describe the structure of teaching activities. All of these things enable more meaningful benchmarks than are available from aggregate department-level data, and in the long run they also will prove more valuable for research purposes.

CHAPTER SIX

Predictive Models and Scenario Planning

Forward planning is one of the most important things a university can do. It enables certain future opportunities and forecloses others, and over the long run it determines the institution's strategic directions and performance. So far, I've considered the application of academic resourcing models to mostly short-term operating and budget decisions. These exercises drive the core functions of a university, but the decisions will be myopic if they are not embedded in a broader conception of the institution and its aspirations. This chapter embeds the short-term decisions into a longer-term planning and budgeting paradigm.

The paradigm involves explicit consideration of

- the university as it is and its probable future environment,
- the university as it would like to become, and
- how the university can best get from here to there.

The first element requires a holistic view of the institution's current status and prospects. This begins with qualitative insights about its academic values, prospects, and concerns—perhaps informed by a formal strengths, weaknesses, opportunities, and threats (SWOT) analysis. I believe SWOTs can be useful, even though research warns us that the outcomes are "never used in any meaningful way."[1] Embedding SWOTs in an AR modeling environment will help solve this problem.

SWOT thinking is not new, but it's not sufficient, either. Any such analysis must be "reduced to practice" by quantifying the evidence and forward-looking assumptions about operations, markets, and finances. We've already seen how AR historical models can quantify information about past activities so they can be assessed against the university's mission, markets, and requirements for financial sustainability. Now it's time to see how AR predictive models can do the same for an institution's forward-looking assumptions.

Envisioning the University's Future

To do a good job of imagining the future, one must think outside the box while retaining an evidence-based grounding in what is both meaningfully probable and operationally and financially feasible. The first consideration refers to creative thought. One searches for ideas more broadly than in day-to-day problem-solving and then uses the results to generate insights and connections with yet more ideas—repeating the process until a satisfactory set of actionable hypotheses has been fashioned and/or the time and energy available for the exercise have been exhausted. The second consideration tests the hypotheses through data analysis, critical conversation, and the application of informed common sense. The two parts must coexist in a delicate balance. Creative but unmoored ideas can lead to disaster, but too much analysis and criticism stifles creativity.

Getting Outside the Box . . . But Not Too Far

The boundaries between creativity and analytics are permeable, but they are also real. Consider the "new industrial legends" of how Steve Jobs and Elon Musk stretched their envelopes, for example.[2] Steve conceived the iPhone without marketplace precedents, yet he brought to bear a career's worth of insight and experience about how people could and would use a mobile device that had not yet been invented. He set cost targets that many judged to be unrealistic and wouldn't accept "can't do" from his engineers, yet the targets were, in fact, based on key items of evidence and proved (just) sufficiently realistic in the end.

Musk did (and does) essentially the same thing—but on steroids. Both SpaceX and Tesla have had near-death experiences driven by his willingness to push things to extremes, possibly beyond the breaking point. The two companies' cost estimates and delivery schedules have been incredibly aggressive but not irresponsible. They generally are grounded in the best data and analysis available, and the risk they embody is due to outsize but worthwhile goals rather than a failure of analytics. Universities should take these lessons to heart. It can be worthwhile to take risks when striving for aggressive goals, but there's no excuse for "winging it" when it comes to data and analysis. Indeed, the more aggressive the goal, the more important it is to avoid ungrounded and wishful thinking about operational and financial factors.

The breakout of Stanford University from a very good regional institution to a world-class research university provides a case in point. I arrived on campus in the 1960s, after the breakout but while its echoes still reverberated. President Wallace Sterling and Provost Frederick Terman had acted on very big ideas about what Stanford could become, and they were able to enlist foundations and donors, as well as key members of the university community, in the effort to "get from here to there." No holistic university model was available to guide the quantitative elements of their thinking, but the moves were of a type that could be analyzed using the tools of the day. This was aided immeasurably by the fact that Terman was an engineer with deep experience in both government laboratories and university academic management. He knew the difference between a dispassionate estimate, no matter how uncertain, and hopeful or self-serving guesswork.

One of my challenges as vice provost for research and vice president for business and finance in the 1970s was to consolidate loose ends left by the Sterling-Terman push forward. I could see the uncertainties they had faced and understood the risks taken, but nowhere in the records was there reason to doubt their commitment to evidence-based assessment. I have no doubt that the Stanford leadership team embraced whatever analytical capacity was available to support their planning. The university continued to do that when it pioneered the use of quantitative models during the 1970s.[3]

So just how does one get outside the box in the first place? It's hard to reconstruct the thinking process of a Jobs, Musk, Sterling, or Terman, but there are some rules of thumb that do seem to help. One is to build on the kinds of ideas that come up naturally in the annual budget process. What if we could boost student demand for this or that program, or a whole collection of programs, for example? What if we mounted a major cost-reducing exercise that eliminated all nonessential course instances with fewer than the break-even number of students and then used some of the savings to reduce teaching loads or adjunct faculty usage? What if we invested in new faculty lines to build a research program in X or Y or Z? What if . . . What if . . . What if?

Scanning through market data of the types discussed in chapter 7 also can produce actionable hypotheses. The program evaluation service offered by Gray Associates, examined there, provides a good example of what can be done. The service offers four deliverables:

1. comprehensive, current, and validated data on student demand, employment, and competition;
2. a custom scoring system to identify programs that fit your school;
3. campus- or market-specific scoring of every current and potential Integrated Postsecondary Education Data System (IPEDS) program in your current and potential markets; and
4. easy downloads so you can analyze the data in Excel.[4]

Gray combines the deliverables with a facilitated process that enables the faculty leadership team to understand the information, agree on a scoring system for program evaluation, and work together to select programs to "Start, Stop, Sustain, or Grow."[5] They recommend the evaluations be refreshed every few years to develop and sustain an optimal program portfolio strategy. The evaluations also fit neatly into the ideation process I'm describing here.

The aforementioned SWOT analysis provides a good framework for organizing both the internal and market data. The planner or planning team tries to identify as many factors as possible under each of the four rubrics. Data can be used to good advantage during this process, but it's less a matter of analysis than it is of stimulating creative thought. The mind connects a different set of thoughts and comes up with different insights when traversing a given thread than it does with a different framework or no framework at all. As in all exploratory processes, it's important to evaluate each insight against the available evidence and subject the results to the test of critical conversation, but the original identification is a matter of creativity. Actionable hypotheses will arise at each stage of the SWOT process, and these, too, can be tested through analysis and conversation.

Evaluation of Actionable Alternatives

AR predictive models can be game changers for evaluating actionable hypotheses developed during the ideation phase of SWOT analysis and planning. This is especially true for Pilbara's full-function (Level III) AR predictive model. Let's use one of the questions given earlier as an example of what such a model can do: "What if we mounted a major cost-reducing exercise that eliminated all nonessential course instances with fewer than the break-even number of students and then used part of the savings to reduce teaching loads or adjunct usage?" The consequences of doing this could be approximated with spreadsheets, but the process would be time-consuming and error-prone, and would produce less accurate results than those attainable with the AR predictive model. Furthermore, this probably would be only one of the actionable hypotheses generated by the ideation process. Building spreadsheets for all of them would be a daunting task that almost surely would force analytical shortcuts. Looking at combinations of the actionable hypotheses, which usually is a good idea, compounds the evaluation task even further.

Application of a predictive AR model is quite simple once the basic implementation is in place. (The predictive model is based on the historical model and thus is updated annually without reference to specific planning needs.) The steps are as follows:

1. Decide on a future year for which you want to target the evaluation. Usually this is three to five years out, which allows time to accomplish the desired transitions.
2. Forecast enrollments to the target year assuming the university continues business as usual. The model then uses internal procedures (described shortly) to distribute the projected enrollments to courses and course instances. Run the predictive model to generate a "base case" for the analysis.
3. Enter data for the changes desired by the chosen what-if question or develop a business rule to do so. The model then uses its internal procedures to calculate the consequences of these changes.
4. Run the predictive model to generate the dashboards described in chapter 4, which now will reflect your what-if hypothesis as applied to the target year. The dashboards will allow you to examine the operational and financial consequences of the proposed action in fine detail.

The last section of this chapter describes how to integrate the resulting data on costs, revenues, and margins into your existing financial planning and budgeting protocols.

The aforementioned list is just one example of an actionable hypothesis. The analyses in chapters 4 and 5 provide many others, as will the proposals for creating, upsizing, or downsizing programs that come from market scanning. The only requirement is that the hypothesis be stated in terms of unambiguous forecasts (especially for enrollments) and responding actions. This is not as onerous as one might think. In fact, it represents a highly desirable planning discipline.

Some hypotheses reflect potential long-term rather than short-term decisions. Planners sometimes call these "strategic initiatives." The predictive AR model can be used to evaluate them, too. For example, teams in Australia and Malaysia have used the Pilbara model in formulating responses to assumed government policy changes and funding cuts, changes in student demand, and other events that would upend the strategic environment.[6] Responses ranged from major realignment of programs and pricing policies to eliminating or consolidating campuses. Many of the actions were tested in combination with one another. The process of evaluating complex strategic actions has come to be called "scenario planning."[7]

Full-Function AR Predictive Models

To appreciate how Pilbara's full-function AR predictive model works in scenario planning, we must again peek under the model's hood. Less comprehensive AR predictive models work the same way but with a lower level of detail. The Pilbara predictive model is installed separately from its historical counterpart, but it can access all the historical data and structural relationships. (I expect the two models to be integrated eventually, but their current architecture and technology are not amenable to that.) What makes the predictive model different is that its analytical engine is configured so users can change some of the historical data in order to do what-if analyses. This may sound simple, but, in fact, it requires considerable modeling prowess.

Doing what-ifs requires predicting the operating decisions of departments and enrollment decisions of students if the changes being considered were implemented. Suppose, for example, that a dean or provost wants to test the consequences of a policy that would change large numbers of course instances. This requires more than simply counting the number of courses that would be affected. One needs to ask what the displaced students will do. (They may enroll in another instance of the same course, in a different course, or not at all.) What will happen to the class sizes in the courses that receive additional students, and how will departments decide when to open new sections as enrollments climb? What will happen as departments decide to open new course instances to meet the shifting enrollments? A good predictive model will resolve questions of this kind and other similar ones. Failure to do so risks unpleasant surprises when reality provides the ultimate test for the predictions. Worse, it deprives the models' users of the opportunity to think deeply about the consequences of their proposed policies.

I'll use three simple what-ifs to show how such a predictive model can work: (1) capping class sizes for existing course instances, (2) eliminating course instances with fewer than a certain number of enrollments, and (3) creating a new course instance in a particular semester or on a particular campus. Each process proceeds in two stages. First, the model uses internal "decision rules" to redistribute the historical enrollments among the newly configured list of course instances. (I'll assume for simplicity that enrollments remain constant overall, but that assumption can easily be relaxed.) Then the model calculates the number of sections required for each instance to see the new configuration's implications for staffing, costs, and margins. Other decision rules can be used to adjust overhead costs to large changes in student, faculty, and staff numbers.

Appendix A describes how these predictions can be structured. Extant Pilbara predictive model implementations do not follow all the logic exactly, but there is nothing to prevent it from doing so. Future predictive models probably will go further.

The decision rules to be described represent more than prowess in model building. They reflect real questions that provosts, deans, and other academic resource managers must answer if they are to predict the consequences of proposed actions. Such predictions often are not made explicitly, but they always lurk in the background and may become important in unexpected situations. A full-function AR predictive model automates the application of decision rules. This drives the incremental cost of testing almost to zero, which means that many more evidence-based predictions will be made.

Planning Scenario Examples

Scenario planning became popular in the 1970s as a way for businesses to think strategically about their futures. Typically, senior leaders develop a small number of narratives, called "scenarios," about how the future might unfold and how this might affect their company. Here's how a 2008 issue of *The Economist* describes the issues for which scenario planning would likely be useful. "The issue could be a narrow one: whether to make a particular investment, for example. Should a supermarket put millions into out-of-town megastores and their attendant car parks, or should it invest in secure websites and a fleet of vans to make door-to-door deliveries? Or it could be much wider: an American education authority, for instance, contemplating the impact of demographic change on the need for new schools. Will the aging of the existing population be counterbalanced by a rising level of immigration?"[8]

Like other commentators, I believe that stimulating conversation is scenario planning's secret sauce. The process brings leaders together for informed and structured consideration of issues, like the aforementioned, that they wouldn't normally think about. Staff members provide data and analysis, but the leaders themselves perform the heavy lifting. The importance of this interaction is underscored by the title of the "Bible" of the field: *Scenarios: The Art of Strategic Conversation*.[9] But as in so many areas we've been discussing, the conversations must be grounded in facts and analytics.

Another book on scenario planning describes that it is "a participative approach to strategy that [uses] diverse thinking and conversation . . . to shift how the external environment is perceived."[10] To this I would add that scenario planners also envision responses to the shifted scenarios as well as descriptions of them and assessments of their likelihood. However, the purpose of the exercise remains to stimulate and guide a multiperson planning process to coherent conclusions.

Speeches and articles about the idea's application to higher education began appearing in the 1990s. James B. Rieley, director of the Center for Continuous Quality Improvement at Milwaukee Area Technical College, provided an early example. He wrote in 1997 that the following kinds of eventualities, among others, can best be analyzed in terms of scenarios: enrollment increases or decreases, heightened or lessened competition, economic upturns or downturns, faculty limitations or unused faculty capacity, funding shortages or surpluses, anti- or pro-education legislation, technology advances, and changes in the need for certain degrees and skills. "By asking the question, 'what do you think the future holds in store for the institution?,'" he said, "a scenario planning team can begin to sort out what futures may be important to look at." In addition, the "richness of the conversation" is a key consideration in scenario planning. The goal is "not trying to predict the future. . . . We are trying to understand the potential futures that we might encounter."[11] Unfortunately, as he notes in a recent blog, the methodology has yet to achieve its potential in universities—which is a problem this chapter seeks to remedy.

Achieving the university's objectives requires leadership and commitment. The required judgments extend beyond the scope of any model, but effective modeling can amplify their effects. Let me emphasize that full-function AR predictive models like the one described here offer, for the first time ever, the ability to perform detailed simulations of significant elements of university operations. Their use resolves the question of whether scenarios should be constructed from the bottom up, usually based mainly on anecdotal considerations, or from the top down, based on principles and central plans.[12] Having a good model allows one to start from both ends and meet in the middle. Among its other advantages, the model can be used to police the consistency of the two approaches. The resulting conversations will help sharpen thinking, coalesce leadership and commitment, and diffuse the vision and plan more widely within the university. I won't dwell on these points, but they should be understood as always lying in the background.

Now it's time to unpack the scenario planning idea and illustrate its use in conjunction with a full-function AR predictive model. Reduced to its essence, scenario planning links envisioned changes in the university's external and/or internal environment ("uncontrollables"), which might materially impact its markets, operations, or financial results, with choices the university might make in response to the envisioned changes ("controllables"). Every run of the predictive model combines both sets of assumptions. Which variables are controllable depends on context—that is, on the scenario being constructed. The model treats the controllable and uncontrollable variables in the same, but the scenario planning conversations depend critically on getting the distinction right.

What remains is to decide on the time frame for applying the predictive model. It's tempting to look at immediate effects, but this doesn't allow for changes that take time to work themselves out. One could run the model for every year of an assumed transition period, but making all the needed assumptions would be an impossible task. What does work is to run the model for a "steady-state" year, where the planning horizon is far enough in the future to allow for transition effects but close enough to predict with reasonable clarity. We'll see that the exact planning horizon doesn't matter much, but setting it at five years provides a common reference point for conversation. The last section of this chapter shows how to handle the transition period and integrate the steady-state results with the university's multiyear financial plan.

The following subsections present examples of how a full-function AR predictive model can ground scenario planning conversations in meaningful data and analysis. The examples are organized around important academic issues rather than the myriad of other factors that affect resourcing decisions. The discussion, which mostly is in narrative form, draws heavily on previous descriptions of how the Pilbara predictive model works. I hope these narratives will convey the qualitative considerations that should go into university planning as well as the technical aspects of the process.

Cope with Revenue Shortfalls

The first narrative deals with revenue shortfalls. This is not the happiest application of scenario planning, but, when the situation arises, it is a very important one. Every university faces the problem from time to time, and many have developed protocols for dealing with it. Use of scenario planning in conjunction with an AR predictive model expands the range of planning alternatives that can be

considered and, importantly, allows provosts, deans, and other academic decision makers to better understand the consequences of each
alternative.

It happens that scenario planning was the context in which I
learned firsthand about the power of Pilbara's full-function AR
predictive model. Working with Pilbara and the University of Melbourne's L. H. Martin Institute a few years ago, I team-taught a
group of Australian university academic leaders in a program called
Leading Universities. The program showed how model-based scenario planning can be used to cope with two then current concerns
in the country's higher education sector. After an initial orientation
and case discussion, we divided the group into teams to develop planning scenarios and structure what-if analyses, to use the model for
scenario evaluation, and to report conclusions based on the model's
results. This approach was fairly close to what a school would do to
apply the model on its own campus. It generated a large amount of
engagement and satisfaction as well as demonstrating the model's
applicability.

We began the process by quantifying the two externally imposed
problems: (1) a fixed percentage reduction in government per-student
subsidies for all subject areas and (2) a drying up of matriculations
from specified countries in reaction to crimes against Asian students
in key Australian cities. The two problems illustrate both general and
market-specific revenue losses caused by events beyond the university's control. The funding cuts were viewed as highly likely and the
market problems as less likely but still a serious worry. The strategies to be described shortly include those initiated by the Leading
Universities teams, but they go further so as to illustrate a broader
range of possibilities.

The number of problems considered should be small because each
problem will spawn multiple what-if responses. (A scenario includes
both a stimulus and a response, and while it's easy enough to test any
given scenario, the total number of tests must remain manageable.)
One also must set the time frame for the scenarios, which should be

far enough in the future to allow transition effects to work themselves out. The main transition effect in this case is the time taken for the loss of student demand to work its way through the system—which, of course, depends on the length of the undergraduate program.

The groups defined the following scenarios for consideration:

- *Base case*: neither worry comes to pass
- *Government funding cut ("intermediate case")*: a clear and present worry, using 10 percent reduction that the planning team believed to be most likely
- *Asian market losses* in addition to *government funding cuts ("worst case")*: the sum of both worries, using program-specific loses equal to 75 percent of demand from the listed countries as calculated from historical first-year enrollment data. This came to a loss of one thousand Asian students in total for the steady state.

Additional scenarios could have been added if time had permitted: for example, different percentage losses for either or both contingencies. Such explorations become practical if the range of response alternatives has been narrowed and one wishes to fine-tune the ultimate plan.

The Leading Universities groups identified the following six strategies for coping with the revenue losses. Details are provided in appendix A.

- *Raise Net Tuition and Fees*. This often is the top-of-mind response for financially strapped universities, even though it can lead over time to affordability and market problems. AR predictive models produce a detailed analysis of effects on the university's internal economy, but the market side is harder to evaluate. (See the discussion of market information in chapter 7, however.) The Leading Universities groups also noted that the differential effects for foreign and domestic students could generate an on-campus equity issue, again as noted in the appendix.

- *Intensify Fund-Raising.* Revenue shortfalls also produce calls for increased fund-raising, although this is more easily discussed than accomplished. Scenario timelines should include opportunities for fund-raising officers and consultants to describe and defend the realism of their plans, and one should be conservative when predicting their results. The AR predictive model cannot evaluate the feasibility of fund-raising plans, but it can help to explore the consequences of different success levels. The model also can explore the effects of donor-imposed restrictions: for example, when significant gift flows are restricted to research in particular schools or disciplines.

- *Boost Class Sizes, Faculty Workloads, and Adjunct Usage.* This approach to coping with financial stringency is as old as the speed-up and substitution of cheap for higher-priced labor in profit-maximizing entities. The full-function predictive AR model easily predicts the consequences of particular speed-up and substitution strategies on an institution's financial performance. What's harder is to gauge their effects on other things the university cares about: for instance, educational quality and research. This is not easy, but the appendix does offer some ideas about how the model can be used to gain insight about them.

- *Boost Enrollments in High-Margin Programs.* Provosts and deans often turn to enrollment expansion as a way to solve financial problems. This can be a good strategy if, but only if, it is accompanied by analyses of markets and margins. Market analysis (described in chapter 7) enables one to judge whether the institution's expansion objectives are likely to work. The appendix illustrates how having good data on margins can avoid the expansion of money-losing programs—which would only worsen the school's financial problem.

- *Close or Merge Courses, Programs, Departments, or Campuses.* This strategy also can be analyzed with a full-function AR predictive model. As with the closure of course instances that was described in chapter 5, the closure of whole courses requires the model to predict how many enrollments will be picked up elsewhere and how many will be lost. Moving up the hierarchy, departmental, school, or campus closure requires predictions about which, if any, programs and courses need to be retained and with what level of capacity. (The appendix describes some of the considerations discussed by the Leading Universities groups.) The behavior of overhead costs, which have detailed representations in full-function AR models, also should be considered when the numbers of faculty, staff, and students are projected to change significantly.

• *Prune Overhead Areas.* This is shorthand for reduction of administrative and support costs. Full-function AR models can help here, too. Detailed cost reduction strategies for the wide variety of overhead operations in a university are beyond the scope of this book. However, the appendix describes how the model can empower deans to participate effectively in the policing of overhead costs. This can be a hugely effective stimulus for overcoming what many faculty members see as an entrenched and dysfunctional defense of the nonacademic expenditures.

Boost Student Learning and Attainment

Boosting student learning and attainment is a more uplifting objective than coping with revenue losses. It has become a high priority at many colleges and universities. I touched on this earlier, but now I can pull the threads together in relation to an AR predictive model. The best place to start is with the WDF (withdrawal, D-grade, fail) paradigm, which I will assume has been included in the AR model's implementation. This enables easy identification of courses where students are having difficulty. A number of important lines of analysis and intervention follow from this important capability.

Searching for patterns in the data is one important line of inquiry. Using the historical model, one can compare the teaching methods, class sizes, teacher types, and teachers' time commitments for courses with high and low WFD rates. Then, virtual experiments using the predictive model can estimate the staffing and cost implications of emulating the low WFD configurations on a large scale. (One might cap class sizes, for example, or reduce the use of adjuncts.) Projecting WDF improvements from the virtual experiments is chancy because they don't control for subject matter or student characteristics, but the staffing and cost estimates are based on solid data. In the end, of course, one would need to change the actual course configurations and observe the actual results. The experiment at a research university's chemistry department that I described in *Reengineering the University* suggests that such experiments have a good chance of success.[13] As noted there, making WDF data available for all course instances would eliminate the time-consuming step of tracking individual student transcripts back to potentially problematic courses.

The predictive model also can be used to evaluate the staffing implications and costs of interventions for reducing bottlenecks in students' progression toward their degrees. The bottlenecks are identified by analytics not based on the AR model: for example, by looking at courses in which capacity constraints cause students to be turned away. Once again, the methods of the previous section can be used to test the addition of sections in the same course instance or the creation of new instances to satisfy the disappointed students.

Expand Teaching Programs

Most universities consider expanding their teaching programs at one time or another. Sometimes this is in response to perceived increases in stakeholder needs or other mission-related values. At other times, it stems from a desire to increase institutional size or reputation. Teaching programs can be expanded in two ways: by boosting the enrollments in existing programs and by the creation of new programs. Scenario development for both approaches should begin with the kind of market analysis to be described in chapter 7 and the analyses based on the AR historical model described in chapter 5. (As noted, Gray Associates offers campus-specific workshops to help institutions scan the market for potential new programs, for example.)[14] The process of adding enrollments to the predictive model for existing programs was described earlier in this chapter.

The predictive model also can help analyze proposed new programs before they are rolled out. The scenario needs to detail the number of new students expected, the amount of cannibalization from existing programs, and the courses the students will take. The new program is added to the predictive model and the data for enrollment and course taking entered. Existing courses are tagged with a link to the new program, and new courses are added in their appropriate departments. The latter is a special case of the course-addition procedure described earlier because most of the enrollment will come from the new program rather than from other courses.

Detailing the new courses and enrollments is a lot of work, but it should be an important part of the planning process whether an AR model is used or not. It's worth noting that the model provides an important discipline (as well as important calculations) that serves to deter dangerous shortcuts and overoptimistic assumptions. The time, energy, investment, and reputational risk inherent in new program creation make such upfront analytics worthwhile in most cases.

Build Up Research

The idea of building up research appeals to universities in a number of institutional segments. Depending on where one starts, the process involves making initial investments in faculty lines and/or reductions in teaching loads, and in various infrastructure and administrative areas. As in other areas, the scenario should be as specific as possible about where research is to be enhanced, the initial investments that will be needed, and the sources and amounts of external support to be anticipated. Then the AR predictive model can be used to test the feasibility of the investments, with and without the expected levels of extramural support.

Most research enhancement programs depend on the efforts of faculty members, and most schools find they must build faculty capacity in advance of getting grants and contracts. Hence the first planning step is to specify one's assumptions about the numbers and types of faculty that will be added to each department's budget. The second step is to evaluate, and perhaps increase, the fractions of faculty effort designated for research—especially for the newly acquired faculty. The costs for these faculty should include ongoing expenditures for special equipment and laboratory operations where applicable. (One-time investments such as for facilities construction and the initial outfitting of laboratories will be added to the analysis at a later stage.) The third step is to add cost to various infrastructure and administrative areas as needed to support the envisioned program. The final step adds the minimum level of externally sponsored research revenue expected within the time frame of the scenario. This will provide a worst-case analysis that helps guard against overoptimistic assumptions.

Running the model with these assumptions provides two kinds of insights. First, decision makers gain understanding about the amount of faculty time that will be made available for new research and scholarship. This is critical because it is faculty leadership that provides the impetus needed for building up research. The model also estimates the worst-case financial outcomes, which may well involve significant losses due to time lags in building new research revenue. The university must be able to absorb these losses without threatening its financial viability.

With the worst case in hand, it becomes appropriate to rerun the model with more optimistic assumptions about research revenue. These scenarios may include greater investments of general funds, but it's important to remember that sponsored research projects usually incorporate nonfaculty direct costs in the restricted portions of their budgets. The model should include these costs, but the fact that they don't materialize without the research project means they don't have to be viewed as a financial risk. (There may be smallish fixed costs to cover research staff between projects.) The model also can track the faculty salary offsets (if any) and overhead recoveries from the assumed sponsored research.

Financial Planning and Budgeting

Imagine now that you have constructed and tested scenarios for describing alternative university futures and have settled on the small subset that you and your team think are the most attractive. What remains is to integrate this information with your spreadsheet models for financial planning and budgeting. (It's rare to find a school that doesn't have some kind of spreadsheet financial model.) As noted, the scenarios refer to a loosely specified planning horizon: for example, about five years out, which for convenience I'll assume is the same as the spreadsheet's planning horizon.[15] This means the planning choices embodied in the scenarios must be cross-walked to the end rather than to the beginning of your spreadsheet. Further, the financial and operating choices for the earlier years must bring the university to the point envisioned in the scenarios.

The university's finance staff will develop the details of the cross-walks, but senior academics will need to understand and provide input for the process. The university's style of budgeting (line item, responsibility center budgeting [RCB], etc.) will affect the process to some extent, but I'll defer that discussion until a little later.

The Multiyear Financial Plan

I described financial planning models of the kind needed for linking up to the scenarios in chapter 5 of *Reengineering the University*.[16] The essentials follow:

1. The university uses multiyear financial forecasting.
2. The forecast begins with the year about to be budgeted and ends with a "terminal year" (as described earlier) where the variables approximate a steady state.
3. Data for the terminal year are cross-walked from one of the chosen scenarios.
4. Data for the intermediate years are interpolated according to the school's desired "transition strategy."

5. The upcoming budget is based on the first year of the resulting forecast.

These steps are consistent with the financial analysis methodology taught routinely in MBA programs, which are as applicable to not-for-profit enterprises as to for-profit ones. Students are taught to calculate present values using year-by-year figures for the first part of the forecast and steady-state formulas for the terminal year. Figures for the terminal year are assumed to be unchanging in constant dollars. I have called the terminal year the "equilibrium period" or "steady state" in some of my writing,[17] but the three concepts are essentially similar.

Table 6.1 presents a summary multiyear financial plan that might result from the revenue shortfall situations described earlier. An actual planning exercise might well start with tables for each school, which then are rolled up to the university level. The column for the terminal year (2023) would be obtained by applying the AR predictive model to one of the short-listed scenarios. (The model provides data at a much more detailed level should one wish to build a more refined financial plan.) The data are expressed in thousands of constant dollars in order to keep things simple, but both the predictive and financial models could be expressed in current dollars, if desired.

The column for 2018 shows the base year: in other words, the one during which the planning work is being conducted. The budget is being prepared for 2019, but in context with the entire planning period. The stub of the table shows high-level figures for income and expenditure, including one-time spending for program startup or closure, plus the resulting surplus or deficit. I've assumed that the surpluses or deficits are added to or taken from the endowment, and the resulting balance is shown on the last line of the table. This is not the way most universities would do it (they would use operating reserves if they had them), but it simplifies the presentation without changing its fundamental logic.

The effects of the intermediate and worst-case situations described earlier are reflected in the boldfaced figures for "Government Block

Table 6.1. The Multiyear Financial Plan (Thousands of Constant Dollars Except for Full-Time Equivalents [FTEs])

	Base Year 2018	Budget Year 2019	2020	Transition Years 2021	2022	Terminal Year 2023
Income						
Tuition Revenue	$400,000	$395,468	$392,385	$388,238	$386,580	$391,550
Original Student FTEs	20,000	19,625	19,250	18,875	18,500	18,500
New Student FTEs	0	50	175	250	450	600
Average Tuition Rates	$20.00	$20.10	$20.20	$20.30	$20.40	$20.50
Government Block Grant	$50,000	$47,500	$45,000	$45,000	$45,000	$45,000
Endowment Spending	$20,000	$20,000	$19,746	$19,391	$19,002	$18,679
Other Income	$25,000	$26,000	$27,000	$28,000	$29,000	$29,000
Total Revenue	$495,000	$488,968	$484,131	$480,629	$479,582	$484,229

Expenditures

Salaries and Benefits	$260,000	$258,390	$255,930	$253,470	$251,435	$251,010
FTE Faculty	1,000	1,000	990	980	975	970
Average Compensation	$85.00	$85.00	$85.00	$85.00	$85.00	$85.00
FTE Staff	2,500	2,477	2,454	2,431	2,408	2,408
Average Compensation	$70.00	$70.00	$70.00	$70.00	$70.00	$70.00
Other Expenditures	$235,000	$234,650	$234,300	$233,950	$233,600	$233,219
Total Expenditures	$495,000	$493,040	$490,230	$487,420	$485,035	$484,229
One-Time Expenditures	$0	$1,000	$1,000	$1,000	$1,000	$0
Surplus or Deficit	$0	($5,072)	($7,099)	($7,791)	($6,453)	$0
Cumulative Surplus or Deficit	$0	($5,072)	($12,171)	($19,961)	($26,414)	($26,414)
Ending Endowment Balance	$400,000	$394,928	$387,829	$380,039	$373,586	$373,586

Note: The boldface figures are predetermined by the scenario definition.

Grant" and "Original Student FTEs." ("Original" refers to the base case.) The illustration uses the aforementioned assumption that the government will cut its block grants by 10 percent and that one thousand Asian students eventually will disappear from the university. Both outcomes are assumed to be phased in: the government's cuts over two years and the student losses over the four-year undergraduate program. If unmitigated, the losses would have produced a $35 million annual deficit in the terminal year—which obviously is not acceptable. This figure, which is not shown in the table, assumes the worst case with no responses from the university.

The university's responses can be described as follows. As noted, those for the terminal year come from predictive model runs for the chosen scenario and those for the transition years from interpolations based on what the planners assume to be reasonable.

- *New Student FTEs.* Six hundred new students have been added to new and existing programs. The buildup begins in earnest in 2020 (after a year of planning) and then percolates forward as students go through their programs and additional new programs are activated.
- *Tuition Increases.* Tuition and fees have been boosted by $500, about 2.5 percent, phased in evenly over the five years. Remember these are inflation-adjusted figures.
- *Endowment Spending.* Calculated as 5 percent of the previous year's ending balance. This spending rate is consistent with the requirements for financial sustainability described in *Reengineering the University* and elsewhere.[18]
- *Other Income.* Increases by $4 million as a result of intensified fund-raising. This 16 percent increase might well be viewed as an aggressive target, but note that it still closes only about one-fifth of the revenue shortfall gap.
- *FTE Faculty and Staff.* Faculty have decreased by thirty FTEs (3 percent) due to utilization improvements and capacity increases to handle new degree programs. Staff have decreased by

one hundred FTEs as the result of overhead reductions offset slightly by incremental program management and fund-raising needs. Once again, note that these changes have been phased in.
- *Other Expenditures*. Decrease by $1.78 million due mainly to efficiency improvement.

The scenario has been designed so the terminal-year budget is balanced: in other words, that sufficient actions have been identified to offset the scenario's $35 million unmitigated loss. This is not the end of the story, however. A cumulative deficit of almost $19 million will be incurred for 2019–2022 because the identified mitigations will take time to implement. These funds will have to be taken from the university's reserves, modeled here as draws from the endowment. This reduces the available endowment spending as shown in the table. The university might wish to run surpluses for a time after the terminal year or make up the difference by intensified fund-raising for endowment. Such actions are beyond the scope of the present analysis, however.

The power of the scenario-driven analysis is easily seen. I have constructed or consulted on many conventional multiyear financial plans (ones that don't incorporate a scenario-based terminal year) and can testify that it's difficult if not impossible to ground their assumptions with enough evidence to have reasonable confidence in the results. This problem is greatly mitigated by the use of scenario analysis coupled with AR predictive modeling. Basing the terminal year on a detailed scenario specification that's quantified using an AR predictive model serves to ground the analysis, and from that point it's not difficult to set policies for the transition years.

The modeled scenario provides a vital end-point discipline. Assumptions are still assumptions, but they focus on actions that academic resourcing managers can understand and evaluate. People can look at the body of assumptions holistically and test their consequences both in detail and in the aggregate. I don't believe it's too much to say that model-driven scenario analysis can, finally, make multiyear financial planning a fully practical proposition for universities.

Applications to Budgeting

The financial plan for 2019 is only an approximation of what will become the actual budget. This remains true even if the scenario, predictive model, and resulting financial plan have been elaborated at the level of individual schools as well as for the university as a whole. Because all the assumed mitigations were interpolated based on modeled results for the terminal year, for example, these year-by-year results could not be based on detailed plans. Such plans can be developed only in conjunction with actual decisions about budget authorizations. Efforts to do so in the abstract would be exhausting and not well grounded in reality.

Existing Budget Systems

One of the things that happens in budget-making is that the provost or other cognizant administrator negotiates with lower-level decision makers to fund the goals laid out for the relevant year of the financial plan—and, perhaps, to downplay areas not related to the goals. These lower-level managers are best able to judge what will happen in their areas. Furthermore, they are the people who will be responsible for implementing and living with whatever changes are decided. The result of these negotiations is to translate the broad strokes of the financial plan to detailed budget choices.

Just who does the negotiating depends on the style of budgeting that the university has adopted. *Reengineering the University* describes the three main styles as line-item allocation, one-line or block budgets, and RCB.[19] With line-item budgeting, negotiations are conducted by the provost or perhaps the provost and the principal officer for nonacademic operations. In one-line budgeting, the provost determines the size of each school's funding block, and the dean negotiates with chairs, and others, about specific expenditure authorizations. In RCB, the responsibility for maintaining school revenue and determining expenses is delegated to the deans. They can "eat what they kill," so to speak, and (except for the subventions described later) they expect little help from the central administration. Whatever the style, effective budget-making depends on a clean handoff between the institution's revenue and expense model and the chosen method of resource allocation. The same is true for results tracking. For example, using different overhead allocations for AR models and RCB reporting will produce no end of confusion.

Designing the university's predictive AR model to provide reports that conform with its style of budget-making turns out to be very important. This means the models' business rules should conform to the rules used for allocating revenue and budget authority. Institutions with well-established RCB systems will have developed software for revenue and overhead allocation, and in this case the AR model should include dashboards based on the same rules.

Conforming the AR models to budget-making is not difficult for line-item systems, which allocate neither revenues nor indirect costs. One-line systems that deal only with direct costs don't pose a problem, either. Problems can arise in the overhead allocation and revenue recognition elements of RCB, however. It seems to me that the first problem is the more difficult to solve. RCB overhead rates are set before the beginning of the fiscal year and then applied to each expenditure as it is incurred. Discrepancies between the recovered costs and those actually incurred are settled up in the setting of rates for subsequent years. The system is easy to implement and produces results that are predictable by academic research managers. Conversely, AR models calculate overhead rates after the year is over. Their purpose is not to "charge out" overhead to operating units but rather to determine the proper allocations after the fact.[20] The two overhead calculations could be reconciled after a fashion by adjusting the AR results by the previous year's RCB carryforward, but whether this is a good idea remains to be seen. The problem doesn't seem terribly important, though, as long as users are aware of what's going on.

The situation is somewhat better when it comes to distributing revenue. First, this applies only to RCB and hybrid budgeting systems, not one-line systems. Second, revenue allocations generally are less complicated than those for indirect costs, and the most relevant ones are tied fairly closely to identifiable revenue flows. In RCB and hybrid systems, for example, much of the revenue that flows to schools is based on tuition, fees, financial aid, and government capitation rates as applied to enrollments generated by the schools. It is not difficult to conform the business rules for these things across the budgeting and AR models. In cases where different views of the data are desired, one can add dashboards to the AR model that display essentially the same results as obtained for RCB. The "bottom line" for both problems is that there is no need for an institution to modify its data systems to conform to RCB before constructing an academic resourcing model.

Budget System Redesign

Full-function AR models open intriguing possibilities for improving both RCB and one-line budgeting systems. In my view, the biggest challenge with RCB is how to determine the subventions needed to balance mission objectives with market forces. Subventions are required because some mission-critical schools can't make ends meet based only on their earned revenues. The need for closing such gaps with university general funds was identified in the earliest stages of RCB adoption, but deciding the size of the subvention always has been difficult. No analytics have been available, so the decisions were based on judgments made in a highly contentious and competitive environment. Decisions about one-line budgets face the same challenges. It should come as no surprise, therefore, that the subventions and one-line allocations change only slightly from year to year and do not necessarily reflect current conditions.

A properly configured AR model can help solve this problem. While this is largely uncharted territory, it seems obvious that comparing a given school's historical cost estimates with the revenue allocated by RCB would provide insight about whether the current subvention is overly or insufficiently generous. Going further, the provost might negotiate with the dean about what programs might be expanded if the subvention were increased and then determine the amount of the increase by testing alternatives with the predictive model. (Running the historical model the following year would show whether the agreed-upon changes had indeed been implemented.) The revenue-driving incentives associated with an RCB system would remain intact, but the vexing subvention decisions would become more evidence based.

Using the AR model for this purpose also would enable conversations between deans and provosts about the relation between the subvention and the university's mission. It would put the provost at the table for negotiating at least some of the school's priorities, but without blunting the dean's incentives to drive revenue. This would go a long way toward solving the often-stated problem that RCB cuts the provost out of priority-setting and gives market forces too strong a role in determining the relative strength and importance of schools.

The same benefits extend to one-line budgeting. The AR models will allow the funding blocks to be "zero based"—built up from estimates of enrollments and research activity—rather than being rooted in the previous year's funding adjusted for salary increases and inflation. Negotiations between provosts and deans would be based on strategy and program offerings, not the minutia of specific budget lines. This was how we conceived the original one-line budgets at Stanford, but our modeling technology was not up to putting it into practice. AR predictive models make it possible to build credible one-line budgets "from the bottom up" based on strategic agreements and enrollment forecasts.

The AR models also may usher in new variants of decentralized budgeting. For example, the revenues for graduate programs and research could be devolved to the deans, while those for undergraduate education are distributed by the provost on a one-line basis. This would mitigate the well-known problem that RCB tends to fragment undergraduate education and produce unnecessary duplication of courses. I proposed the development of such systems in my 1996 book, *Resource Allocation in Higher Education*,[21] but, as for the RCB subventions, there was no satisfactory evidence-based way to make the one-line allocations. Now, however, the model-driven, zero-based approach makes such hybrid systems practical. I know of no research on this subject, but I believe it is quite promising.

The Australian National University

In a late-breaking development, the Australian National University (ANU, in Canberra) has embarked on a major budget redesign project that incorporates the Pilbara predictive model. ANU was one of the institutions I interviewed while preparing to write this book. The redesign was "a gleam in the eye" of the university's most senior officers, and we discussed it at some length during my visit. ANU is a large, prestigious, and complex institution. (It is Australia's top international university and among the top fifty universities in the world according to London's *Times Higher Education*.) Therefore, it's highly significant that the university has adopted Level III AR modeling as a key element of its budget redesign.

ANU's current budget system allocates income to its faculties and other major academic units using a variant of RCB. However, its leaders have concluded that this process does not take proper account of the actual costs of teaching and the institution's objectives with respect to research. I noted earlier that the standard mitigation for these problems in RCB involves provision of subventions, that properly sizing the subventions is extremely difficult, and that AR models can be used to good advantage in subvention-setting. ANU is going a step further by allocating its resources on the basis of relative cost as informed by AR modeling, rather than in terms of income. Incentives for income improvement and other goals will be provided separately.

The new system applies a somewhat simpler approach than the model's application to scenario planning that I described earlier but retains its essential elements. (Stated in the terms of that discussion, ANU cross-walks the model to the first year of the multiyear planning period rather than to the terminal year.) The ANU historical model informs development of a "base case" for budget allocations in the upcoming year. These allocations are adjusted based on various what-if analyses using the predictive model and then projected forward to the end of the planning period—probably three to five years out. What-ifs will include changes in student numbers, changed research strategies, or desires to increase or trim the university's investments in particular program areas. Level III predictive AR models like the one installed at ANU are designed to explore these kinds of situations.

I was particularly intrigued by one of the scenarios described by my contacts at the university. It assesses the possibility of upgrading educational provisions in a number of language-related areas—"not to a Rolls-Royce standard, but to a level more appropriate than at present to the quality of its students and its aspirations." The model evaluates variables such as online versus face-to-face teaching, class sizes, adjunct utilization, and (importantly) the mix between teaching and research. Then it costs out the new configurations and recalculates the margins for the course and programs. Stakeholder groups have been convened to help work out the scenarios, and they are reported to be both enthusiastic and realistic in terms of aspirations. Among other things, the process gives departments an opportunity to present their cases for improvement and also a scaffold for working through the details of their proposals. It appears to be working as I have envisioned in this book.

Finally, use of AR models in combination with planning scenarios provides central administrators with an opportunity to evaluate important risks—many of which they have been aware of for some time but lacked the tools to analyze. Examples include international and domestic political changes that will affect student demand and research funding. Policy questions such as admission levels for degree programs can be evaluated as well, as can the magnitude and treatment of overhead costs. ANU has evaluated four complete scenarios so far, and more are coming over the horizon. The university is looking forward to extending the reach of these scenario models in the years to come.

Part Three
Other AR Tools

We now turn to a collection of academic resourcing tools that complement the AR processes and models discussed so far. These include deep dives into the use of modern market information systems, the assessment of teaching quality, and what it means to be a value-driven, not-for-profit university as opposed to one that pursues financial profit. Finally, we will look at the "way forward" toward implementing all kinds of AR tools.

Chapter 7 introduces new ideas about program review, a subject that we first encountered in the prologue, and that has arisen in many forms since. The key idea is that program review can and should be more than the narrowly focused "academic health checks" that so many institutions now perform. Taking stock of market information is one such extension. I describe the kinds of information that now are available and how they can be used in program review. Evaluating the program's performance in the university's internal economy is the second extension we shall examine, based on the groundwork already laid in previous AR modeling discussions. The efficacy of program review also will benefit from a closer look at teaching and learning quality. I describe a method for nonintrusive quality evaluation that works well in many settings, and that I believe will fit nicely into a program review format. The chapter ends by putting the three elements of new information together with the traditional ones, in a process that can be used for single programs or an institution's whole portfolio of programs.

Chapter 8 expands on one of the key themes of the book: that traditional not-for-profit universities are value-driven enterprises, and that AR processes need not and should not undermine this core value. It begins by describing what I call the "not-for-profit paradigm," which provides a needed alternative to the familiar way of thinking about for-profit enterprises. Instead of maximizing profits, not-for-profits maximize attainment of their mission, which we can think of as the academic and social values that motivate traditional universities, subject to limitations imposed by the marketplace in the university's internal economy. The remainder of the chapter presents a practical model for applying the not-for-profit paradigm to university budget-making. The tool's introductory version comes on a spreadsheet and is easy to use. My proposal for a more complicated version is described in appendix C.

CHAPTER SEVEN

Comprehensive Program Review

The term "program review" has two meanings in higher education. The traditional meaning calls out an in-depth study of a particular degree program or department. Many colleges and universities perform these reviews, often on a recurring schedule of about five to seven years. The term can also mean comparative evaluation of all the university's programs: for example, as described near the end of chapter 5. (Robert Dickeson refers to this as "program prioritization,"[1] but I prefer to recognize it as a form of program review.) The individual evaluations are much less detailed than the traditional reviews, but this is offset by the advantages stemming from the ability to compare. Moreover, some universities are beginning to think of "program portfolios," where the synergies and shared risks of the whole collection of programs are taken into account.

Traditional program review is defined by the Western Association of Schools and Colleges (WASC) as a faculty-driven "cyclical process for evaluating and continuously enhancing the quality and currency of programs."[2] The idea can be elaborated, as Northwestern University puts it, to "enhance each unit's quality and effectiveness, to stimulate planning and continuous improvement, and to encourage strategic development in ways that further the university's priorities."[3] (As noted, the "units" referred to may be individual degree programs or academic departments housing multiple degree programs.) In some cases, as at Northwestern, for example, administrative departments are reviewed as well. This chapter asserts my belief that program review also should include the university's "internal economy" (measured by AR models) and "external economy" (measured by market information systems) insofar as they impinge on the program in question. They also should include systematic assessments of teaching quality using modern tools.

This chapter describes how the expansion of program review can be accomplished. The addition of "comprehensive" to "program review" in its title calls out the need to use the market, AR model, and quality data simultaneously. I'll describe the three components separately before bringing them together in the last section of this chapter.

Adding market and economic information to traditional program review will face cultural headwinds. The idea is not really foreign to academic thinking, however, as indicated by the WASC guide's[4] description of program review as a comprehensive analysis based on a wide variety of data. Such reviews often involve formal self-evaluations followed by assessments by reviewers from outside the department or even the university itself. There is much to gain by asking both types of reviewers to consider the "wider variety of data" in tandem with their usual analysis. If experience is any guide, useful and perhaps surprising insights will be forthcoming once the reviewers' initial skepticism has been overcome.

Market Information

Academics usually are surprised when they learn how much market data are available for their programs. These data don't cover every question that might be asked, but they do cover a great many. Institutions can collect considerable market information on their own, but processing these data can be complex. As with the academic resourcing models discussed earlier, it's usually better to hire experts to build the models. Gray Associates of Concord, Massachusetts, provides the best example I know of an integrated system. I have no financial stake in the company, but its people have been generous about sharing their insights and examples.

Program review presents an excellent platform for using market data. What kinds of students are being served, and where are they located? Who are the employers of these students? Do the courses mesh well with the stated needs of these employers? What other programs serve the same students and meet the same needs, and how intense is the competition? Are these things trending upward or downward? How good is the program's strategic fit with the institution's other activities? All these questions arise naturally in comparative program review. Traditional program reviewers invest time and energy learning about what's being taught, how, by whom, and very occasionally the quality of learning. (The quality of scholarship usually does get evaluated in research universities.) Doesn't it make sense for reviewers to seek insight about what's happening in the marketplace? Wouldn't their reports be better if they included recommendations that could help sustain student interest and thus improve the program's market position? Looking at these things is essential for a mission-driven institution like a university. It does not mean sacrificing academic values on the altar of the marketplace.

Overview of the Newly Available Data

The market profiles, which are compiled from many different sources, are designed to meet a particular institution's specific needs. This section describes the data one item at a time. The next one describes how one can view the data holistically—to see the forest instead of the individual trees. Sidebars in each subsection ground the narratives by listing the specific variables that Gray believes to be important. I'll revisit these variables when I discuss the holistic scoring and display systems.

STUDENT DEMAND

The geography of student demand has obvious importance for evaluating a program's reach and therefore its market strength and prospects. This is easily obtained by arraying the addresses of applicants in terms of zip codes or census tracts. (The addresses of current students are problematic because they may well change residences as a result of enrollment.) Reach varies by institutional segment and also by program type. Most if not all programs in what Robert Zemsky calls "medallion and name brand institutions"[5] have national or international reach, though the geographic distribution of applicants varies greatly. Typical schools in the convenience segment get 90 percent of their applications from within thirty or thirty-five miles, though this depends on the availability of public transit and similar factors. Scarce and highly valued programs such as nursing will reach farther.

Program reviewers may come up with fruitful insights when viewing these data, especially when they can be arrayed over time and compared to similar programs the university offers. Adding demographic and socioeconomic trends can provide additional insights. Mapping software can display these data in ways that stimulate interest and understanding, especially among professionals who know the programs intimately. The goal is to detect signals that may suggest turning points in student demand.

External data sources also provide valuable information about student demand. The Integrated Postsecondary Education Data System (IPEDS) degree completions data track the demand for particular programs offered by individual schools and campuses, which, of course, are situated at known locations that can be compared with the source of one's own applications. As with the other demand data, the display shows the chosen output units (completions in this case), growth in units, and percent growth over the past two years. These data cover all degree recipients, but they measure demand only with long lags. For example, bachelors' completions in 2020 reflect student choices in, say, 2013 to 2015: a year's lag in data publication plus at least four to six years as an enrolled student. Still, the data may stimulate insights by providing context for the institution's own data on applicants.

Student Demand

- *Applications*: By geography
- *Completions*: Units, unit growth, and % growth
- *Search Volume*: Indexed growth and % growth
- *Student Inquiries*: Units, unit growth, and % growth

Source: Gray Associates

Google provides two additional sources of insight about trends in student demand for particular programs: *search volume* and *student inquiries*. For the first, one enters keywords into the appropriate Google tool and observes the number of times users have searched on that term. Inquiry data result from users clicking through and requesting further information on a school or other construct. Searches and inquiries represent different stages of an applicant's interest-development process. Both results are up-to-the-minute in terms of currency and can be broken down geographically to the census tract. (Fine-grained geographic breakdowns may produce unusably small returns, however.) These data may be reported by geography, if desired. For example, certain countries, states, counties, or zip codes might score higher or lower on search initiations or inquiries.

The web-based data are tedious to obtain without special software (e.g., getting good search data may require many different keywords), and they also require careful normalization. But when properly processed, they provide a more forward-looking picture of demand changes than obtainable from IPEDS completions.

EMPLOYMENT

The employment prospects of graduates are important for many programs. The Bureau of Labor Statistics (BLS) collects wide-ranging statistics on employment and wages. The data are free, but it's not easy to make them relevant for particular programs. Mappings between BLS occupation categories and the academic program categories used in the IPEDS completions data are far from precise, especially for more generalist-oriented programs and those that feed into graduate work rather than directly into the labor force. Further problems arise because the BLS data are survey based and thus not fine-grained geographically, and comparable data are available only on a biennial basis. (The surveys include self-employed individuals on alternate years.) Still, they can provide insights about current demand, as well as forecast information about employment and wages. The latter are particularly noteworthy because they report wage percentiles (not just averages or medians), which allows programs to be calibrated to particular market strata. Data also can be obtained on wages by bachelor's degree major and career stage, as well as wages for certificate and associate's degree holders.

Job postings provide a detailed and up-to-date picture of current employment prospects for particular fields, including the ones used in IPEDS and also by location down to the zip code. One can obtain these from commercial job posting websites or, better yet, by aggregating individual postings by employers. (The latter give a more accurate picture, because the sampling is more representative and filled jobs are promptly removed.) Job postings are available from Burning Glass Technologies and a number of sources. Current postings tend to correlate highly with future postings, which make them good forecasting tools. Placement rates also provide valuable information. Federal rules require two-year schools to post them on their websites, from which data suppliers can harvest them for fields and geographies. Unfortunately, nothing equivalent is available for the four-year sector.

Program reviewers can benefit from an additional data source that is not shown in the sidebar: qualitative information about what employers are looking for when they post a job. A website called "Skill Center" (at Dice.com) uses artificial intelligence algorithms to collect such data for particular skill areas (e.g., "accounting management") and makes them freely available by simply typing in the name of the skill. One of the quality principles described later calls for consideration of just this kind of data.

Employment

- *US Employment*: Total, % growth, forecast job openings, and 10th percentile wages
- *Wages*: By bachelor's degree major and career stage. Associate's and below wages
- *Placement Rates*: % of graduates employed (associate's and below)
- *Job Postings*: Units, unit growth, % growth, and job postings per graduate

Source: Gray Associates

COMPETITIVE INTENSITY

Higher education is no longer a growth industry, so the main challenge for most programs is to defend their market share, take share from competitors, or find a new and unique market niche. Reviewers need to understand the intensity of competition in order to opine on a program's health and prospects, and to make judgments about how it should move forward. A few of the many metrics for competitive intensity are described in the sidebar.

The most straightforward competitive metric comes from the familiar IPEDS completions data. Simply download the relevant statistics for competitors active in the geographies (e.g., states, counties, zip codes) from which your school receives significant numbers of applications. These might include the number of competitors, median program sizes, and completions per college-age student in the geography—and also the percent changes in these figures. Online programs are treated similarly but without the geographic dimension. How to display these data for maximum clarity can be tricky, but the data themselves are readily understandable and available.

The web search and student inquiry data discussed earlier also provide insight about competitive intensity. Statistics on cost per click and inquiry are helpful because it generally costs more to reach people in saturated markets. Too few interested people generate a larger search cost, and too many competitors will boost the cost per inquiry.

Competitive Intensity

- *Completions*: Number of competitors, change in number of competitors, median program size, unit and % change in program size, completions per capita
- *Programs Offered Online*: % of programs offered online, % of completions in online programs
- *Search*: Cost per click, competitive index
- *Student Inquiry*: Cost per inquiry

Source: Gray Associates

Reports on share of inquiries also are useful. (This is an area where expert knowledge is especially helpful in constructing appropriate indices and interpretations.) Program reviewers may well view programs in a different light when they operate in a saturated or near-saturated market.

STRATEGIC FIT

The question here is whether a program's market continues to match the institution's core competencies with respect to degree levels and costs. The fractions of completions at the associate's, bachelor's, master's, and doctoral levels can change dramatically over time, for example, and schools should be aware of these changes. I once advised a university on the market for its physical and occupational therapy programs, for example, at a time when the field's emphasis was shifting from master's to professional doctorates. The question was whether the school should try to compete at the higher degree level given its faculty, facilities, and the mix of degrees offered by its other programs.

BLS data on the distribution of degree levels in the current workforce provide another view of employers' needs. These data change at a much slower pace than do completions, which represent the leading edge of workforce changes, but they can be valuable neverthe-

Strategic Fit

- *Degree Level*: % of completions by degree level
- *Degree Level*: % of current workers by level of educational attainment
- *Cost per Degree*: Associate's and below national instructional cost index, student-faculty ratio

Source: Gray Associates

less. You don't want to overeducate someone preparing for a given career, but, as Bob Atkins of Gray Associates likes to say, "don't send someone with a knife to a gunfight," either.

A similar observation can be made about average cost per degree. The National Higher Education Benchmarking Institute's data on associate's degrees and below provide insights about how recent graduates' pay compares to the institution's own cost-quality structure. Among other things, this can help calibrate program reviewers to the level of educational quality and intensity being demanded in the marketplace.

Summary Market Metrics

We've seen that there is no lack of meaningful data about the higher education marketplace. The current menu surely will be improved upon as more institutions look carefully at the marketplace and suppliers rise to meet the demand. Indeed, the main problem is not the availability of data but its interpretation. Institutions and their suppliers must summarize the data before they can use it effectively in academic resourcing. This is not unlike the situation for teaching activities before the advent of AR models. University systems contained a plethora of data, but they could not be accessed and used effectively before a structural model for teaching was developed.

Higher education lacks a structural model of the marketplace. I started my academic career as a market modeler and can state unequivocally that, despite much-publicized developments in "big data" analysis, no marketing equivalent to the structural teaching model exists or is likely to exist anytime soon. Yet the marketplace data don't speak for themselves. They must be displayed in ways that are meaningful for users: including, importantly, people who are much more familiar with the program as it exists within the university than they are with its markets. This requires some kind of summarization and scoring system.

The marketplace data are too voluminous to be assimilated without some kind of summary scoring. Table 7.1 illustrates the scheme used by Gray Associates in their Market Mapping System. The system was designed to solve three problems: the need for summarization noted earlier, the apples-oranges incommensurability of the various measures, and the highly nonlinear character of each metric (where equal changes in a metric don't produce anything like equal

Table 7.1. Sample Scoring System for Market Variables

	Past Year Inquiries	Year over Year Percentage Change
Set Targets	Maximum > 6,000	Maximum > +50%
	Medium > 2,000	Medium > +25%
	Low > 500	Low > −25%
	Minimum < 1	Minimum < −50%
Set Scores	Maximum = +5	Maximum = +2
	Medium = +3	Medium = +1
	Low = +1	Low = −1
	Minimum = −3	Minimum = −2
Base Market Percentiles	100%: 59,473	80%: +86%
	98%: 5,043	70%: +24%
	95%: 1,698	50%: +24%
	90%: 445	20%: −98%
This Program	50,473	−28
	5	−1
	Overall Score = 4	

effects). It shows the system as applied to two variables from the student demand dataset described earlier: past year inquiries and year-over-year percentage change in inquiries. Mapping starts by setting targets and scores as shown in the table's first two sections. For example, situations with more than six thousand inquiries get mapped into the "Maximum" target category, those between two thousand and six thousand go into the "Medium" category, and so on. The scores for the two categories have been set at +5 and +3, respectively. The third part of the table, "Base Market Percentiles," gauges the inquiries and percent changes for various points on the variables' underlying frequency distributions. To continue the example, the maximum inquiry level in the dataset is 59,473 (100 percent of cases are below this figure), 98 percent of the cases are below 5,043, and so on.

Results for the program being scored ("This Program") are shown in the bottom section of the table. Its inquiry level of 50,473 falls into the "Maximum" category, well above the ninety-ninth percentile of the distribution for all such programs. This gives it a score of +5. The value of year-over-year percent change is −28 percent, which puts it in the "Low" category for a score of −2. Adding the two figures together produces an overall score of +3. The scores, which are dimensionless and nonlinear in the underlying data values, reflect the relative importance of the variables as judged by the user.

Figure 7.1 illustrates how Gray Associates combines the scored marketing information into a one-page, four-quadrant composite display. The actual display is color-coded such that the excellent, good, bad, and ugly stand out clearly for users. Additional displays can be prepared as needed for specific purposes: for example, direct comparisons of different student types and geographies.

The four quadrants in the display correspond to the sidebars presented earlier. Starting in the upper left-hand corner and moving clockwise, they are "Student Demand," "Employment," "Competitive Intensity," and "Strategic Fit." The actual metric is presented in the "Value" column and the resulting score in the right-hand column. The

Category	Criterion	Value	Score	Total
Inquiries	Total	571,464	5	
	Online	43,804		
	Unit Change	-137367	-2	
	% Change	-0.194	0	
	Certificate	73.4%		
	Associate's	26.6%		
	Bachelor's	0%		
	Master's	0%		14
	Doctoral	0%		
Google Search*	Total	1,333,620	3	
	Unit Change	56,910	2	
	% Change	5.8%	0	
Completions	Total	80,572	8	
	Unit Change	-8,044	-2	
	% Change	9%	0	
Institutions	Total	1,446	0	
	YoY Change**	-44	0	
Cost per Inquiry	Average**	$44	0	
Market. Saturation	Completion per Capita**	1.07	0	0
Google Search*	Cost per Click**	$26	0	
	Comp. Index**	0.69	0	
Program Size	Average	56	0	
	Median	11	0	
	Unit Change	0	0	
	% Change	0%	0	
National Distance Education Competition	DE Institutions**	70	0	
	% of Institutions	8%	0	
	DE Completions**	4,946	0	
	% of Completions	6%	0	

Percentiles:	<40%	40%+	70%+	90%+	95%+	98%+
Overall Score:	<17	17+	25+	37+	42+	47+

Category	Criterion	Value	Score	Total
Job Postings* (Burning-Glass)	Job Posting	101,214	3	
	JP w/ EDU	55,952		
	% JP HS	95%		
	% JP AA	5%		
	% JP BA	0%		
	% JP MA	0%		12
	% JP Doc	0%		
	Unit Change	4,626	2	
	% Change	4.8%	0	
	JP per Grad	1.3	-1	
BLS*	Total	576,208	5	
	Job Openings	17,881	3	
	CAGR	2.3%	1	
	Wages	$22,429	1	
Nat'l ACS Wage (Bachelors)	Age <30		0	
	Age 30–60		0	
Nat'l GE (2-Yr)	Wages	$19,167	-3	
	Certificate	72.9%		
Placement Rates	Associate's	78.4%	1	
National Percent of Workforce	No College	25%	0	
	Certificate	43%	0	
	Associate's	22%	0	
	Bachelor's	8%	0	
	Graduate	2%	0	
Percent of All Completions	Certificate	81%	0	
	Associate's	19%	0	
	Bachelor's	0%	0	
	Master's	0%	0	0
	Doctoral	0%	0	
NHEBI National 2-Yr	Cost Index**	0.94	0	
	Stu:Faculty Index**	0.95	0	

* Google search and employment data do not filter by award level.
** Color scale in reverse.

N/A: No data available.
2-Yr: Associate's and certificate programs only.

Figure 7.1. Scored Marketing Information Results. Courtesy of Gray Associates

results are color-coded for easy reading, such that better scores render here as more intense shades of gray in the figure. Each quadrant's overall score appears in its right-hand panel, and the sum for all the quadrants appears at the top of the figure.

The example shows that the program being reviewed has a score of 26, which, as indicated in the key at the bottom, places it near the center of the possible range. Student Demand, with a score of 14, turns out to be its strongest attribute, and Employment is a close second with 12. However, the program is only average in terms of Competitive Intensity and Strategic Fit. Displays like figure 7.1 are proving useful when scanning multiple programs and also for guiding deeper analysis into specific dimensions of the market.

Gray's scoring scheme can be criticized for its step-function transitions: for example, from −3 to +1, as shown in table 7.1, for only a small change in the underlying variable. However, this is easily remedied if one feels concerned. I have worked out a "smoothed" procedure using the principles of fuzzy logic, which is presented in appendix B. Certainly, many other such procedures are possible.

Relation to the University's Internal Economy

The WASC guide's list of things program review should consider includes several items that bear on the economics of academic resourcing. Not surprisingly, financial resources tops the list. WASC calls for operational budget (revenues and expenditures) and trends over a three-to-five-year period. Also, under "Allocation of Resources," the guide lists faculty workload, sufficient time for course development, research, and so forth, and a series of items pertaining to facilities. What's missing is consideration of how the program fits into the university's internal economy. Does it make or lose money, for example? What synergies does it have with other programs? The era in which the WASC guide was written tended to consider individual programs in isolation, but that view is no longer appropriate.

The full-scale AR models detailed in part II can help both traditional and comparative program reviewers answer many questions related to resource availablility, enrollment capacity, teaching quality, and synergy with other programs. For example, getting good data on faculty workloads allows reviewers to determine whether there is adequate coverage of teaching programs and to ensure the sustainability of both teaching and research. For example, the reviewers may be able to comment on the model's profiles for faculty time spent on advising, student evaluation and assessment, and other "soft" factors that affect program completions and quality. Measures such as student-faculty ratios, the ratios of full-time to part-time faculty, and regular faculty teaching loads allow inferences about the quality of teaching and learning. The degree of course sharing among programs speaks to questions of synergy.

Department-level statistics on the aforementioned are readily available without the use of AR models, but they suffer from serious drawbacks. Should one look at the department "owning" the given major, or more broadly at all the departments offering courses that are taken by students in the major, and if the latter, how should the various departmental figures be weighted? The mismatch between department and program as the unit of analysis is basic. As noted at the end of chapter 6, this cannot be resolved without starting at the course rather than the department level.

Whether unfunded faculty research time (so-called departmental research) is a necessary input for teaching quality has long been a subject for debate. It's hard to be categorical about this, but what's beyond doubt is that research effort dealing with pedagogy and the adaptation of content to student needs does contribute to teaching. Modern AR models provide estimates of unfunded research (as well as sponsored research) for each of the university's departments, and program reviewers are likely to find these data interesting. They may have insights on how much the unfunded research and scholarship actually contributes to teaching.

Gaining better understanding about the possibilities for improved teaching delivery options, and the degree to which courses in the major have implemented such options, should be another program review goal. AR models compare the cost of conventional and nonstandard teaching methods on a routine basis. These data will attune reviewers to the importance of teaching innovation and provide a basis for deeper dives as part of the program review process.

The same is true for understanding classroom utilization. Program reviewers may consider the availability of appropriate classrooms, but they rarely ask whether the school's classroom inventory is being used efficiently. As with many questions at the interface between academic quality and economics, classroom utilization efficiency can erode due to the reluctance of administrators to micromanage what they see as being in the faculty's domain. If nothing else, the inclusion of classroom utilization efficiency in program review can yield guidelines for helping administrators manage the room scheduling process.

The reviewers also might comment on the courses that students registered in the major actually take, as compared to, say, the expectations laid down during curricular development. They can compare actual enrollments with catalogue-suggested distribution options, for example, or look at how students deploy their free electives. Either approach can provide insight about the curriculum and how it might be improved. AR models allow this to be done in a flexible and seamless way, which should help sustain the interest of program reviewers.

Identifying candidates for course redesign or elimination is a major challenge for programs subject to the dictates of institutional budget stringency. Sometimes redesign options arise organically as faculty reflect on their teaching, but good economic data can tee up the question even when attractive options have not surfaced on their own. Readers who have followed my arguments to this point will not be surprised to learn that margin, measured at the individual course and program levels, is a key data element for this purpose.

An important tenet of this book is that margin needs to join academic considerations in decisions about whether to retain or eliminate programs. One needs to ask whether it's worth spending large sums of money to retain the academic benefits of particular low-enrollment courses. Such decisions are never easy, but they should be made by faculty and not left to administrative decree. Program review provides a good opportunity for faculty to dig deeply into the question. They also allow faculty to weigh in on criteria for their colleagues to use in making these quality-viability trade-offs.

Finally, program reviewers are well known for recommending new university investments to take advantage of opportunities they have identified. AR models can provide evidence that is useful for buttressing such proposals. However, these data also allow the university to compare the evidence for the reviewed program with that for other programs. The reviewers will become more effective advocates for improvement, *and* administrators will become more effective evaluators.

Quality: The Elephant in the Room

Why emphasize quality in a treatment of academic resourcing, and in particular on program review? There are two reasons. First, the improvement and assurance of quality is a quintessential academic resource management objective. Second, one of the biggest concerns about the use of AR models is that such widespread use may lead to quality diminution. These subjects should be of great interest in academic resourcing and, therefore, to program reviewers. I'll concentrate on teaching and learning quality because that's the greatest focus of concern for most schools. Research quality is important, too, but it's generally policed through peer review of publications and grant applications.

Teaching and learning quality should be integral to many of the resourcing decisions described in the prologue. I have chosen to treat it here because quality improvement and assurance processes fit logically into comprehensive program review. I don't mean they should be limited to these episodic events, however. Quality processes should pervade routine academic work. A mature culture of quality, as defined later, will ensure that an invigorated focus on program economics won't become unduly influential in academic resourcing decisions.

As with so many matters in academe, resolving the problem of teaching quality requires a careful look at processes. Good processes don't guarantee high-quality learning or conversely, but they provide pretty strong indications if one cares to look at them. The following definition, based on the work of David Dill and Frans van Vught, describes what I have in mind.

> *Academic quality processes are organized activities dedicated to improving and assuring education and research quality. They systematize a university's approach to quality instead of leaving it mainly to unmonitored individual initiative. They provide "a framework for quality management in higher education . . . drawn from insights in [quality pioneer] Deming's approach, but grounded in the context of academic operations."*[6]

The conventional wisdom conflates academic quality processes with the levels of teaching and learning quality actually achieved. This is clarified by extending the quality process definition as follows.

> *Academic quality processes should not be confused with the acts of teaching and research themselves. Course development is not the same as teaching, for example, nor is improving the department's research environment the same as doing one's own research. One might say that* quality processes plan and govern the improvement and monitoring *of teaching and research.*[7]

The concept of academic quality processes emerged from the higher education quality assurance movement, particularly in work by the Hong Kong University Grants Committee (UGC). The UGC's subcommittee on teaching quality, which I chaired during the 1990s, surveyed worldwide best practice to determine what would work best in Hong Kong's eight Western-style universities. This was a time of worldwide debate between advocates of "hard" quality measurement, as exemplified by intrusive assessment visits and normed testing, and advocates of less intrusive, "soft" methods like quality process review. Believing that faculty are the only people who can assess, assure, and improve the quality of their programs, we opted to look at the processes by which they did so rather than to engage in independent evaluations that all too often second-guess the on-the-ground decisions.

The method we evolved was a variant on then current practices in the United Kingdom, New Zealand, and (slightly later) Australia. Our approach was successful, and the Hong Kong Quality Assurance Council has continued along the same lines even as the approach in other countries has tended to harden. I later implemented academic quality process review at the University of Missouri and the Tennessee Board of Regents and, with colleagues Steven W. Graham and Paula Myrick Short, described the methodology and results in *Academic Quality Work: A Handbook for Improvement*. Among other things, this work led us to expand the original Hong Kong work on teaching and learning quality to include the processes institutions use for improving and assuring research quality. My references to "academic quality processes" apply to both sides of the teaching–research nexus. Coverage in this chapter is limited to the former, which I refer to as "education quality processes." The analogous research processes are covered in the aforementioned handbook.

Institution-wide education quality process reviews look at two things: (1) how departmental faculty discharge their collective responsibility for managing teaching and learning quality, and (2) how school deans and the central administration hold departments accountable for good work in this area. Department-level reviews address the first area. They cover both the courses taught by faculty in the department and the degree programs "owned" by it. Interdepartmental governance committees conduct the reviews for interdisciplinary degree programs. I recommend that department-level evaluations be performed as part of the program review cycle, and that discussion of the results be included in the reviewers' agenda.

Quality Process Focal Areas

"Quality" is too broad a concept to be assimilated all at once. Hence the UGC found it useful to divide the problem into five focal areas, each of which reflects work that faculty are or should be doing to discharge their fundamental academic responsibilities. Each area is defined in terms of a short list of questions that faculty can fruitfully ask themselves as they reflect on and improve their courses and programs. The objective of the quality process reviewers is to determine whether faculty do, in fact, reflect on these or similar questions, or whether they "fly by the seats of their pants" by relying on traditional practice and intuition. Just as in the use of AR models, the objective is to improve the conversations about teaching and learning quality.

The questions are similar to those asked by Derek Bok in his 2006 book, *Our Underachieving Colleges: A Candid Look at How Much Students Learn and Why They Should Be Learning More.*[8] The particular formulations presented here emerged from research on teaching quality at Stanford's National Center for Postsecondary Improvement (NCPI)[9] and then refined in the Hong Kong quality process reviews. As noted, my colleagues and I used them successfully in Missouri and Tennessee. There is no magic in the particular focal areas or questions, however. Schools should ask their own questions. The important thing is that faculty reflect deeply and holistically on the processes they use to instill learning.

- *Learning Objectives.* What knowledge, skills, and values should students acquire from each of their courses and cumulatively from their degree programs? How will this experience pay off in employment, societal contribution, and quality of life? Are the objectives based on the needs of actual or potential students rather than of some idealized student?
- *Curriculum.* How does the curriculum relate to the program's learning objectives? What is being taught, in what order, and from what perspective? Does the curriculum build cumulatively on students' prior knowledge and capacity? To what extent does the co-curriculum support the curriculum and the program's learning objectives generally?
- *Teaching and Learning Methods.* What teaching methods are used in each course: for example, for first exposure to materials,

for interpreting material and answering questions, for stimulating student involvement, and for providing feedback on student work? Is learning active? Is it collaborative? Is technology being used, and if so, is it exploited effectively? Are students exposed to a variety of different teaching methods during their study for the degree?

- *Student Learning Assessment.* Is the assessment of student learning based on evidence rather than impressions and anecdotes? What measures are used to for the assessments? Are they constructively aligned with the program's learning objectives? Do the metrics for individual courses compare beginning and ending performance to ascertain value added? Who is responsible for program-level learning assessment? Are the assessment results trending upward or downward? Do they inform quality improvement efforts, and if so, how? Because the faculty's development of student learning assessments is so important, table 7.2 reports WASC's "Evidentiary Principles" for learning assessment in full.

- *Quality Assurance.* How do faculty and departments assure themselves and others that the designs for curricula, teaching and learning methods, and student assessments are being implemented as intended? How do they assure themselves that research and other priorities don't push education quality improvement and assurance to the sidelines?

Quality process reviews ascertain the degree to which faculty in a department think hard about these questions, discuss them in faculty meetings or other fora, and take steps to remediate shortfalls when they find them. Some professors already take the questions seriously, but most don't spend much time on them. (Question 2, about the curriculum, may be an exception, but the recent book by Robert Zemsky and Susan Shaman, *Making Sense of the College Curriculum*, casts doubt even on that.)[10] Nonengaged faculty say informal individual initiatives are sufficient to do what needs to be done, but field experience demonstrates that this claim is mostly wishful thinking.

Table 7.2. Evidentiary Principles for Learning Assessment

1. Cover knowledge and skills taught throughout the program's curriculum. The unit of analysis should be the cumulative experience of the student at the time of graduation, not simply averages based on work done in individual courses.

2. Include multiple judgments of student performance. Program-level assessments should represent the considered judgment of a faculty team, not a single individual. They should be discussed by the team members before finalization.

3. Provide information on multiple dimensions of student performance. Program-level student assessment should include more than a single summative performance measure. Information should instead be collected on a variety of performance dimensions. Reports should include profiles of the relevant student population, not simply averages or data for the top few percent of the class.

4. Include more than surveys or self-reports of competence or growth by students. Surveys asking students to rate their satisfaction, strengths and weaknesses, and/or areas of perceived growth, though helpful, are not adequate as the primary metric for a program's teaching and learning quality.

Source: Adapted from Western Association of Schools and Colleges (2002).

Addressing the questions is tough. It requires deep reflection, conversation, and usually the collection of evidence—plus some kind of documentation to make sure that follow-up actually takes place.

The faculty's ability to assess student learning in particular courses will evolve with experience in using the education quality processes. I mentioned earlier that full-function AR models provide a scaffold for recording such assessments in the profiles for courses and course instances. I suggest that institutions make provision for these data during the design of these profiles. Then departments can encourage teachers to record their performance data. The primary objective is to give faculty and departments the wherewithal to compare performance with model-derived, course-level data (e.g., on class size and teacher type). In time, this will build insights that can be used for quality improvement or low-impact cost-containment. The ability to do such comparisons also will inform future research.

Education Quality Principles

My NCPI colleagues and I worked with the American Productivity and Quality Center[11] to identify seven principles of good

quality-related practice in business, government, and healthcare—
which we then adapted for use in university teaching and learning.
Subsequently, the seven informed the quality reviews in Hong Kong,
Missouri, and Tennessee. Brief summaries of them follow.

1. *Define Quality in Terms of Outcomes.* Learning outcomes
   should pertain to what is or will become important for the
   department's students. Exemplary departments carefully determine their students' needs and then apply their disciplinary
   knowledge in the service of those needs. They know that student
   learning, not teaching per se, is what ultimately matters.
2. *Focus on How Things Get Done.* Departments should carefully
   analyze how teachers teach, how students learn, and how both
   parties approach learning assessment. Departments should consult
   their discipline's pedagogical literature and collect data on what
   works well and what doesn't. They should stress active learning,
   exploit information technology, and not hesitate to experiment
   with new teaching and learning methods. Faculty should be quick
   to adopt their colleagues' successful innovations, which should
   become part of the department's modus operandi and form the
   baseline for future experimentation and improvement.
3. *Work Collaboratively.* Professors should demonstrate collegiality
   in education-related work just as they do in research. For
   example, working in teams brings an array of talent to bear on
   difficult problems, disseminates insight, and allows members to
   hold each other accountable for results. This makes the department a learning organization, not only for disciplinary content
   but also for academic quality processes and outcomes.
4. *Base Decisions on Evidence.* Departments should monitor
   outcomes systematically. The evidentiary principles in table 7.2
   can be used to evaluate student learning, and department
   members also can collect data from graduates and employers.
   Data on student preparation and learning styles can be helpful
   as well. The data should be analyzed carefully in light of disci-

plinary standards and the faculty's professional experience, and findings should be incorporated in the design of curricula, learning processes, and assessment methods.

5. *Strive for Coherence*. Departments should view learning through the lens of the students' entire educational experience. Courses should build on one another to provide the desired depth and breadth. Students' portfolios of educational experiences also should reflect coherence. For example, a mix of large lectures and small seminars may produce better overall learning than the succession of medium-sized classes that consume the same amount of faculty time.

6. *Learn from Best Practice*. Faculty should identify and analyze good practices in comparable departments and institutions, and then adapt the best to their own circumstances. They should compare good versus average or poor practices within their own departments, assess the causes of the differences, and seek ways to improve the subpar performers.

7. *Make Continuous Improvement a Priority*. Departments should strive regularly to improve teaching and learning. Although many professors will continue to place a strong emphasis on research, they should spend enough discretionary time on education quality to maintain an impetus for improvement. Personnel committees should consider the results of such work, along with research and teaching performance, as important evidence for promotion and tenure.[12]

No department, or individual professor for that matter, should be expected to follow the principles in a formal or slavish manner. Reference to the principles is likely to improve performance, however, so considering them in the context of particular decisions (e.g., within each of the five focal areas) represents a worthwhile goal. Doing this requires awareness and understanding, so quality-conscious schools and departments should find ways to inject the principles into faculty thinking.

Maturity of Quality Processes

Experienced quality process reviewers can size up the maturity of a department's academic quality processes in an hour or less of discussion with representative faculty members. Engaged departments present many examples of their thinking, if not organized according to the focal areas, then in terms of another relevant framework. They will table action-oriented documentation and be able to describe the results of interventions they have made. Respondents in departments that have yet to embrace education quality improvement and assurance will be unable to rise above vague generalities.

Rough quantification of the reviewers' judgments turns out to be easier than one might think. My UGC colleagues and I adapted Carnegie Mellon University's Capability Maturity Scale, for advanced development software teams, into a rubric for assessing education quality processes. The scheme asks reviewers to characterize a department's quality process maturity into one of the five categories listed below. Reviewers using the scheme report relatively few difficulties with the categories, although sometimes their ratings span two adjacent ones (e.g., a 2.5 instead of a 2 or a 3)—which poses no problem.

1. *No Effort.* The department asserts little responsibility for education quality and does not have systematic quality processes. Quality improvement and assurance are unmonitored and approached mostly in traditional ways.
2. *Firefighting.* The department responds to problems, but mostly with ad hoc methods. The five focal areas are not covered systematically, and the quality and evidentiary principles receive little if any attention.
3. *Informal Effort.* Individual professors experiment with the quality principles, but few colleagues pay much attention. Coverage of the focal areas remains spotty, and the department has yet to become a learning organization with respect to the quality and evidentiary principles.

4. *Organized Effort.* The department plans and tracks quality process initiatives in all five focal areas. Emergent norms encourage consideration of the quality and evidentiary principles, and methods for gauging performance are under development.

5. *Mature Effort.* The quality principles have become embedded in the department's culture. The idea of regular improvement in all five focal areas and application of the quality and evidentiary principles are well accepted ways of life. The department has accepted planning, tracking, and performance evaluation of quality processes as important elements of peer accountability, and has developed effective methods for doing so.

Making judgments about a department's quality process maturity is not simply an exercise in quantification. Imagine the tough-minded conversations that would occur between department chairs and deans, or between chairs and professors, if performance has been judged to be unsatisfactory. For example, what chair would feel comfortable defending "no effort" or "firefighting" to a concerned dean? What dean would like to defend poor departmental maturity ratings to the provost? What institution would like to defend them to trustees or a state coordinating board, or to accreditors, students, and the public? In other words, the ability to judge a department's quality processes, even approximately, can be a powerful force for improvement.

Embedding Quality Processes in Academic Routines

How does a department climb the maturity scale? I'm reminded of the proverbial question asked by a visitor to New York: "How do I get to Carnegie Hall?" The answer is "Practice, practice, practice!" (Of course, it helps to have some coaching, too.) Figure 7.2 shows how departments can learn good quality assurance and improvement practices, and then, importantly, embed them in their faculty's regular academic routines. The paradigm has been tested in the field at multiple Tennessee Board of Regents campuses and found to be appropriate and helpful.

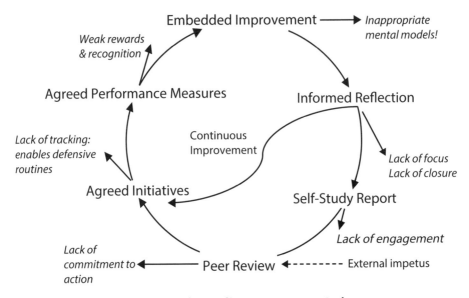

Figure 7.2. The Quality Improvement Cycle

As the figure's title suggests, quality assurance and improvement should be viewed in cyclic terms, with each year's improvements building on the experience of the previous year. In fact, there are two cycles: one embedded within the other. The outer cycle, ideally activated every three to five years, is a deep review of the department's quality processes: informed reflection followed by a self-study, peer review of the self-study, and agreement on specific initiatives to take and performance metrics to adopt. (Readers should consult the aforementioned *Academic Quality Work* volume for detailed descriptions of the steps.)[13] The deep dive provides opportunities for faculty to exercise their thinking about the focal areas and quality and evidentiary principles discussed earlier. Hopefully, one outcome will be progress on developing course- and program-level student learning metrics that can be incorporated into an AR model.

Each step in the process mitigates one or more problems, as depicted by the centrifugal arrows in the figure. For example, "informed reflection" sometimes ends in "lack of focus or closure," but this

problem can be mitigated by a self-study with its need to write coherently to a deadline. Similarly, "lack of engagement" is mitigated
by the prospect of peer review, and "lack of commitment to action"
is mitigated by the need to agree on initiatives. Near the top of the
diagram, "weak rewards and recognition" can be mitigated by embedding the improvement into departmental expectations and routines, which should include provision of appropriate rewards and
recognition for good work.

The outer cycle describes what I've referred to as a "quality
process review," ideally performed every three to five years. This organizational learning and problem-solving exercise produces immediate payoffs. Additionally, it aims to motivate and inform continuous
improvement during the off years as depicted by the inner cycle. Sustaining continuous improvement without formal self-study and peer
review means that quality has become embedded in the department's
processes and culture: in other words, the "organized effort" or "mature effort" levels of capability. The "embedded improvement" step,
at the top of the diagram, represents both a beginning and a culmi-
nation. It is the job of departmental leadership to keep the wheel
spinning.

Using the Market, Economic, and Quality Information

The new market, resourcing, and quality information has many
obvious applications in both traditional and comparative program
review. I'll discuss only one in each category. They illustrate the kinds
of things that can be done to make the program review conversations
more comprehensive.

Program Portfolio Analysis

Portfolio analysis emphasizes the totality of a set of activities rather
than the attributes of each activity separately. Balancing risk and
return in an investment portfolio probably is the best-known example. Here the "totality" depends on the correlations among the investment vehicles as well as each one's expectations for total return

and standard deviation of return (which is the usual metric for risk). A business firm's "product portfolio" also seeks to balance risk and return, but with the added twist that managers' ability to change the mix of products depends on market forces and internal economic factors rather than on a low-cost "buy" or "sell" decision. This puts a premium on identifying market trends in relation to profitability: for example, the famous classification by the Boston Consulting Group of products as stars, dogs, cash cows, and question marks. Stars are products that are profitable and growing, and thus candidates for additional investment. Cash cows are profitable but in static or declining markets and thus are more likely to be "milked" than enhanced. Dogs are both unprofitable and declining, and thus may be on the way to elimination. Finally, question mark products are growing but unprofitable; they have possibilities, but success is uncertain. Variations on the model use different measures of market potential and demand, but profitability is the common denominator.

Figure 7.3 applies these concepts to academic program portfolios. It is built around five broad indicators of a program's academic and financial sustainability, which I have adapted from analogous charts offered by Gray Associates and the Pilbara Group.

1. *Program Size*. Large programs tend to be more stable than small ones, but the variations that do occur are likely to have more important financial consequences. Therefore, institutions typically concentrate on the financial sustainability of their large programs. The exception occurs when multiple small programs are losing money, which may require remedial action.

2. *Margin/Credit Hour.* "Per credit hour" figures provide significantly different information from aggregate ones. They are used for comparing courses and programs to identify potential areas for expansion and contraction, and/or potential operating efficiencies. For example, large programs with relatively low margins/credit hours may be candidates for redesign, even though they make significant money overall. These data and the

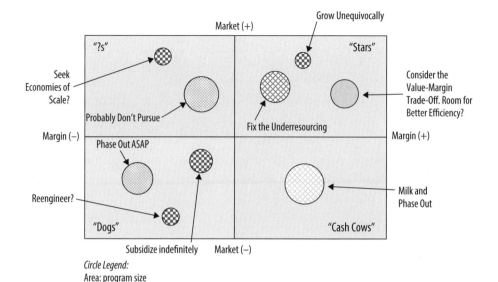

Figure 7.3. Program Portfolio Chart

data for Indicator #1 are obtainable from the new breed of AR models that are changing decision makers' perspectives about how their institution's "internal economy" affects academic as well as financial performance.

3. *Market Performance and Prospects.* Both student demand and competition matter. Modern market information systems provide detailed, forward-looking, and customized data about each program's actual and potential student demand and competitive environment. This promises to do for the university's "external economy" what the AR models do for its "internal economy."

4. *Contribution to Mission.* This refers to alignment with the university's goals, values, and roster of activities. It is the "business of the business." Delivering on mission should be a primary and articulatable institutional goal, even though the contributions of particular programs are and will remain matters of judgment. Assessments of contributions can be obtained from

statements by advocates, program reviews, and previous conversations about university priorities. These data cannot be codified,
but they can and should be organized in ways that are meaningful to senior academic resource allocators.

5. *Sufficiency of Resourcing.* You need to consider whether the
assigned human, physical, and financial resources are fit for
purpose. Data can include average class sizes; teacher types;
room configurations for plenaries, breakouts, and labs; and the
demands on faculty effort for different kinds of teaching tasks.
For example, programs where class sizes, teaching loads, and
adjunct usage are growing relative to benchmarks show evidence
that may point to resource insufficiency. Forcing professors to
work beyond their comfort levels or students to work under
suboptimal conditions undermines academic sustainability.

All the data needed to calculate these indicators are available from
today's academic resourcing and market information systems. The
academic resource management models also provide data on the
courses that students take as they complete their degree requirements,
which are essential for interpreting and acting on the indicators.
Many of the available interventions with respect to program sustainability require attention to curricula or the individual courses that
make them up. (Pure program-level decisions include admissions targets, pricing, and financial aid.) A good academic resourcing system
will make this information available along with data on the indicators themselves.

Briefing Books for Program Reviewers

I have argued that program reviewers should add market, economic, and teaching quality information to their repertoire of evaluations. But how can this process be initiated? One simple approach is
to summarize both the old and new information in a briefing book
for the reviewers and organize an orientation session for discussing
it. Overseers of the process should pose whatever questions occur to

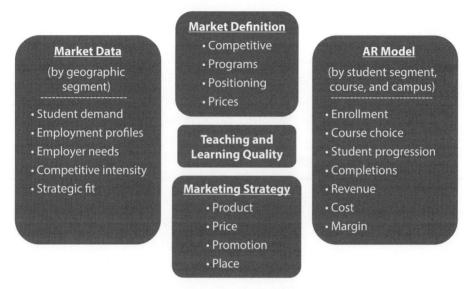

Figure 7.4. Briefing Book Content

them and also ask the reviewers to formulate their own questions. This won't necessarily jump-start the needed conversations, but it is a way to get the ball rolling. Hopefully the natural inquisitiveness of academics will cause at least some reviewers to engage with the new material.

Figure 7.4 presents my thinking about the data that should be considered for inclusion. It calls out five categories of information, as follows:

1. *Market Definition*: a concise description, prepared by the program's governing faculty, of intended content, target market, significant competitors, and positioning with respect to the market and competitors. Such information is the minimum necessary for thinking about markets and the institution's internal capacities and politics. It is essential for decisions about potential new programs and for comprehensive review of existing ones.
2. *Marketplace Data*: externally obtained information about student demand, employer needs and wants, competitive

intensity, and strategic fit. The variables and displays were described earlier in this chapter.

3. *Data from AR Models*: internally generated information about teaching processes and their financial outcomes. The organizers of program reviews may select from the various displays and dashboards discussed in earlier chapters, or they may provide access to the interactive dashboards themselves (perhaps limited to the program in question and to certain variables).

4. *Quality Assessments*: brief narratives describing the available information about teaching and learning quality, including executive summaries of assessment team reports and capability maturity scores, if available. I recommend that appropriate quality process evaluations be conducted in the run-up to comprehensive program review.

5. *Marketing Strategies*: descriptions of the institution's efforts to market the program, so reviewers can relate these to the program's activities and marketplace data. It's desirable for reviewers to have such data even when they are not specifically charged with evaluating the marketing strategy.

I envision an attractively presented briefing book that makes the data accessible in a single place. The objective, as always, is to stimulate deep conversations about the important issues. Exactly how the information will improve these conversations remains to be seen, but one thing is certain: the desired improvements won't occur without the new data. It's possible that much of the material won't get used initially. However, with an appropriate agenda and nudges by the university, both the briefing book and the conversations will improve over time.

CHAPTER EIGHT

Universities as Mission-Driven Enterprises

One of the biggest barriers to the adoption of academic resourcing models has proved to be concerns by faculty that doing so will "turn the university into a business." As a former professor myself, I can understand that concern. Part of this stems from the view that margin, which plays such a central role in AR models, equates to profit, and that profit has no place in a traditional academic institution. The case against the proposition is very strong, but its demonstration requires considerable explanation. The case is presented in the first half of this chapter. The second half describes a model I have developed for reducing the ideas to practice in the context of university budgeting.

The Not-for-Profit Paradigm

Traditional universities are not-for-profit institutions. The goal of these institutions is to serve the public interest rather than the private interests of owner-shareholders. This means that no one outside the university can claim its surpluses from operations. That's not the only difference, though. A well-run business will respond more strongly to the demands of the marketplace than will a not-for-profit university, which seeks to balance these demands with "intrinsic values" derived from its own mission. Both types of entity also must take account of the technical and behavioral laws that govern people's ability to produce (what economists call the "production function"), and also the governmental regulations and political objectives that both enable and constrain the entity's decision makers. It is the balancing of mission, market, and money that distinguishes a not-for-profit from a profit-maximizing organization.[1]

Figure 8.1 compares the not-for-profit paradigm with its better-known for-profit counterpart. Not-for-profit entities maximize mission attainment, but their ability to do so is not unlimited. They must observe the operational, governmental, and market constraints referred to earlier. They also must ensure that their overall margin (revenue minus cost for the institution as a whole) isn't persistently in the red—which eventually would drive the school to bankruptcy. Conversely, for-profit entities maximize total profit (i.e., overall margin) subject to the aforementioned operational and market constraints. For-profits can go bankrupt, too, if they suffer large sustained losses. The "not-for-profit difference" comes from dislodging margin as the maximizing objective and putting it on the same basis as the other constraints. Money remains crucially important to not-for-profits, but in a very different way than for for-profits. It's a means for mission attainment in universities, whereas it is the overriding objective in business firms.

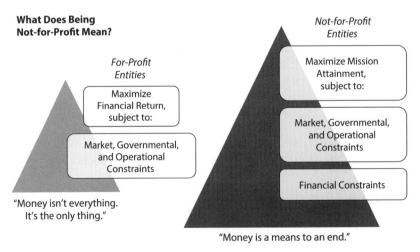

Figure 8.1. The Not-for-Profit Difference

The aforementioned can be summed up by comparing the basic decision rules that guide for-profit and not-for-profit behavior. The profit-making rule, taught in elementary microeconomics courses, is that programs should be expanded until marginal revenue equals marginal cost: that is, until $MR = MC$. What's different for not-for-profit entities is that (1) mission-related values must somehow enter the picture *and* (2) total revenues always must equal total costs.[2] The first point causes the left side of the $MR = MC$ rule to become a weighted average of marginal revenue and marginal value (contribution to mission). The new rule is $MR + \lambda\ MV = MC$, where λ is the aforementioned weighting factor (to be discussed later). We shall see that the difference produces profound results.

The not-for-profit model has more moving parts than its for-profit counterpart, but the following provides an informal sense of how it works.

Imagine a "classic" liberal arts college that offers two kinds of courses: the traditional humanities, arts, and sciences courses for this kind of institution, and a program of business courses. First, suppose the college is in financial equilibrium with both programs at their optimal size according to the not-for-profit decision rule, and that this has resulted in surpluses from business that cross-subsidize the liberal arts courses. One might ask why the college doesn't expand business to increase its operating surplus, which then would allow it to expand or improve the quality of its liberal arts program.

The answer (based on the aforementioned equilibrium) is that expanding business would reduce the college's values more than expanding liberal arts would increase them. In other words, business's incremental contribution to mission is negative and larger than the incremental positive contributions of the liberal arts programs that benefit from the cross-subsidies. It's business's negative incremental mission contribution that deters the college from enlarging it despite its positive margin. The argument goes like this:

"Our business courses are profitable, but we don't want them to dominate the college's sense of itself."

Now suppose the college falls on hard times financially due to sharp losses in the value of its endowment, but that neither its margins nor its fundamental values have changed. Getting to a new equilibrium may well involve expanding the business program in order to minimize the consequences for the liberal arts. What's happened is that the weighting of value in the college's decision rule ("λ") has gotten smaller as financial urgency has increased, which has made the revenue term more important.

Economist Estelle James and I independently developed this theory of not-for-profit behavior in the late 1970s. Using the same rigorous tools as in the for-profit case, we showed how market forces are "buffered," so to speak, by balancing them with the university's mission: that is, by adding marginal value to the not-for-profit decision rule. This is not a case of limited rationality but a conscious and entirely proper exercise of judgment as provided for by law and in the entity's not-for-profit charter. The effect of this buffering is very important. It should permeate the academic resourcing conversations of a traditional university.

Differences between For-Profit and Not-for-Profit Enterprises

The most important differences between the economic behavior of for-profit and not-for-profit entities follow. (See appendix C for more formal statements.)

- For-profit entities expand programs (or products) as long as their incremental revenue exceeds their incremental cost, whereas not-for-profits also consider the programs' incremental contributions to their mission.
- Cross-subsidies are suppressed in for-profit entities because the money is paid out as dividends. No such payments are made by not-for-profits. The money funds cross-subsidies, which reflect the very important differences between what the market wants

and what the university wants based on its mission. (See the business–liberal arts trade-off in the previous narrative, for example.) Defining and acting on these differences is a defining feature of not-for-profit entities.

- Extreme financial stringency (short of bankruptcy) depresses for-profits' share prices and increases the likelihood of hostile takeovers. These are nonissues in not-for-profits, but what does happen is that mission becomes less important relative to the possibilities for making money.
- Both types of entities have strong incentives to raise prices to the extent permitted by the marketplace: in for-profits because they want to distribute bigger dividends and in not-for-profits because they want to fund more and better academic programs.
- Both types of entities have incentives for efficiency and productivity improvement. Savings fall to the bottom line in for-profit entities. They relax the financial constraint in not-for-profit ones, which enhances the funds available for cross-subsidies.

In summary, traditional universities must pay close attention to their margins because money is what permits them to fund their programs. Cross-subsidies, which play the role of dividends to shareholders in for-profit entities, enable not-for-profit institutions to fund programs at levels that would not be supportable in the marketplace alone. Financial stringency reduces traditional universities' ability to subsidize programs to the point where markets, and only markets, dominate their program offerings. In other words, universities teetering on the edge of bankruptcy must prioritize moneymaking over their mission-based values in order to survive. Ironically, academics who try to "purify" their university by eschewing the management of margin risk hastening the day when money must be prioritized over mission.

The differences between mission- and market-based values are important in other ways as well. I described in *Reengineering the University* how the market is more likely to value the teaching of pragmatic skills, abilities, and experiences, and how it has a relatively short-term horizon. Conversely, traditional universities tend to have a broader perspective and a longer-term horizon.[3] Universities put higher value on furnishing the mind for a lifetime of thinking, by requiring humanities and basic science study, than do most undergraduates. Universities also consider the needs of nonmarket stakeholders, including the society as a whole. In research, for example, they value basic research more than most corporate sponsors and many government agencies. Goals related to diversity, affordability, degree attainment by disadvantaged students, and the preservation of culture also come to mind. I find it hard to understand why some market-oriented critics of higher education so vociferously discount these mission-related values.

We see examples of not-for-profit behavior everywhere in the traditional university sector. Universities eliminate or limit teaching and research programs that, while laden with profit potential, fail to pass muster in terms of academic mission. Professors sometimes override the preferences of their students, the students' employers, and donors when they make value-based judgments about what should be taught. Deans and provosts provide long-term cross-subsidies for some programs by using surpluses from others. All require bucking the market to some degree—the kind of buffering described earlier. These actions are taken unapologetically. They are deeply embedded in the university's culture. More importantly, they are consistent with the purposes and incentives built into the not-for-profit organizational form. They always should be front and center in academic resourcing conversations.

More about Margins

In well-run universities, margin is more than an accounting metric. It provides insight into the relative contributions that programs make to the institution's mission. There is, in fact, a strong inverse relationship between margins and academic values. Appendix C shows this synergy can be summed up by the relation:

Effective value contribution = −Margin

where both are expressed in per-student or per–credit hour terms. What this means is that mission contribution is inversely proportional to margin in a not-for-profit institution that has optimized the size of its programs.

What emerges from this relationship is that money-losing programs have positive value contributions, and conversely. This was illustrated by the business–liberal arts example presented earlier, and we will see it again in the model for reducing not-for-profit theory to practice that is presented in the next section. It goes back to the commonsense notion that programs with positive margins should be expanded until nonfinancial factors, in this case mission-related considerations, cause the expansion to be halted.[4]

Figure 8.2 illustrates the value curve as a function of program size. The curve's rising portion reflects an appetite for increasing size, but after a while the appetite becomes sated and further increases are viewed negatively. Business studies as used in the example given earlier provide a classic case: initially they add needed diversity to the curriculum, but if too large they unbalance the institution's academic program portfolio.[5]

The slope of the value curve represents the value added or subtracted by a one-unit change in program size: what I am calling its

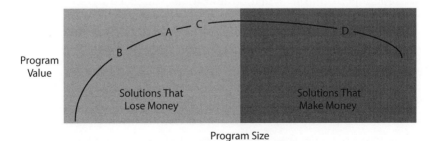

Program Value

Program Size

Figure 8.2. Relationship between Mission Contribution and Size

marginal (or incremental) value at that point on the size scale. Maximizing the value function requires the function's slope to equal minus the program's incremental margin at the optimum point. This
means the solutions for programs that lose money must lie on the
left-hand side of the diagram, and conversely. Suppose a program's
margin/unit happens to equal $-\Delta$ *Value* at the output represented at
point A. This is the output level at which mission contribution is at
its maximum given the university's current funding limit. A solution
at point B would be too small because, when all the other activities
are considered, money could be made available to support a larger
subsidy. Similarly, a solution at point C would be too large because
that would draw a larger-than-optimal subsidy.

The causal drivers are reversed on the right-hand side of the diagram. Consider point D, for example. The budget poses no problem
because increases in program size make money. However, the university's sense of mission tells it that such an increase would detract
from the mission. The aforementioned business program example is
instructive once again: for instance, increases from point D would
unbalance the program portfolio more than could be compensated
for by the larger earned margin.

Considerations like the aforementioned inform decisions about
items 6 and 11 ("Program investment or disinvestment" and "Improving program review") in the list of AR model applications given in the
prologue. I don't mean to suggest that academic resource managers do
or should perform the actual optimizations suggested by this reasoning. That would require unattainable information about the mission
contributions of all programs, not to mention about how they interact
in the context of the school's overall program portfolio. Yet the reasoning does explain what well-run universities tend to do in practice. It
also clarifies what the not-for-profit paradigm says they should be trying to do. Hopefully this will improve academic resourcing conversations about reducing the chaotic character of decision-making.

The idea that moneymaking programs have negative incremental
value in well-run universities may seem esoteric or counterintuitive,

but, in fact, it is filled with meaning. Overdoing the pursuit of margin can have serious, deleterious effects on mission. This may not be as obvious as the opposite problem of overreaching in terms of mission, which can seriously damage an institution's financial health, but it is equally true. I have asserted the need to balance mission and margin throughout this book. That balance requires one to avoid overreaching in either direction. Additionally, as I have stated repeatedly, the correct balance can only be determined by people with deep academic knowledge who also are well informed about the money side of their university's operations. Academic resourcing models provide academic officers and faculty with the data they need to work (with business officers) on achieving the right balance.

Institutional versus Local Values

I noted earlier that my one-time colleague Jim March described university decision-making as organized anarchy. Misunderstandings about the not-for-profit decision paradigm contribute significantly to this anarchy. First, there is the great confusion about the paradigm itself—about what constitutes proper not-for-profit behavior. This spawns a cacophony of arguments and decision interpretations that do look anarchic. I hope a wider understanding of the not-for-profit paradigm, coupled with the advent with better tools for implementing it, will mitigate this problem over time.

Different perceptions about the relevant facts of a situation provide a second explanation for March's anarchy. Universities are complex organizations—often more so than the largest business firms. Different data and perceptions lead to different conclusions. They make it harder to find common ground or discuss compromises. The resulting chaos contributes to the sense of anarchy. This problem can be mitigated through provision of better data and more coherent academic resourcing conversations.

Lack of agreement about values is perhaps the most important contributor to the seemingly anarchic behavior. Academic resource managers, and especially faculty, differ vociferously about what's important and how it should be pursued. Universities are neither monoliths nor hierarchical, management-driven organizations, and how the interests of the various players should be weighed is always a fraught subject. Different schools and departments, and teaching and research programs, may well have distinct missions. Self-interest plays a role as well. Faculty careers depend on the resources allocated to their programs by academic resourcing processes.

In *Reengineering the University*, I described how a professor's human capital tends to be more specific to his or her program and university than is the case for, say, professionals in other fields.[6] This arguably confers "property rights" that can make academic resourcing a blood sport, especially when the facts of the situation and the applicable decision-making principles are controversial. The answer lies in the ability of these groups to negotiate their differences through informed conversation. And this, in turn, requires the kind of AR models described in this book.

An Approach for Balancing Mission and Money

We now come to what might be called "the last mile problem" in university budgeting: how to link the powerful information systems and models that increasingly support economic and market analysis with the "soft" judgments about mission contribution that lie at the center of budget-making. The term was coined to describe the connections between local telecommunication switching centers, with their powerful computer and fiber technologies, and customer sites— connections that for a long time represented the weak link in a rapidly evolving system. How to assess mission contribution and balance it with margin and market have become the weak links in university budgeting. Every traditional university must do this balancing once a year, or more often if responsibility center budgeting or another decentralized system devolves budget-making responsibility to schools or faculties.

In *Reengineering the University*, I introduced a new approach for bridging this last mile. I will review and extend that discussion here and in appendix C. The approach makes maximal use of the information available to the budget process and brings consistency and rationality to what has too often been an ad hoc process. Perhaps most importantly, it ensures that budget makers keep mission firmly in mind when making their choices. This is especially important in situations where highly quantitative financial and market analytics, and the advocates for their more extensive use, can come to dominate the conversations. The proposed method ensures that "soft" mission considerations get their proper emphasis and helps users process the subjective judgments required to do so.

The basic method is powerful yet easy to apply. Add-on algorithms for enhancing certain aspects of the process are described in appendix C, but the basic method can stand on its own.[7] Technically, this is a multi-attribute constrained choice system with judgmentally determined preferences. ("Preferences" refer to estimated mission contributions.) However, I'll just call it the "constrained choice system." As noted, it represents an attempt to reduce the not-for-profit decision paradigm to practice in the context of university budgeting.

How to Make Better Choices

Let's start with first principles. Sooner or later, even the most sophisticated university budgeting systems boil down to the problem of choosing from a list of options according to subjectively determined preferences, subject to a predetermined limit on resources.

Remember what it was like as a child to walk into a penny candy store with a quarter in your pocket and an insatiable longing for all you saw? All the items look good, but some look better than others. Each has a different price, and your coin will only go so far. One's natural tendency is to muddle through by selecting what appear to be the most preferred items, one at a time, until the money is exhausted—but this turns out to be a bad strategy. It's all very complicated, but that's what it's like to set a university's budget. Worse, in a university there always are people (deans or chairs, for instance) who urge you to accept their proposals and predict dire consequences if you fail to do so.[8]

Let's formalize the situation. One starts with a list of proposed funding and/or budget reduction options, each of which is characterized by a priority (contribution to mission) and a financial outcome (estimated margin, which may be positive or negative). The problem is to choose the sublist of options that maximizes total mission contribution, subject to a fixed limit on new spending (budget limit).[9] Data about market and perhaps other factors also may affect the decisions, but they'll be brought in later.[10]

The problem of making rational choices among options is of more than passing difficulty. (It's easy enough to muddle through as in the candy store example, but we should not be satisfied with muddling if its avoidable.) Consider the following highly simplified example from outside higher education. You are asked to choose among high-value items for shipping to a far-off destination, subject to a strict weight limit of two hundred pounds. The list of items appears in table 8.1. Your goal is to select the most valuable combination of items whose combined weight does not exceed the specified limit. The

Table 8.1. A Simple Shipping Problem

Item Number	Value (Dollars)	Weight (Pounds)
1	1,000	150
2	850	100
3	800	80
4	500	70
5	400	50
Feasible Combinations of Items		
3, 4, 5	1,700	200
1, 5	1,400	200
2, 3	1,650	180
2, 4	1,350	170

solution, easily obtained in this case by eyeballing the data, is to choose items 3, 4, and 5 for a combined value of $1,700 and a weight of exactly two hundred pounds. Unfortunately, solutions by enumeration aren't practical for the dozens or hundreds of options that arise in real university budgeting. Established computer algorithms can solve the shipping example as illustrated,[11] but they don't work well with judgmentally determined preferences.

As noted, the university's assessment of the options' relative contributions to mission are and must be subjective. These preferences take the form of a rank-ordering from best to worst; it does not appear to be practical to judge how much better one alternative is to another. Let's assume the rankings are set by a group of senior leaders (let's call them the budget group), headed by the president, provost, a dean, or in some governance structures a senior faculty member. (I'll describe the ranking process later.) Budget groups can state their preference for one option over another, but they can't specify a formula that covers all the options. There is no way to get to a set of cardinal numbers like the dollar figures in table 8.1.

Budget groups usually address the choice problem by proceeding iteratively using "rules of thumb": for example, by deciding judgmentally on the best option, putting it on the "funded" list, judging the next best item, and so on until the spending limit is reached. Or the group reverses the process by judging and eliminating the worst option, then the next worst, and so on until the remaining options fit within the spending limit. Then they go back through the lists and perhaps make fine-tuning changes. It's hard to apply either method in a way that seems satisfying if the list of options is long, but at least the process comes across as logical.

The problem arises in foreseeing the consequences of choices in one iteration on those that come later. In the shipping illustration, for example, the most preferred item was so costly that selecting it would have precluded choosing others that in the aggregate are worth more. (Creating a weighted average of the preference rankings and costs doesn't work, either.) Among other things, budget makers should avoid overemphasizing the financial outcomes in relation to mission just because the financial data are stated in numeric terms.

Other strategies include eliminating options that can be supported using restricted funds or given one-time approval only. (The latter aren't added to the budget base.) My colleague Ray Bacchetti, Stanford's longtime vice provost for planning and budgeting, called this "migration analysis"—the idea being that some options "could be induced to migrate" from the "requested" column in his spreadsheet to the "restricted fund" or "one-time funding" column. But while restricted and one-time funding strategies should be considered in budgeting, neither can solve the underlying choice problem.

My proposed constrained choice model offers just such a solution, which is described under the following headings:

- Codifying preferences by *rank-ordering* the options' contributions to mission.
- Adjusting the options' margins to take account of *time-varying financial consequences*, in cases where these occur.
- Selecting which options to adopt by judgmentally balancing their attributes (intrinsic value, expected market outcomes, and financial consequences) with the aid of a "new constrained choice app."

Two additional procedures are described in appendix C. They are more complicated analytically and not fully reduced practice, but I present them in hopes of stimulating future research and development.

- *Quantifying the preference structure*, as revealed by the budget group's selections in the third point, in terms of an algebraic formula.
- Using the formula to perform *quick what-if analyses* if the spending limit or other elements of the options' dataset change.

Taken together, I hope that the five procedures will point the way toward solving the last mile problem in university budgeting. As noted, the first three can be used with good effect, at the present time, by any institution.

RANK-ORDERING MISSION CONTRIBUTIONS

Budget groups must confront the subjective value assessment problem if they want to bring mission contribution into budgeting in a systematic way. Both common sense and the not-for-profit paradigm provide incentives to get the maximin contribution possible in light of the budget limit. Maximizing financial return or some other metric not specifically related to mission violates the fundamental tenets of not-for-profit universities. Decision makers must grapple with mission on its own terms, as daunting a task as that may appear.

The first step is to rank-order the options' mission contributions. Mission should be construed broadly to include societal and ethical values as well as narrowly defined academic ones. I have sat in many budget group meetings where these values swirl together in debates about what the university should or should not do. Written mission statements can inform these conversations, but they never include enough detail to be dispositive. My advice to those who judge these matters is that, in the end, you must trust your judgment about what is right. The ability to do this well is a prime criterion for choosing senior academic officers in most if not all not-for-profit universities.

One principle must be observed, however: the ranking process must be performed without reference to the economic data. To judge the options' mission contributions even partly on the basis of their margins would contaminate the process. (Don't worry, margin gets into the analysis later.) Hence my strong recommendation is that budget groups should hide the data on financial consequences when judging mission contribution.

The next question is how to do the rank-ordering. This subject has been studied for more than fifty years, and there is a large literature that covers many different situations. The general view is that peoples' judgments are most reliable for the top-ranked three and bottom-ranked three items in any list, and that it's hard to keep more than

Suggested Ranking Procedure for Individuals

1. Create a set of mission contribution categories, ranging from "best" to "worst," each of which eventually will contain nine items.
2. Remove the best three items from the list and place them in the top category; remove the worst three items and place them in the bottom category. Repeat this two more times, augmenting the top and bottom categories until they are filled.
3. Repeat step 2 for the second-best and second-worst categories, and again for the next-best and next-worst categories. Repeat again and again until the original list is empty.
4. Reclassify pairs of options near the boundaries of the categories if, upon reflection, the ranks appeared to be inverted. For example, an option near the bottom of the best category might be interchanged with an item near the top of the second-best category.
5. Rank-order the items within each category, proceeding iteratively from the top and bottom to meet in the middle. (Recall that options within the original tranches of three were not ranked, and that inversions of ranks near the tranche boundaries remain possible.) Tied rankings are acceptable and probably will occur fairly often.
6. Repeat steps 4 and 5 until you are satisfied with your judgments. At this point, the whole list has been sorted and the contribution categories become irrelevant.

seven to nine items in mind at any one time. My colleagues and I applied a few methods from the literature to university budgeting in the 1970s. This convinced me that the simplest methods work best, and that group processes need to be simpler than ones used by individuals.[12]

The sidebar lists six steps that individuals can use to sort decision options according to mission contribution. They're based on the so-called Q-sort method, which has been applied to a wide variety of situations but not, so far as I know, to the ranking of mission contributions. The approach is grounded in the general understandings about human mental capacity mentioned earlier. Steps 1 through 3 move tranches of options from the original list to a coarsely sorted list, and steps 4 through 6 refine the judgments to produce a more finely sorted list. Users should not feel bound to the details, however, as experience surely will lead to useful modifications.

My experience with budget groups suggests the aforementioned process is too complicated for group work. It would grind to a halt as too many people weigh in with minor objections at each stage. Instead, a group may be able to process more information at once than a single person can. Thus the group might combine steps 1 through 3 by assigning options directly to the mission contribution categories. For example, members might agree on the top ten options, then the bottom ten, and so on until the list of options is empty.

The individual and group approaches are easily combined.[13] The provost or dean might ask a few knowledgeable and respected people, perhaps members of the senior staff whose job it is to support the budget group, to rank the options individually. The rankers might be asked to report directly to the budget group or try to reconcile their rankings before reporting. The budget group would then apply step 5 to one or more ranked lists or start with an earlier step if it wished to make more extensive changes. In the end, of course, it is the provost or dean who is accountable for the university's academic performance, so that person should have the last word on setting the rankings.

FINANCIAL OUTCOMES THAT VARY OVER TIME

The financial impacts of some options vary over time, even when measured in constant dollars. Hiring professors who need laboratories and starting new degree programs incur start-up costs, for example, and budget reduction initiatives may incur termination costs or need to be phased in over time. University budget makers face a quandary in these situations. Should they budget such items on a pay-as-you-go basis or smooth the financial effects in some way that allows them to recognize eventual losses on a current basis or obtain immediate credit for long-run gains?

Business firms solve the problem by capitalizing major start-ups and setting aside reserves, usually in ways that don't count against current profits, to handle the one-time costs of downsizing. Both businesses and universities capitalize the cost of construction and software development projects and then depreciate or amortize them over time. A growing number of universities analyze the time paths of revenue and expense for ordinary budget options, but few build these data directly into go–no go decisions. They think of the consequences as benefits or liabilities for future budget cycles. This is fine as far as it goes, but it would be better to address the whole range of consequences at the beginning rather than let them overhang the future.

Most university budgets are built around the base revenues and expenditures that derive from their various activities. These financial flows are expected to continue in constant dollars unless the underlying activities are reengineered or rescaled, or until changed external conditions require their elimination. Any method for smoothing revenue and expense transients should fit smoothly into the base-budget analysis. And because universities must choose among start-up and phaseout situations that are intermixed with conventional options, the smoothing method should integrate seamlessly with the choice process—which should operate in its usual manner once the needed financial smoothing has been done.

The constrained choice system requires the sum of margins for selected options to fit within a predetermined spending limit. The implicit assumption was that the margins pertain to the current year, but the preceding paragraphs explain why this is a bad policy. The model puts the problem into sharp focus and thus motivates the search for a solution. I'll propose two such solutions: one involving some financial engineering and the other a workaround that leaves the heavy lifting to users' judgment.

My proposed financial engineering solution is based on the revolving fund concept that some schools use for facilities renewal. The basic idea is simple: one finances initial deficits from a revolving fund and pays them back with an annual budget base allocation that is determined at the project's outset. The calculations are best done in constant dollars. Appendix F of *Reengineering the University* briefly introduces the idea as an interesting enhancement of choice modeling, but I have come to believe it addresses a broader problem. This is the disconnect between the cash accounting that's typical of university budget-making and the net present value (NPV) calculations used to evaluate proposals with time-varying financial consequences.

Adding an item to the budget base means its expenditure or revenue will carry forward to future years unless further action is taken to remove or change it. (Year-to-year inflationary cost rise can be handled by financial staff and need not concern us here.) For options with time-varying financial consequences, however, neither the first-year margin nor the NPV can be compared "apples to apples" with the university's annual spending limit. Use of current margin requires one to set up a system of recordkeeping that will adjust the budget for the expected cash flow changes in each subsequent year.

My proposed procedure eliminates this requirement by converting the time stream of varying revenues and expenses into a time-invariant summary figure I call "adjusted margin." This figure is added to or subtracted from the budget base just like the margin for an ordinary option, whose inflation-adjusted costs or net revenues remain constant over time. Indeed, applying the conversion procedure to an option with unvarying constant-dollar financial consequences yields the original margin figure. This allows options with time-varying and time-invariant financial consequences to be intermixed freely in the budget process.

Table 8.2 presents two examples of how the conversion procedure works for options that lose money early and produce surpluses later. The top panel describes a new master of science (MS) program that eventually will be profitable but where initial revenues grow more slowly than costs. The lower panel describes a downsizing initiative where initial termination costs are followed by expenditure reductions that are phased in over time. Year-by-year forecasts are provided

Table 8.2. Two Examples of Margin Adjustment (Dollars in Thousands)

New Master of Science Program				
Adjusted Margin	Fiscal Year			Steady
47	1	2	3	State
1. Revenue	0	200	325	375
2. Expense	(100)	(200)	(300)	(300)
3. Budget Base Allocation (Contribution)	(47)	(47)	(47)	(47)
4. Interest/Amortization Payment		(6)	(8)	(28)
5. Profit or Loss Net of Adjusted Margin	(147)	(53)	(30)	0
6. Owed to the Revolving Fund	147	199	229	

Downsizing Initiative				
Adjusted Margin	Fiscal Year			Steady
224	1	2	3	State
1. Revenue	0	0	0	0
2. Expense	(200)	100	200	300
3. Budget Base Allocation (Contribution)	(224)	(224)	(224)	(224)
4. Interest/Amortization payment		(17)	(23)	(76)
5. Profit or Loss Net of Adjusted Margin	(424)	(141)	(47)	0
6. Owed to the Revolving Fund	424	566	613	

Note: Assumptions: Amortization period = years; Annual interest rate = 4%.

for three years, followed by a steady-state column where the figures remain unchanged in constant dollars. Lines 1 and 2 contain the forecasts for revenue and expense, respectively. (The downsizing example does not involve revenue.) There is nothing unusual about the display so far, but things change when we get to the calculation of adjusted margin.

Let's start by assuming that the new MS program's adjusted margin equals $47,000, as shown in the upper left-hand corner of the table. The assumption is used at line 3, where the negative of adjusted margin (−$47,000) is inserted into the cash flow for each planning year and the steady state. The negative sign appears because positive margins represent money earned by the activity, and negative margins represent subsidies from the central university. The activity's initial negative margins are financed from the revolving fund mentioned earlier. Line 6 shows the outstanding loan balance at the end of each year of the planning period, and line 4 shows the interest charged on these balances (4.5 percent per year). Line 5 shows the activity's profit or loss after taking account of the assumed adjusted margin.

The key to calculating adjusted margin lies in the boldfaced figure at the end of line 4 ($28 for the new MS program). It is the annual payment needed to amortize the amount owed to the revolving fund at the end of the planning period ($229,000) over the specified re-payment period (fifteen years). Put another way, line 4 shows that the loan is interest-only until the end of the planning period (year 3) and then is subject to a level payment during the steady state that combines principal and interest as in a home mortgage. The calcula-tion uses Excel's PMT function and SOLVER add-in procedure. The software amortizes the loan balance while requiring the profit or loss net of adjusted margin (line 6) to be zero for each year of the steady state: for example, $375 - $300 - $47 - $28 = $0 for the new MS pro-gram. SOLVER searches through alternative assumptions for ad-justed margin until it finds the one that causes all the figures to come out right—a process that requires only a second or so of computa-tion. Interested readers can verify that any other value of adjusted margin will produce a different amortization payment and, thus, a non-zero value for the steady state's bottom line.

The new MS program has an adjusted margin of +$47,000, which is much larger than its initial loss and much smaller than its steady-state annual profit. The procedure has smoothed out the variations by using the revolving fund as a buffer. The positive adjusted margin is an artifact of the data in the illustration: revenue reductions and/or expense increases could easily produce negative figures. The down-sizing illustration works the same way, with the initial loss and later gains producing an adjusted margin of +$224,000. As with any re-volving fund, the university will need to supply the initial capital and consider adding to it from time to time as experience is gained and conditions change: for example, if unexpected setbacks make it necessary to write off the outstanding balance for some previously selected option.[14]

The workaround method mentioned earlier is less powerful, though it may appeal to schools that don't wish to adopt the financially engineered solution.[15] Each option's NPV is calculated using conventional methods (essentially based on the first two lines in table 8.2) and then considered to be just another descriptive attribute. The budget limit is applied to a conventional margin figure, which may be the first year's figure or one that's modified slightly to exclude "special start-up" or similar expenditures. The budget staff must remember to adjust future budgets as activities come fully onstream, just as they do today.

A PRACTICAL METHOD FOR CHOOSING

To review matters briefly, the budget group must choose items from a rank-ordered list of dozens or hundreds of proposed options, so as to maximize total mission contribution subject to a fixed spending limit. We've already seen that humans (even the astute members of a university budget group) can't process that much information at once. Something must be done to reduce the cognitive load—and, as I've noted, ad hoc approaches don't work very well.

Algorithms exist for solving the choice problem when the options' values are expressed in a metric like dollars, but they fail when the valuations consist of rankings. For example, reanalysis of table 8.1 shows the best solution based strictly on rankings is to choose items 2 and 3, which isn't even close to the dollar-maximizing solution (items 3, 4, and 5). This is because the options' dollar values do not vary uniformly with changes in the rankings. There is a $150 difference between items 1 and 2 but only a $50 difference between items 2 and 3, for example. This kind of nonlinearity is the rule rather than the exception in preference analysis.

Happily, two commonsense principles, applied iteratively, will simplify the constrained choice problem to the point where the judgmental process becomes practical. The choice process will proceed by moving items from the "available" list to the list of already-budgeted items and then proceeding iteratively until the sum of the budgeted items' margins hits the spending limit: in other words, it is "selection without replacement." Now imagine that you stand ready to select your first option. The whole daunting list stretches before you, but it turns out that there is no need to consider all the available items together at this or any other stage of the choice process. The principles are as follows:

- *Affordability Principle.* You need consider only the available options that are affordable given the currently available funds, which equal the original spending limit adjusted for the net cost of all the options selected so far. Options that are not currently affordable can be ignored for now, although they may become available in subsequent iterations.
- *Dominance Principle.* You need consider only the available and affordable options that are not "dominated" by any other such option. One option dominates another when it is better, or at least as good, in terms of both preference and margin. For example, figure 8.3 shows that option B is dominated by A (and all other points in the shaded area) because B is both lower ranked and has a smaller margin than A. Conversely, option C does not dominate B because the latter has a better margin.[16]

Applying the two principles produces the short list of options that fall into the shaded triangle in figure 8.3. The short list is much more manageable than the available-and-affordable list as a whole. What remains is for the budget group to select their preferred option from the short list. They can proceed with high confidence that options outside the affordable and undominated short list can be ignored for the time being.[17] The process still requires difficult trade-offs between mission contribution and margin, but these judgments are vastly easier given the smaller list of options. Moreover, the short list usually gets shorter as more options are selected.

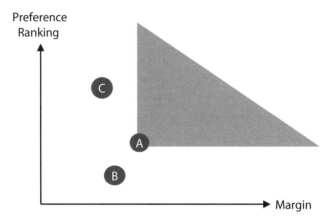

Figure 8.3. Illustration of the Dominance Principle

An Easy-to-Use Tool

While the choice process is fairly easy to conceptualize, it involves a fair amount of tedious bookkeeping: that is, maintaining the running total of available funds and determining the dominance status of the available options at each iteration. The bookkeeping is easily handled by a computer, however, and I have developed a "Constrained Choice Tool" to do just that. The tool is programmed in Excel, and the resulting app has been made available on the Johns Hopkins University Press website. The tool displays the current short list of options and the available funds at each iteration. It also records the sequence of choices made, which can be useful for discussing results or restarting the iteration at some point along the way. Double-clicking on an available, affordable, and undominated option selects that option for inclusion in the budget.

The tool includes several other features that I've not discussed so far. First, double-clicking on an already-selected option removes it from the budget list and puts it back into the available pool. This is important because budget groups may have second thoughts about their selection of a particular option: for example, because doing so has precluded the selection of other objects that in retrospect seem more important. Removing the option takes the iteration back to that point and allows the group to proceed in a different direction.

Second, the tool can handle more than mission and margin, the two attributes discussed up to this point. The illustration to be presented includes a third attribute, "Market and Brand," which I will define shortly. This capability derives from the fact that the affordability and the dominance principles can handle any number of attributes. I illustrate the third attribute to suggest the kinds of discussions that may be elicited, although I have not had an opportunity to try this formulation in practice.

Finally, the tool can require the selection of certain options to be deferred until others have been selected. This allows "continuous" options to be divided into tranches—as when, for example, a program can be developed to various degrees of intensity. For example, one can divide an option like "investing in program X" into several options, such as "make a basic investment, increase that investment by a certain amount, and increase it again by a further amount." (An example will be given shortly.) The tool includes a "prerequisite" variable that requires first option to be chosen before the second, second before the third, and so on.

ILLUSTRATIVE INPUT DATA

The remainder of this section presents a worked example of how the Constrained Choice Tool and its associated app operate. Table 8.3 defines the twenty-six hypothetical options that will be used in the example. The column headings are as follows:

- *ID*: an arbitrarily assigned identification number that will be carried across all of the app's screens.
- *Prerequisite*: the ID number of the option, if any, that must be selected before choosing the item under consideration. For example, option 25 cannot be selected before option 15 has been put into the budget.

Table 8.3. Illustrative Budget Options

ID	Prerequisite	Short Description	Comment
1		Launch a major research initiative	New faculty, infrastructure, seed money will (hopefully) move research to a new level.
2		Increase financial aid: Increment 1	Socially responsible; will improve selectivity and student diversity.
3		Start a new master's degree program in biotechnology	A new area that is included as a priority in the university's strategic plan.
4		Reduce faculty teaching loads	Hopefully will improve both teaching quality and research.
5		Reduce use of adjuncts	Will improve teaching quality and departmental coherence.
6		Create a social science research center	Dean is enthusiastic; costs to be partially offset by sponsored research.
7		Expand the neuropsychology program	Identified in program review as having good quality and strong market potential.
8		Start a summer program in world politics	Boosts the political science program; marketplace is somewhat uncertain.
9		Cap university-funded student loans	Socially responsible and improves diversity but not strongly visible in the marketplace.
10		Open a new undergraduate specialty in financial auditing	Strongly desired by the accounting faculty but not a top university priority.
11		Boost student recruiting staff	Hopefully will improve the applicant pool, yield rates, and perhaps student quality.
12		Add a faculty position in engineering	Will strengthen the program; moderately important to the dean.
13		Add a professional doctorate in physical therapy	Excellent market potential, but the school's ability to deliver quality is not certain.
14	2	Increase financial aid: Increment 2	Intrinsically valuable, more marketplace effect than the first tranche.
15		Expand the patent licensing office	Would make money and help faculty researchers but still somewhat questionable.
16		Add a part-time vice provost for student diversity	Strongly desired by some students and faculty but of questionable priority overall.
17		Grow fund-raising staff	Additional gifts would be welcome, but the payoffs from additional staff are uncertain.
18		Software certification and training: Increment 1	Good market prospects but somewhat off the university's mission.

ID	Prerequisite	Short Description	Comment
19		Build a fitness facility	Attractive as a student amenity but questioned by academics.
20		Eliminate a faculty position in geology	Departmental enrollments have declined, and there's been a retirement.
21	15	Software certification and training: Increment 2	Same as item 15, but even harder to reconcile with mission.
22		Cut administrative clerical staff	Difficult to accomplish but easier than cutting academic-related activities.
23		Downsize the School of Fine Arts	Enrollments have been dropping, but the school is important for mission and brand.
24		Eliminate three major graduate programs	Very expensive programs with weak demand but important for the research program.
25		Major cuts to the student services operation	Many view the operation as bloated, but opinions differ dramatically.
26		Lease an underused campus building to local business	Lucrative, but may disrupt the university's operations, culture, and image.

- *Short Description*: serves to label the item on the tool's screens. Eventually, the tool should include links to longer descriptions and possibly to arguments for and against the options.
- *Comment*: brief elaborations of the short descriptions to remind users of what's in the aforementioned longer descriptions.

The options, though not unrealistic, are fabrications designed to illustrate the tool's features and breadth of applicability. Some options represent simple line items of expenditure (e.g., an additional assistant professor or secretary), others eliminate items from the budget base, and still others involve the creation, enlargement, or downsizing of whole programs (e.g., a new master's degree in computer science). Thus, as in a typical budget exercise, we see a mixture of costs, budget savings, and net program revenues.

Options are characterized in terms of attributes. Table 8.4 shows the ones used in the example.

- *Preference Ranking*: the agreed valuations of mission contribution as described earlier (option 1 is best, and there can be a significant number of ties). As noted, the rankings should be constructed without regard to the market or margin data. Some institutions may wish to rank high-risk options lower than ones with equivalent intrinsic appeal but lower risk.
- *Market and Brand*: an index that reflects what's expected to happen as market forces, triggered by the option, play out over time. Positive figures imply marketplace success for programs and other market-facing options, and conversely. The index for other options reflects expected impact on the university's overall

Table 8.4. Attributes of the Budget Options (Dollars in Thousands)

		Attributes			
ID	Prerequisite	Preference Ranking	Market and Brand	Adjusted Margin ($)	Short Description
1		1	5	(5,000)	Launch a major research initiative
2		2	3	(2,000)	Increase financial aid: Increment 1
3		3	4	1,750	Start a new master's degree program in biotechnology
4		4	1	(4,000)	Reduce faculty teaching loads
5		5	2	(2,600)	Reduce use of adjuncts
6		6	1	(200)	Create a social science research center
7		7	3	(1,250)	Expand the neuropsychology program
8		7	2	200	Start a summer program in world politics
9		8	2	(350)	Cap university-funded student loans
10		9	2	(500)	Open a new undergraduate specialty in financial auditing
11		10	2	(1,050)	Boost student recruiting staff
12		11	2	(200)	Add a faculty position in engineering
13		12	5	2,750	Add a professional doctorate in physical therapy
14	2	13	3	(2,000)	Increase financial aid: Increment 2

ID	Prerequisite	Attributes			Short Description
		Preference Ranking	Market and Brand	Adjusted Margin ($)	
16		14	1	(150)	Add a part-time vice provost for student diversity
17		14	0	1,250	Grow fund-raising staff
18		15	4	2,000	Software certification and training: Increment 1
19		16	5	(1,500)	Build a fitness facility
20		17	(1)	150	Eliminate a faculty position in geology
21	15	18	3	800	Software certification and training: Increment 2
22		18	0	1,500	Cut administrative clerical staff
23		19	(3)	2,750	Downsize the School of Fine Arts
24		20	0	2,600	Eliminate three major graduate programs
25		21	(2)	2,300	Major cuts to the student services operation
26		22	(5)	2,500	Lease an underused campus building to local business

brand image. It encodes market information such as that described in chapter 6 into a single number between −5 and +5.

- *Adjusted Margin*: the options' expected financial impact on the ensuing year's budget. This may be a budget base charge or credit, or a present value of time-varying financial outcomes, as described earlier. Negative adjusted margins reduce the running balance of available funds, and positive ones add to the balance.

The year's spending limit (i.e., the available funds before the first option has been selected) is the final data item needed to run the model. It appears on the model's main display screen, which will be presented shortly.

The value ranking and adjusted margin attributes are required for the constrained choice procedure to work. The market and brand index is not required, but it demonstrates that more than two attributes can be accommodated. The three variables reflect the subtitle of *Reengineering the University: How to be Mission Centered, Market Smart, and Margin Conscious.*

The data in table 8.4 are hypothetical, but I have tried to include some realistic and interesting relationships. The new master's program in biotechnology (option 3) has strong value with good market and financial potential. Building a fitness facility (option 19) offers strong market appeal, but it's ranked relatively low in terms of mission. Launching a major research initiative (option 1) has the highest possible value ranking and promises great benefits in the marketplace, but it is very expensive. Using the model motivates careful consideration of trade-offs among attributes. They are extremely important but not easy to process without a model's organizing template.

A real budget exercise would, of course, have many more than twenty-six options. In most cases, the options would be more like those in the upper three-quarters of the illustrated list than those near the bottom, which were included to show the logic of a hypothetical choice termination before all options had been selected. The mix of options with positive and negative mission contributions probably would depend on the degree of financial pressure faced by the institution. Hard-pressed schools would tend to surface more money-making options than those with larger spending limits.

THE TOOL IN ACTION

Users experience the model's affordability and dominance relations through the screen in figure 8.4: in this case, the display for iteration 1, the start of the choice process. The "Status" column reports each option as "Available," as "Dominated" by at least one other item, as in need of a "Prerequisite" item, or as "Unaffordable" given the currently remaining funds. Iteration history reports the sequence of selections prior to this iteration. (The column is blank because this is the first iteration.) Other panels show the option's labels and

| | | | | | Budget Limit $4,900 |
| | | | | | Remaining $4,900 |

AVAILABLE OPTION SELECTIONS [RESET]

ID	LABEL	Rank	Mkt	Margin ($)	Status
		* Attributes — Available options shown in large boldface.			
1	Launch a major research initiative	1	5	(5000)	Unaffordable
2	Increase financial aid: Increment 1	2	3	(2000)	Available
3	Start a new master's degree program In biotechnology	3	4	1750	Available
4	Reduce faculty teaching loads	4	1	(4000)	Dominated
5	Reduce use of adjuncts	5	2	(2600)	Dominated
6	Create a social science research center	6	1	(200)	Dominated
7	Expand the neuropsychology program	7	3	(1250)	Dominated
8	Start a summer program In world politics	7	2	200	Dominated
9	Cap university-funded student loans	8	2	(350)	Dominated
10	Open a new undergraduate specialty in financial auditing	9	2	(500)	Dominated
11	Boost student recruiting staff	10	2	(1050)	Dominated
12	Add a faculty position in engineering	11	2	(200)	Dominated
13	Add a professional doctorate in physical therapy	12	5	2750	Available
14	Increase financial aid: Increment 2	13	3	(2000)	Prerequisite
15	Expand the patent licensing office	14	0	250	Dominated
16	Add a part-time vice provost for student diversity	14	1	(150)	Dominated
17	Grow fund-raising staff	14	0	1250	Dominated
18	Software certification and training: Increment 1	15	4	2000	Dominated
19	Build a fitness facility	16	5	(1500)	Dominated
20	Eliminate a faculty position in geology	17	(1)	150	Dominated
21	Software certification and training: Increment 2	18	3	800	Prerequisite
22	Cut administrative clerical staff	18	0	1500	Dominated
23	Downsize the School of Fine Arts	19	(3)	2750	Dominated
24	Eliminate three major graduate programs	20	0	2600	Dominated
25	Major cuts to the student services operation	21	(2)	2300	Dominated
26	Lease an underused campus building to local business	22	(5)	2500	Dominated

Figure 8.4. Initial Choice Availabilities with a $4,900 Budget Limit

Table 8.5. Chronicle of the Status Tableaus

ID	Short Description	Iteration 1	2	3	5	7	8	11	13	17	Iteration History
	Remaining Funds	$4,900	$4,900	$1,650	$600	$50	$2,800	$100	$3,350	$100	
1	Launch a major research initiative	⊗	○	◈	◈	◈	◈	◈	◈	◈	2
2	Increase financial aid: Increment 1	○	○	⊗	⊗	⊗	○	◈	◈	◈	8
3	Start a new master's degree program in biotechnology	○	◈	◈	◈	◈	◈	◈	◈	◈	1
4	Reduce faculty teaching loads	×	×	⊗	⊗	⊗	⊗	⊗	⊗	⊗	
5	Reduce use of adjuncts	×	×	⊗	⊗	◈	◈	◈	◈	◈	13
6	Create a social science research center	×	○	○	○	◈	◈	◈	◈	◈	6
7	Expand the neuropsychology program	×	○	○	◈	◈	◈	◈	◈	◈	4
8	Start a summer program in world politics	×	○	○	◈	◈	◈	◈	◈	◈	3
9	Cap university-funded student loans	×	×	○	○	◈	◈	◈	◈	◈	5
10	Open a new undergraduate specialty in financial auditing	×	×	×	×	⊗	○	⊗	◈	◈	10
11	Boost student recruiting staff	×	×	×	⊗	⊗	×	⊗	⊗	◈	16
12	Add a faculty position in engineering	×	×	×	○	○	○	◈	◈	◈	9
13	Add a professional doctorate in physical therapy	○	○	○	○	○	◈	◈	◈	◈	7

14	Increase financial aid: Increment 2	□	□	□	□	□	□	⊗	⊗	⊗
15	Expand the patent licensing office	×	×	×	×	×	×	×	×	◆ 14
16	Add a part-time vice provost for student diversity	×	×	×	×	⊗	○	⊗	⊗	⊗ 11
17	Grow fund-raising staff	×	×	×	×	×	○	○	○	◆ 11
18	Software certification and training: Increment 1	×	×	×	×	×	○	○	○	◆ 12
19	Build a fitness facility	×	×	×	⊗	⊗	○	⊗	⊗	⊗
20	Eliminate a faculty position in geology	×	×	×	×	×	×	×	×	◆ 15
21	Software certification and training: Increment 2	□	□	□	□	□	□	□	□	○
22	Cut administrative clerical staff	×	×	×	×	×	×	×	×	○
23	Downsize the School of Fine Arts	×	×	×	×	×	○	○	○	○
24	Eliminate three major graduate programs	×	×	×	×	×	○	○	○	○
25	Major cuts to the student services operation	×	×	×	×	×	×	×	×	×
26	Lease an underused campus building to local business	×	×	×	×	×	×	×	×	×

Key: Selected ◆   Passed over ○   Dominated ×   Unaffordable ⊗   Available □

attributes, the original budget limit, the currently remaining funds, and the number of the upcoming iteration.

The decision maker's task is to choose the "Available" option that offers the best combination of rank, market, and margin. Double-clicking the chosen item's status cell records the choice. Clicking on an already-selected option removes it from the list of chosen items. Pressing "Reset" cancels everything and returns the model to its initial status.

Table 8.5 chronicles the choice strategy of our hypothetical budget group. "Selected" means the option was put in the budget prior to the iteration shown in the column heading, "O" means it's available, and "X" means it's dominated. (The full key appears at the bottom of the figure.) The group's main preference judgments involve balancing mission contribution with market and brand. Exceptions occur when a moneymaking option would fund a highly desirable but unaffordable option at the next iteration (what I call a "look-ahead")—in which case the moneymaker is chosen over the immediately preferred alternatives. I've illustrated the results for a series of representative iterations, followed by the full iteration history in the last column. Note how the "Remaining Funds" figure changes as options are selected, how various options become unaffordable as funds become scarcer, and how the list of dominated options shrinks as the iterations proceed.

The choices in this illustration tend to follow the preference ranking, although this is by no means necessary. Early exceptions include choosing the profitable option 3 at the first iteration so that option 1, by far the highest priority, can be chosen next. That made option 2 unaffordable, which illustrates the Hobson's choices sometimes encountered in budget-making. The successive judgments eventually reached the point, at iteration 7, where only option 13 (the professional doctorate in physical therapy) remained available. I imagined that our hypothetical budget group was split on whether a move was consistent with the university's mission, but that the program's profitability had become too important to forego. Similar trade-offs can be identified through the remaining iterations. Note that option 14 entered the dominance and affordability calculations only after option 2 had been selected, at which point its status changes from "Prerequisite" to "Unaffordable."

The process was halted just before iteration 17, despite the availability of multiple options that could have been selected. A glance back at table 8.4 shows that the remaining available options had positive margins—which means they were affordable no matter what the remaining funds. But affordability does not necessarily confer desirability, even when the profits can be used to fund higher-ranked but currently unaffordable options. This illustrates the point, discussed in connection with the not-for-profit paradigm, that all moneymaking programs do not have positive mission contributions. In this case, for example, the budget group could have downsized the history department (option 22) and used the proceeds to reduce the use of adjunct faculty (option 5).[18] That they chose not to do so shows that the pain of downsizing history would have been greater than the gain from reducing adjuncts. Leaving a moneymaking option on the table indicates that it conflicts with the mission, that its intrinsic value is negative. This means that the contributions of all lower-ranked options must be as bad or worse.[19]

One additional observation may ease concerns about the procedure's practicality. It's that the path chosen to reach a particular end point is of no consequence. For example, it wouldn't matter whether the budget group selected desirable moneymaking options early in the choice process or (as in the illustrated example) waited until just before they were needed. Therefore, users need not worry about the exact sequence of decisions provided they end up in what feels like the right place—which in this case is the choice tableau before iteration 17.

Budget group members can work with the tool on an individual basis and then come together to compare ideas and make final decisions.[20] This will sharpen discussion and perhaps aid in achieving consensus. The tool also facilitates organizational learning by allowing decision makers to explore various options and strategies in a systematic and documentable way. This will stimulate mutual understanding about the university's mission in relation to market and margin. Finally, the greater scrutiny that comes through more systematic thinking will motivate deeper analysis of the market and financial variables. Over the long run, such organizational learning may be as important as the immediate benefits from using the tool.

The Way Forward

The preceding chapters have described how universities can harness the power of information technology to improve their academic resourcing management so as to deliver better on their student attainment and knowledge creation missions. The new economic models, quality review processes, and market information systems can inform faculty and staff judgments in profound ways. They can change the conversations that precede important decisions, and over time this will transform the academic culture itself. The new culture will be more purposeful and mission centered, more evidence based, and—perhaps most importantly—will make faculty full partners in the critical process of balancing academic values with market forces and financial realities. I said in chapter 1 that these are ideas whose time has come. The confluence of technological capacity and the need for better university management make this a time of great opportunity and excitement.

This chapter summarizes the book's key takeaways and outlines the steps required for adopting the models and achieving the transformations needed for institutional change. We will examine the adoption and transformation process from two points of view: a university officer (say, a president, provost, dean, or CFO) who wants to improve his or her institution and an external policy maker, overseer, philanthropist, or other stakeholder who wants to improve the higher education sector generally. The chapter ends with an appeal for research, development, and training on academic resourcing tools and processes.

Takeaways from Previous Chapters

While the wealth of detail discussed in the previous chapters defies quick summarization, the overall paradigm is relatively easy to fathom. Part I provided an introduction to the concept of academic resourcing and the kinds of academic resourcing models discussed in the book. How the models can be used to change important academic conversations was the main topic of chapter 1, basic descriptions of the models themselves and what it takes to install them in a college or university were covered in chapter 2, and the problem of building trust in the models was examined in chapter 3. The three chapters of part II examined the current state of the art in full-function models of a university's internal economy (a type of AR model). Part III considered the use of AR models in program review (chapter 7), the so-called not-for-profit paradigm that distinguishes universities from businesses (chapter 8), and a number of topics related to the way toward propagation of AR models across higher education. I'll elaborate on some of these below.

The Need for New Conversations

Academic resourcing conversations focus on specific decisions or, more generally, on opportunities and threats to the university's mission, markets, financial sustainability, or culture. True conversations involve engagement on important issues rather than transmission of information from one participant to others. That's the way things are supposed to happen in universities, especially when it comes to teaching, research, and their supporting administrative and support activities. Some of the most critical, and difficult, conversations involve the tension between resource constraints and judgments about institutional mission, teaching and learning quality, and the tenets of academic disciplines.

I noted the disconnect between faculty and academic leaders below the level of deans (and sometimes the deans themselves), on the one hand, and the people responsible for financial sustainability, efficiency, pricing, and other money-related activities, on the other. This role differentiation is deeply embedded in the academy's culture. It is understandable given the differences in background among the parties. This wasn't a problem when resources were relatively plentiful—indeed, it enabled more creativity, quality improvement, and collegiality. But those days are long gone. Now the world's not-for-profit universities must scramble for competitive advantage and public support. To be successful, they must examine their academic value-creation processes, particularly in the area of teaching. This requires an intimate partnership between people with on-the-ground academic knowledge (the involved faculty) and those with deep knowledge of the university's internal economy—including its market, productivity, and financial situations.

The conversations discussed in this book aim to bring all the parties together around a common evidentiary base. I believe academic leaders such as provosts, deans, department chairs, and program heads should drive, and in some cases personally lead, these conversations. Ultimately, it is these leaders who are responsible for delivering on the university's mission. Both common sense and the tenets of shared governance argue for strong faculty involvement, and it would be irrational to exclude staff with financial-, market-, and productivity-related expertise. Therefore, academic leaders should feel a strong responsibility for bringing the requisite people together and ensuring that they embrace the concepts and tools necessary for quality decision-making.

Access to accepted concepts and tools is not enough, however. The participants in each set of conversations must climb a sometimes-steep learning curve before the benefits can be achieved. This, too, requires sustained and engaged conversation. Successful academic leaders will motivate and nurture these conversations, provide the resources needed to inform them, and push them forward where necessary.

Three Academic Resourcing Models

The best way to change academic resourcing conversations is to confront the participants with significant new data with clear relevance to the decisions being considered. For colleges and universities, that requires some radical new tools. This book considers three types of academic resourcing models: (1) models that describe the university's internal economy and its activities, costs, revenues, and margins; (2) market information models that describe the external economy; and (3) a model for choosing among alternative budget options that are defined by subjective mission-related values, market data, and margins.

The internal economic models receive the most detailed treatment: to the point where I often sometimes refer to them simply as "AR models." Such models are becoming available from a number of different vendors. This book discusses two such offerings: Gray Associates' implementation of the core AR functionality and the Pilbara Group's full-function AR model. Readers should view these as good examples of what can be done rather than exclusive endorsements. Indeed, no current AR model has reached what Harvard professor Clay Christiansen calls a "dominant design"[1] in the sense that no significant changes in structure or capability should be expected.

The internal economic AR models provide comprehensive representations of a college's or university's operations, with emphasis on the teaching and research functions. An extension of activity-based costing, they model an institution's teaching and, if desired, research activities. They track operating details, revenues, direct and indirect costs, and direct and burdened margins down to the level of individual courses and programs. Historical AR models are used to analyze current and trend information, and AR predictive models are used for what-if analyses and the evaluation of planning scenarios.

Chapter 2 introduced AR by describing Gray Associates' economic model. It explained the model's structure and presented a number of examples about the kinds of data it produces and how the data can be used. Part II (chapters 4, 5, and 6) described the Pilbara full-function model in considerable detail. This allowed me to unpack the ways their data can be applied to all of the economic decision areas described in the prologue. As noted, the model's depth and breadth of detail make it a game changer in most of these areas.

The Gray Associates Program Evaluation System combines extensive marketplace information with a simple but useful economic model for program costs, revenues, and margins. I described the power of combining these data genres, whether from the Gray, Pilbara, or any other vendor. Such a combination will add value to an institution's periodic program review process, and also to its annual budgeting. This is the kind of connection that I envisioned in chapter 5 of *Reengineering the University*, which emphasized the importance of holistic thinking about academic resources.

My own Constrained Choice Model for University Budgeting allows academic resourcing managers to place mission contribution at the center of budget-making. It starts with the list of budget proposals ("options") put forward by deans, other operating unit heads, and members of the budget staff in an annual budgeting cycle. Each option is characterized by its margin, adjusted as necessary for financial consequences that vary over time, and its market potential and probable effect on the university's brand. The provost and other senior decision makers rank-order the options in terms of mission contribution and then use a supplied software tool to facilitate the choosing of options subject to an overall spending limit. The tool, which currently exists in beta form, solves the problem of deciding how to weigh mission contribution, market, and financial factors when making budget decisions.

Four Concepts to Remember

To be truly effective, the conversations and tools need to be grounded in a conceptual structure that makes sense to academic professionals as well as to the people responsible for the university's financial affairs. A good structure is important for all kinds of decisions, but particularly in academe, where the principals think deeply about what they are doing and why they are doing it. The book describes four general concepts that I have relied on for many years in my work as a university officer, professor, and consultant. I'll recap each briefly.

THE NOT-FOR-PROFIT ECONOMIC PARADIGM

The literature on university administration abounds with advice about how to make academic resourcing decisions, but very little of it recognizes that universities are fundamentally different from counterparts in the for-profit world. Much of the advice centers around the "money" side of administration: for example, downsizing or getting rid of money-losing activities or searching for new programs that will be profitable. Such statements are not wrong, but they miss the point of what's important in a university and raise the specter that academic values will be eroded. These fears upset academics, and rightly so. The economic paradigm of a not-for-profit enterprise resolves these concerns, I hope once and for all.

The paradigm, which appears in chapter 8, briefly describes how universities maximize contribution to their academic and societal missions subject to three constraints: production (relations between inputs and the quantity and quality of outputs), market (the preferences of people who purchase the outputs and provide subsidies), and financial (the sustainability of costs in relation to revenues). In contrast, for-profit entities maximize the difference between revenue and cost (profit), subject to the same kinds of market and production constraints as universities. The difference is fundamental, and universities ignore it at their peril.

THE DISTINCTION BETWEEN HARD AND SOFT MANAGEMENT

The conversations that loom so large in this book represent "soft management," participatory processes that seek to get the best from everyone involved. "Hard management" is necessary in some situations (e.g., when dealing with regulations or financial imperatives), but it should be the exception rather than the rule in universities. It's dead wrong to consider the models discussed here as reflecting a hard management philosophy. In fact, they enable the kind of informed conversations that make soft management effective. The best academic resourcing processes, enabled by the availability of good AR models, solidify incentives that further soft management.

TEACHING AND LEARNING QUALITY PROCESSES

Chapter 7 makes the case that improving and assuring educational quality provides a quintessential example of effective soft management. Faculty are the only people who can define quality in the context of a particular department and program, let alone improve and assure it. Comprehensive program review provides an ideal vehicle for addressing these goals in relation to the aforementioned production, market, and financial constraints. Quality depends importantly on resource availability, for example, and resourcing information of the kind discussed in this book can be a motivator for initiatives to improve teaching and learning.

DECISION SUPPORT MODELS

All the models discussed in this book are of the "decision support" genre: that is, they aim to help people charged with deciding important issues rather than making decisions or asserting the truth of any particular point of view. I'm often asked how the models can be "proven wrong," but that misses the point because decision support models seek only to produce more informed choices than could be made without them. (All models are abstractions and thus "wrong" in an absolute sense; the question is whether they are useful in the sense of leading one in the right direction.) As noted, the models may be "historical," in which case they provide information to help decision makers analyze situations, or "predictive" in the sense of forecasting the consequences of particular actions.

Adoption by a University

I have argued that the responsibility for spurring AR model adoption lies mainly with provosts, deans, and other academic officers of the university or college. If an institution's senior academic officers don't provide leadership, chances are that nobody else will. Others responsible for academic resourcing, including faculty, will continue to operate in their own silos, and the disconnect between academic processes and the institution's internal economics—which lies at the core of higher education's cost and quality problem—will continue.

Financial officers also have an important role, of course. Theirs is the staff job of developing high-level financial strategy, supplying data and analyses to drive the academic resourcing models, and in some cases being the custodians of the models themselves. Senior financial officers sit on the executive councils of most universities. They are in a position to promote the use of economic data for decision-making and indeed the use of evidence generally. As I maintain throughout this book, however, they are neither capable nor empowered to drive the all-important academic decisions that link financial factors with teaching and research.

Presidents and trustees are critical, too. Ultimately, they bear responsibility for the AR models' successful adoption, but their main role should be to motivate and facilitate rather than to get involved with day-to-day operations. At the front end, this means they should question academic resourcing officers about the due diligence behind their decision-making. They should press the questions with increasing urgency until the requisite priorities for information provision become manifest. They also should take a real interest in the results, not for purposes of micromanagement but to reinforce the importance of good information. And they must provide support and "political" cover when the inevitable pushbacks occur. Failure to play any of these roles well can doom the adoption of AR models and cost the institution dearly over the long run.

I'm well aware that the responsibility for implementing the new breed of academic resourcing models may not be welcomed by provosts, deans, and other academic officers. Partly this stems from a lack of knowledge about what the models are, how they work, and the kinds of benefits they deliver. But there's more. The reasons are well described in Ronald A. Heifetz and Marty Linsky's *Leadership on the Line: Staying Alive through the Dangers of Leading.*[2] They point out that people do not resist change, per se, but that they do resist loss. AR models conjure up a variety of threats: some philosophical, like the undermining of academic values, and some eminently practical and self-interested: for example, that one's budget might get cut. Yet freezing in the face of threat produces a huge opportunity loss. This book offers considerable advice about how to move forward while protecting one's position to the greatest extent possible.

Barriers to be Overcome

Simple inertia is a barrier to institutional renewal, but it's not the only one. Chapter 1 described the Survive + Thrive behavior channels that seem to explain individuals' and organizations' responses to environmental threats and innovation opportunities. "Survive" detects threats and responds with emotions like fear, anxiety, and anger, which tend to drive out the "Thrive" channel's positive energy that helps so much in achieving change. I have noted frequently that talk of financial analytics (including the money side of AR models) can be a put-off for many academics. Such talk activates "Survive" and thus inhibits the very behavior we seek to encourage. Successful innovators will appeal to positive emotions like the excitement of exploring something new and the challenge of solving complex problems, which are associated with the thrive channel and also with faculty's inherent creative instincts. The approach should be about enabling better conversations rather than adhering to externally imposed standards, especially financial ones, that seem to be embedded in the models.

Fear that the new models will undermine academic values activates major triggers for Survive. I've done my best to show, both in theory and with practical examples, that this concern is unfounded—provided that faculty are fully engaged in the decision-making process. Failure to engage will force administrators to develop and use the new models on their own, which will risk precisely the outcomes that academics fear. The modern era of resource scarcity will force one outcome or the other because the status quo is not sustainable.

Faculty impatience with what faculty call "administrivia" represents another barrier to adoption. Administrivia refers to the unrewarding and often deadly boring tasks that professors must perform as they navigate their school's administrative and financial processes. I hope it's clear by now that the use of AR models by academics is not administrivia, and that model use does not need to be boring or unrewarding. I have seen faculty groups dig into the model with great enthusiasm. They are thrilled to finally be getting answers to questions that have concerned them for some time, and they are challenged by fresh questions triggered by the new insights.

Other barriers to adoption are not unique to colleges and universities. For example, the classic problems of turf and what former Stanford president Donald Kennedy called "function lust" can arise when dealing with academic resourcing models. This takes many forms, but perhaps the most frequent one is the claim by IT or accounting professionals (or their consultants) that "the university's data are not ready for serious modeling of the kind described in this book." I described the problem in chapter 2: the argument is that clean datasets, or better yet a good data warehouse, is a prerequisite for such models. The fact, however, is that model-building projects like those used by the Pilbara Group and Gray Associates are designed to take data as they are. They perform any needed data organization and cleaning work in context of the model's actual requirements rather than as a generalized precursor exercise. My experience as a Stanford vice president convinced me that this "just in time" approach works better and costs less than conventional "just in case" approaches, where one must consider every eventuality rather than only those relevant for a particular application. Modern software tools allow datasets to be revised as necessary, which enables iterative development rather than trying to make everything perfect the first time.

Concerns about the cost of developing and using the academic resourcing models represent another important barrier to adoption. These costs certainly aren't negligible, but often they are less than expected. My experience is that out-of-pocket expenditures for full AR model development run in the low to medium six figures for large and complex institutions, and can be held to the five-figure range for smaller and simpler ones. Larger expenditures may be incurred if the precursor data are enhanced before proceeding, or if an institution wants a particularly complex model, but those choices are strictly discretionary. Annual maintenance and update expenditures are considerably less than the cost for the initial installation. Institutions also need to make internal personnel assignments to support model construction and ongoing usage. These aren't show stoppers, however. The ancillary benefits for data improvement and analytical prowess would make the effort worthwhile even if no AR model was constructed.

Lack of a sense of urgency is perhaps the biggest barrier to adopting the new academic resourcing models and principles. I recognize the biases that I bring to the table, but I believe the evidence points to the extreme importance of bridging the gap between academic decision-making and the university's internal economics. The people responsible for colleges and universities, and the higher education sector as a whole, ought to feel a sense of urgency about effecting the needed transformations.

Strategies for Overcoming the Barriers

My first direct encounter with barriers like the aforementioned occurred when I was Stanford's vice president for business and finance. This was an era when administrative and support service productivity had become a hot topic in universities. Being an economist, I started touting the virtues of productivity improvement to my senior staff and others in my 1,500-person organization. The response was, well, underwhelming. Instead of sharing my view that productivity is an intrinsically exciting thing to work on, most respondents saw it as code for speed-ups, budget cuts, quality degradations, and threats to the organization's goals and culture. I was a popular leader, but not popular enough to carry the day.

I went back to the drawing board aided by a few trusted lieutenants and an organizational consultant. The business literature at that time discussed quality circles on the factory-floor and other productivity-improving techniques that seemed to have little applicability to universities. However, a closer look revealed the common denominators of responsibility diffusion, conversation, and the need to kindle a sense of excitement and pride in achieving change. We settled on what we called our Quality, Service, and Productivity (QSP) Program, which challenged a cross-section of people through several levels of the organization to come up with creative ideas, work on pilot implementations with unit-level QSP teams and locally available resources, and report results to a central QSP Council. Notice that the infamous "P-word" was relegated to last place behind quality and service—the latter being goals my staff found it easy to rally around. The process was structured to generate engaged or even passionate conversations, locally driven initiatives, quick wins throughout the organization, and opportunities for "show and tell" and celebration with senior managers including myself. It spawned a good many successes, not the least of which were heightened knowledge and concern about Q, S, and P, and agreement about metrics to measure performance on a continuing basis.

It is only now, some thirty years after the fact, that I can fully articulate the dynamics that drove QSP. The breakthrough came in a short book by John Kotter, the originator of Strive + Thrive referred to earlier, which describes what he calls the "dual operating system" for achieving change in mature organizations.[3] New and highly innovative organizations, he says, are best characterized as networks where people connect and reconnect as needed to identify and solve problems. Conversely, mature organizations rely on hierarchies that are designed to achieve reliability, efficiency, and accountability. The problem is to inject network-type problem-solving without undermining the hierarchy and its needed benefits.

Kotter describes the dual operating system as consisting of the mature organizational hierarchy *plus* a semiformal and dynamically changing network that can innovate and solve problems without disrupting the hierarchy's ongoing focus on current routines. The network must mesh closely with the hierarchy but is separate from it. Top management creates the network initially, then turns it over to a "guiding coalition" that reports to management but has considerable latitude to recruit volunteers, to obtain the resources needed for problem-solving, and, above all, to act. It is this network that drives the change process, not simply through information and exhortation but by actually doing key elements of the job. These interventions solve problems associated with the new solutions, demonstrate effectiveness, and help get results imbedded in the hierarchy's regular routines.

Kotter's concept of networks for achieving change applies directly to the problem of transforming academic resource management in universities. Changing these conversations requires lots of effort, over months or even years, by respected, informed, and passionate people who share the academy's values and are integrally familiar with the decision-making process. The hierarchy, responsible as it is for managing the university's ongoing operations, isn't likely to sustain the transformation effort by itself—no matter how good its intentions may be at the start. However, this can be done by a network of change

agents who also function within the hierarchy, energized and supported by senior university leaders and its own guiding coalition.

Five Principles for Achieving Change

Kotter offers considerable detail about how to "seize opportunities with a dual operating system," but the most essential points are
embodied in his five principles and eight accelerators. They are summarized in this and the next section, together with brief callouts on
their application to the transformation of academic resourcing in universities. I can think of no better strategies for initiating and sustaining the adoption of AR models in universities.

- *Many people driving important change, and from everywhere,
  not just the usual few appointees*:[4] getting boots on the
  ground—lots of eyes to see, brains to think, and legs to act on
  accelerating the identification and solution of problems throughout the organization. For academic resourcing, this means
  engaged faculty, staff, and officers across the university.
- *A "get-to" mind-set, not a "have-to" one*: the desire to work
  with others for an important and exciting shared purpose, and
  the realistic possibility of doing so, are key. People who feel they
  have the privilege of being involved in an interesting and important activity have shown, throughout history, that they will
  volunteer to do so in addition to their normal activities. In our
  case, this taps the intrinsic creative energy that's the hallmark of
  a good university.
- *Action that is head and heart driven, not just head driven*: logic
  isn't the only motivator for organizational change. One also
  must appeal to how people feel. Providing a vehicle to give
  greater meaning and purpose to people's efforts can produce
  amazing results. That's especially true in a university, where
  professionals usually care deeply about the academic enterprise.
- *Much more leadership, not just management*: coordinating
  routine tasks performed by numbers of people requires effective

management, but for generating change the name of the game is leadership. That game is about vision, opportunity, agility, inspired action, passion, innovation, and celebration. Changing the conversations about academic resourcing requires all of these things and thus effective leadership at all levels of the university.

• *An inseparable partnership between the hierarchy and network, not just an enhanced hierarchy*: the two systems, network and hierarchy, work as one—in part because the people who volunteer to work in the network already have jobs within the hierarchy. This is quintessentially true in universities, because the network required to bridge the gap between mission and money must include, in key roles, the academic decision makers themselves.

Eight Accelerators for the Change Process

The accelerators represent steps that can be taken by senior leadership to engage people in the transformations that are essential for renewal. Keep in mind that the goal is not simply a one-time change but rather a shift in culture that results in new routines that never stop.

1. *Create a sense of urgency around a Big Opportunity.*[5] As used here, urgency is not about meeting immediate deadlines but rather about strategic threats and possibilities. I have spoken often about these and believe that traditional universities face watershed decisions. In our context, the "Big" lies in renewal as made possible by the adoption of AR models and their associated processes. Leaders should do everything possible to create a sense of urgency about this, both through what they say and by role modeling the kinds of attitudes and thinking that will be needed.

2. *Build and evolve a guiding coalition.* The guiding coalition should include the initial champions for change plus people from across the organization who have come to share the aforementioned sense of urgency. These should be people who want to lead, to be change agents, and to help others do the same. They

will represent the core of the network, then later help it evolve into a stronger and more sophisticated form. I encountered such people in every university I visited when writing this book and in pilot testing my earlier models. The leadership challenge is to bring them together, empower them to act, and then support them through thick and thin.

3. *Form a change vision and strategic initiatives.* An early test of the guiding coalition is to clarify a vision about the Big Opportunity and identify initiatives that can move the organization toward it. Let's assume the university already has decided to install one or more academic resourcing models discussed earlier, so that the Big Opportunity lies in realizing their potential. The vision will describe the needed transformations, and the initiatives might target application areas and groups or individuals where quick wins appear possible. Again, successful adoption in these as in all areas is fundamentally the responsibility of line decision makers, but energy supplied by the network may be needed to tip the scales toward action.

4. *Enlist a volunteer army.* The guiding coalition, and others who wish to help, communicate the change vision and initiatives across the organization in ways that, hopefully, will bring larger numbers of people on board. This is the nature of an interest-based network: it consists not of people who were appointed to do certain tasks but of those who truly want to do so. And because no appointment to the network is required, as many people as want to may join in. For example, there should be no limit on the number of conversation-changers in the university's academic and administrative ranks.

5. *Enable action by removing barriers.* A successful network will involve talking, thinking, inventing, and testing—all in the spirit of an agile and swift entrepreneurial start-up. Much of the action here involves identifying and removing barriers. Some of this will involve established systems, models, and data: in these cases, technical support people must be available and willing to

make the desired changes wherever possible. Failure to green-light such changes will have a chilling effect on adoption, especially if the problem occurs early in the process. Other barriers involve established policies and routines. Here is where the university's top management may need to weigh in on behalf of the network and its guiding coalition, so that the needed changes can be accomplished quickly.

6. *Generate (and celebrate) short-term wins.* These wins demonstrate the transformation's feasibility and benefits. They are satisfying for the people involved, who then become energized and perhaps eager to discuss their accomplishments with others. This process becomes amplified when the network finds ways to celebrate each new accomplishment. Sometimes informal recognition does the trick, but this can be enhanced through formal meetings, social events, or perhaps what the British Navy used to call "mention in dispatches" sent up the line.

7. *Sustain acceleration.* The problem here is to maintain momentum once the sense of newness begins to wear off. Many wins come from small actions and interpretations that by themselves may be neither substantial nor particularly useful in a strategic sense. The network and its guiding coalition can recognize and reinforce both large and small wins, and maintain a drumbeat of enthusiasm for renewal even when the hierarchy wants to move on to other priorities.

8. *Institute change.* The ultimate goal of the renewal process is to integrate the new models, processes, and culture of evidence into all relevant academic resourcing conversations. The network and guiding coalition are in a good position to gauge progress toward this goal. Hopefully the day will come when the new culture is sufficiently robust to persist on its own—at which time the network can disband or move on to other areas of innovation.

Readers may recognize my account of Stanford's QSP program in some of the principles and accelerators. This is no accident. Our work predated Kotter's by many years, and we did not begin to develop his powerful generalizations. Our approach was consistent with his, however, and the success we achieved demonstrates that his ideas can indeed work in academe.

Improving the US Higher Education Sector

Imagine a world where many colleges and universities have successfully adopted the concepts and models discussed in this book. I hope I have convinced you that this world would be better than the one in which we currently live. Resources would be deployed more effectively in support of teaching, research, and essential support services. Institutions would be more attentive to market forces, and more consciously balance these forces against their intrinsic, mission-based values. Problems would remain, of course, because people disagree about values and the interpretation of even the best available evidence. But the conversations about academic resourcing in such a world would be better informed and more coherent than most such conversations are today.

The benefits of AR models extend beyond the improvement of decision-making in particular institutions. A world that has achieved critical mass in the adoption of such models would be able to support the benchmarking of operational detail, revenues, and costs for individual programs. Cooperative arrangements would have to be worked out, but the underlying data would exist. Competitive problems could be surmounted by classing institutions according to segment and providing access to an institution's own data plus average data for the segment. A database like this also would be extremely useful for researchers who study the higher education production function, particularly the one for teaching, and the returns on investment in higher education for different fields. For example, the fact that no such database now exists makes it difficult to study the production function at a sufficiently micro level to answer important questions like "Why Is Math Cheaper Than English?" (to quote the title of a recent working paper).[6]

Many external policy makers and overseers of higher education advocate these kinds of improvements, and significant numbers of philanthropists are demonstrating a willingness to facilitate them. The consulting industry should not be forgotten, either, as such firms often play key roles in furthering the adoption of innovations. All these parties are well positioned to encourage and support the actions of individual institutions—and I very much hope they will do so at every opportunity.

In addition, there are some high-leverage interventions that I believe would spur adoption across the higher education sector. It is to these that we turn now.

More Boots on the Ground

The experience of the past few years has underscored the importance of hands-on advocacy and support in helping institutions commit to the kinds of changes discussed here and then carrying the process through to a successful completion. The innovation-adoption literature is replete with references to change agents, even in cases where effective opinion leaders exist within the target population. The world of higher education is a cluttered place, and it often takes an informed and committed external party to drive even the most desirable changes.

The Bill and Melinda Gates Foundation and the Lumina Foundation have been very active in this space. The former, especially, has an ongoing program to further virtually all the goals espoused in this book—or, to describe the situation more accurately, this book seeks to further the Gates Foundation's objectives. (I have worked with both foundations.) Hopefully they will be joined by other foundations and philanthropists in a national effort to change the conversations that swirl around academic resource management and thus transform institutions for the better.

At present only a few commercial organizations have demonstrated the interest and capacity to play a change-agency role. These include the Pilbara Group and Gray Associates, whose efforts I have discussed at some length. Grant Thornton (a large accounting and consulting firm) works closely with Pilbara, and Deloitte has been involved to some extent as well. While not exactly a commercial form, the Educational Advisory Board's model that I mentioned briefly in chapter 2 should be counted as well. These firms are defining the state of the art in AR model development. Write-ups and ads from a few other consulting, modeling, and training firms appear from time to time, but the proprietary nature of their products make it hard to determine whether they have adopted the principles discussed in this book. Despite the fact that it's early days, however, I have little doubt that other firms will emerge in the not-too-distant future as the adoption of AR models accelerates.

Higher education's many associations and consortia also can play an important role. These tend to be membership organizations, and as such they tend to follow and amplify trends rather than create them. Once there are some successful adoptions, however, they can become powerful disseminators of best practice—a kind of "super opinion leader" for their members. I'm seeing signs that this process is beginning to occur. For example, the National Association of College and University Business Officers (NACUBO) has launched a new Economic Models Project for the purpose of helping institutions "navigate their mission, structures, strengths, and resources to create viable models for economic sustainability."[7] The language echoes the ideas in this book, and I am pleased to be participating in the project. NACUBO also collaborated with the Association for Institutional Research (AIR) and EDUCAUSE on a "2019 Enterprise Summit: Analytics." These developments augur well for the adoption of analytics by academic as well as business officers, and they will help spur adoption of the models discussed in this book.

The concept of critical mass is very important in the innovation-adoption literature. As noted, innovation moves faster when innovators are able to communicate with one another and have occasion to do so. The associations, consultants, grant-making organizations, and overseers all facilitate such communication. In Australia, for example, the government's decision to require more detailed cost data than it has previously has jump-started new conversations about activity-based costing, which Pilbara and other firms have been quick to support and amplify. Foundations and associations can do the same thing. More boots on the ground, and indeed anything that gets people talking more often about the opportunities for improvement will spur the innovation process.

Accelerated Research and Development and Training

The other need, and it's a pressing one, is to accelerate the research and development process on academic resourcing information and its associated tools and processes. Much has been accomplished in recent years, but these are still early days. Consulting and software companies can be expected to continue developing services and products, but there also is an urgent need for research within the academy itself.

There are several reasons for this need. First, because academic research is not motivated by short-term market and profit considerations, it is more likely to produce fundamental breakthroughs. Second, some of the research needs to be on how the models can upend long-established norms, how academics react to these challenges, and what can be done to make adoption easier and more likely to achieve success—all subjects better addressed within the academy than by outsiders with less academic insight.

There is a long history of academic research on the aforementioned questions as they apply to business, government, healthcare, and other aspects of university behavior. Now that serious transformation opportunities exist in academe, there's no reason why academic resourcing shouldn't become the target. Finally, research about the academy that's done by academics usually is more credible than work done by commercial suppliers and other external advocates. Credibility is a terrifically important factor in the faculty's adoption of new ideas. Hence peer-reviewed academic research can be expected to generate leverage that's out of proportion to its cost.

What's needed is for foundation and government grant makers to prioritize research and development on academic resourcing tools, how they are best used in decision-making, and how to surmount the barriers to their adoption. Gates and Lumina have done so already, and I hope and trust they will do even more in the future. However, the work has yet to achieve critical mass. Most research on higher education remains focused on macro issues like affordability (who pays and how), diversity (the served and underserved), university governance (basically, setting the mission), the sociology of decision-making (which organizational theories are correct and appropriate), and highly specific questions of teaching efficacy (perhaps involving controlled experiments on alternative methodologies). These all are very important, but they don't address the matters discussed in this book—which are equally important, interesting, respectable, and worthy of attention and financial support.

Once more, the Australians are ahead of the United States, although not by as much as it once appeared they would be. Ten years ago, the Australian government provided some well-funded grants to establish the L. H. Martin Institute at the University of Melbourne's Graduate School of Education. The objective was to further research of the kinds described herein and also to run an ambitious array of degree, certificate, and outreach programs to stimulate transformation in the country's higher education sector. I have taught in L. H. Martin Institute programs and have worked on a few of their research projects—in some cases alongside people from the Pilbara Group. Funding cutbacks and perhaps market saturation caused by the institute's own success on the training front (Australia has relatively few universities) have led to a period of financial austerity. The approach has proven its worth, however. Good research has been performed, and a generation of doctoral students and university leaders has been educated in philosophies and approaches like the ones I've been advocating here. Nothing like the L. H. Martin Institute exists in the United States, though programs at Harvard, the University of Pennsylvania, and a few other places do possess some of its attributes.[8]

In my view, the biggest single action that could be taken to spur higher education transformation would be to create an L. H. Martin

Institute–like entity in the United States. The entity most likely would be attached to a university—perhaps one of those with a history of higher education research—or it could be free standing like the National Center for Higher Education Management Systems in Boulder, Colorado. Wherever housed, the new entity should be separate enough from existing education research traditions to develop a fresh culture around the support of academic resourcing and related topics. The initial funding should be large enough for the entity to reach and sustain a critical scale of operations without waiting for the emergence of reliable revenue streams from sponsored research, training programs, and advisory roles—though such activities should be part of its longer-term mission. Such independence and staying power will be critical for overcoming the higher education sector's legendary resistance to change.

Probably the most urgent need is for seminars and workshops on academic resourcing as discussed in this book. Academic Impressions, an important higher education training organization, has entered this space with multiple high-quality programs. Institutions are encouraged to send teams of academic and financial decision makers in order to develop common values and understandings. I have contributed to these programs and in the process have learned a great deal from Academic Impressions' staff, other presenters, and the participants themselves.

The development of degree and certificate programs should be another early priority. As with the L. H. Martin Institute in Australia, this might include a certificate program by which early- to mid-level university staff members could develop analytical and change-agency skills in the economic and market analysis space. A focused master's program on concepts and tools such as those discussed in this book also would be valuable. I believe there would be a brisk and sustained market for such programs, and that building a cadre of well-trained staffers would be of great help for spurring renewal in higher education.

Finally, an institute attached to a research university could develop an interdisciplinary doctoral program that would attract high-quality people to the field. Depending on the host university's areas of specialization, this could cover information systems, microeconomics, management science as needed for tool development, and the organizational behavior skills needed to understand and overcome barriers to adoption. The work would include hands-on involvement with universities in a participant-observer relationship, just as I have done over the years. Creation of the envisioned institute would improve the intellectual base for AR models and increase the number of boots on the ground for their adoption.

Creating such an entity is well within the capacity of foundations, or consortia of foundations, and well as state and federal governments and perhaps even individual philanthropists. This action would build a cohort of experienced administrators, faculty, doctoral students, and advisors who will help develop the new protocols, tools, and organizational cultures needed to change the conversations around academic resourcing. I can think of no better way to embed, expand, and enhance the tools and thinking I have espoused in this book.

More on Full-Function AR Models

Activity Analysis Detail

Chapter 4's discussion of how full-function AR models work places much emphasis on their representations of teaching and research. This appendix elaborates on three aspects of that discussion: the structural teaching model, summaries of teaching activity, and research.

The Structural Teaching Model

Reengineering the University described the structural model I constructed when first demonstrating how full-function AR models can support academic decision-making. That work has been incorporated in the Pilbara Model described in this book. Structural models seek to capture the details of particular processes in enough depth to inform real decisions. Table 4.1 illustrated the main physical descriptors on which the model is based. My original model involved the following identities, which apply separately to each column of that table.

$$\textit{Teacher Hours} = \textit{Sections} \times \textit{Hours per Section} + \textit{Students} \times \textit{Hours per Student}$$

$$\textit{Sections} = \textit{Students} \div \textit{Average Class Size}$$

$$\textit{Hours per Section} = \textit{Contact Hours per Section} + \textit{Out-of-Class Hours per Section}$$

$$\textit{Regular Faculty Share} = \textit{Sections by Regular Faculty} \div \textit{Sections}$$

Timetabling and student registration systems supply data on course enrollments (students), section counts (sections), and teacher type (regular faculty or other). These enable the calculation of average class size. All the other variables, which are treated as constants in the model, are supplied by judgment or taken from ancillary systems as discussed later. The scheme captures the variables that departments use in planning their course offerings and administrators use in deciding the adequacy of budgets. Fieldwork with my prototype model verified that faculty understand and care about these things.

The distinction between hours per section and hours per student is important. The former includes tasks, such as in-class contact and preparation for class, for which effort does not vary with enrollment as long as the number of sections remains constant. In contrast, the effort reflected by hours per student does vary with enrollment regardless of sectioning. The identities can be stated separately for regular faculty, adjuncts, and any other teacher type—which, again as discussed in *Reengineering the University*, is important for decision-making.

The identity is nonlinear because it includes a step function: that is, the section-related portion of total effort increases in discreet steps as a course's enrollment grows. Step size depends on the maximum tolerable class size, which may or may not be limited by classroom size. Class size is a key variable that needs to appear explicitly in the model. Class size limits also are profoundly important for calculating the incremental cost of enrollment. Proportional allocation models based on enrollments or student credit hours do not include section counts and class sizes. They are not structural models, which by itself can account for their lack of acceptance by faculty.

To anticipate material covered later, full-feature AR models allocate regular and adjunct faculty cost using drivers derived from the identities presented earlier. The allocations are linear in the drivers, but the drivers themselves are nonlinear functions of the descriptor variables. The Pilbara model looks different from my stated identities, but, in fact, the two are mathematically equivalent.[1] My statement is more intuitive, but the Pilbara implementation is easier to program, more flexible in dealing with variations in data availability, and more robust in operation.

Nonfaculty operating costs for courses can be allocated using the same method. Examples include teaching assistants, technical support people, and expendable materials and supplies. Such costs typically are accumulated in departmental accounts, but they go to individual courses in proportion to section counts, enrollments, and applicability factors stored in the course profiles to be described shortly. Costs that are charged to courses are applied directly with no need for allocation.

Teaching Activity Summaries

The course instance and profile data produce ground-level views of departmental teaching activities, which then can be rolled up to get profiles for degree programs, schools, and the whole university. The results are comparable across the university and are routinely available on a semester-by-semester basis. They help chairs manage their operations and provide important information for academic resource managers at all levels.

The instance and profile data enable calculation of measures such as these for each course in the curriculum:

1. *Mode(s) of teaching*: for example, in person, online, or hybrid
2. *Enrollment head count and credit hours*: in total and by student characteristics such as the program in which they are enrolled
3. *Section counts by section type*: for example, whether an in-person course has breakouts and/or labs or is freestanding
4. *Average class size by section type*: or equivalent measures for online teaching
5. *Percentage of teaching by faculty type*: for example, regular or adjunct faculty, by type of section
6. *Hours of teacher effort required*: by task and faculty type

These results flow directly from the data. No allocations are needed except where gaps in the university's data systems require some kind of workaround. One benefit of the modeling process is to call attention to such gaps and spur efforts to fix them. The most common gap is failure to maintain accurate faculty assignment information in the timetabling system as needed for item 6, the fix for which usually is more a matter of management than IT development. A lesson of modeling is that a system's input data are more accurate when the data providers also are users—who benefit from good data and directly experience the consequences of poor data.

Several uses for these data come to mind immediately, and, of course, there are many others. Low-enrollment courses can be culled, in a particular semester or overall, with due regard for the degree programs of the enrolled students. Average class size and adjunct faculty usage can be monitored regularly to ensure against the unintended quality erosion discussed in *Reengineering the University* and chapter 5 of this book. Faculty effort can be estimated for both courses and degree programs. Regular faculty teaching hours can be monitored with respect to the concerns raised in chapter 1 and discussed again shortly. Portfolios of class sizes can be considered, in which the effort required to teach many small interactive courses can be balanced against a few larger ones in which intense faculty–student interaction is not crucial—a so-called barbell strategy.[2]

The Research Model

As noted in the text, step 1 is to map faculty research into the chosen fields and subfields. The Australian model classifies professorial outputs like publications, citations, and conference attendance according to the established field and subfield definitions (mostly to the four-digit level). This task is facilitated by work of the national research community, which has defined criteria for doing the mapping or in some cases has done the mapping already in connection with their funding and publications review processes. This yields a profile for each research-active faculty member, which can be used to distribute that person's output to the agreed-upon fields and subfields. While the task might seem daunting, it has turned out to be eminently practical given the stakes involved. Refinement of the mapping scheme should significantly involve faculty, which is essential for gaining acceptance and generating improvements over time. Importantly, the scheme's efficacy should be judged against the crude current mappings represented by assignments to schools, departments, and other organizational units—which confound the data for research subfields or even whole fields.

With the faculty research profiles in hand, it's a simple matter to allocate effort and revenue to the fields and subfields. Absent specific data to the contrary, all faculty and staff full-time equivalents associated with projects flow proportionately to the research profile(s) of the principal investigator(s). To anticipate the next section's revenue discussion, the same is true for funding from sponsored projects. Unfunded faculty research effort flows in proportion to the individual's research profile. The result is a comprehensive picture of the resource usage and revenue associated with the identified fields and subfields: in other words, just what's needed for an institution's strategic decision-making.

Figure A.1 presents representative research data on the "two-digit" level for a typical Australian university. The two-digit level describes "broad fields" of research; similar data are available for more detailed levels. The lightly shaded bars show direct total revenue, and the dark ones show total expenditure, which include overhead recoveries and allocations, respectively. As noted, the expense figures include estimates of unfunded "departmental research" as well as charges to organized research activities. In other words, this simple diagram captures the economics of the university's research program in a holistic way.

Figure A.1 also presents the faculty's weighted publication output for each two-digit field. The university developed this weighting well before AR model development, and the data were simply added into the research subfield profiles and included on the graph. The data suggest that the university is "punching above its weight" in information technology, for example, and below its weight in

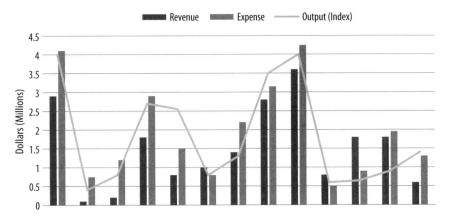

Figure A.1. Revenue, Expense, and Outcomes by Broad Field of Research

psychology—although one can't be sure without knowing something about the relative unit costs of research in each field. As in many areas of model interpretation, the value of these data becomes greater once time series have been accumulated for analysis. What is beyond argument is the importance of departmental research, which can be inferred from the difference between the revenue and expense bars. University investment is a substantial factor for many fields, and this shows up in the outcomes data. Our interviews demonstrated that data about these investments are very important for setting research investment strategies.

Cost Savings from Closing a Course Instance

The discussion in chapter 5 also describes decisions about what course instances to offer in a particular course. The top panel of table A.1 summarizes the instance-level data for CSI 4363. These data, not given in the text, are readily available in the model. The course is doing well overall, but the summer semester is losing a significant amount of money, especially on a per-credit-hour basis. The two primary instances have about twenty students each, but the summer instance has only one student. We don't need a model to conclude that the latter isn't viable as it is, but it's instructive to do the analysis using this simple case.

Does maintaining students' progress toward their degrees require the course to be available during the summer session? If so, we might wish to promote it more strongly for that semester (e.g., to students from outside the university) while working hard not to cannibalize enrollment from the other semesters. Having exhausted that possibility, we then ask what would happen to the single enrolled student if we were to stop offering the course. Results for the two logical possibilities are shown in the lower panels of table A.1.

In option A, the student enrolls in the first or second semester instead of in the summer. In this case:

- The university retains the income related to the student.
- The fixed costs associated with teaching the summer course remain constant (and will be reallocated over the department's other courses).

Table A.1. Course Delivery Instances for CSI 4364, Systems and Database Design

When, Where, and How Taught	Total Revenue ($)	Total Expense ($)	Net Margin ($)	Enrollment	Margin/ Enrollment ($)
All Instances	80,052	54,768	25,284	39	648
Semester 1, Sydney, Face-to-Face	41,505	27,219	14,285	20	714
Semester 2, Sydney, Face-to-Face	35,937	22,641	13,297	18	739
Summer, Sydney, Face-to-Face	2,610	4,906	(2,298)	1	(2,298)
Option A: Summer Students Enroll in Either Semester 1 or 2					
All Instances	79,497	50,375	29,122	39	747
Semester 1, Sydney, Face-to-Face	41,505	27,227	14,278	20	714
Semester 2, Sydney, Face-to-Face	37,992	23,148	14,844	19	781
Option B: Summer Students Don't Enroll at All					
All Instances	77,443	49,897	27,563	38	725
Semester 1, Sydney, Face-to-Face	41,505	27,230	14,276	20	714
Semester 2, Sydney, Face-to-Face	35,937	22,649	13,289	18	738

- The classroom costs will be shifted to the "unutilized" pool and reallocated over other courses.
- A portion of the direct costs associated with the course may be saved: for example, if casual staff had been employed to teach.

The AR predictive model can be used to analyze the scenario. This produces a margin of $29,122, which is $3,838 more than with the summer instance in place.

In option B, the student doesn't enroll in anything at the university. The effects are the same as in the first example except that the university loses the income associated with the student. The resulting margin is $27,563. This is $2,279 less than the base case and $1,559 less than for option A. The differences aren't eye-catching, but they would become so if overall enrollment in the course was larger or a somewhat higher percentage had enrolled in the summer. And it's worth observing that most efficiency gains are built up from multiple small improvements.

The chair might consider the likelihood of each outcome and calculate the expected values of the two.[3] The result is $28,342, or $3,058 more than the base case if the two options are equally likely, so the decision would be to go ahead unless there are significant academic reasons to the contrary. Alternatively, she might simply note that money is to be made under either outcome and there is no financial downside. Similar analyses can be done for blended and online delivery, the latter possibly being handled by an external partner who would recruit and manage the students (but not actually teach them) on a fee-per-student or percentage-of-revenue basis. (The only requirement is that there be instances of each delivery mode in the university's database.) Failing that, one must redesign the course as described in chapter 4 of *Reengineering the University* before estimating the cost savings.

Some Predictive Model Decision Rules

The text states that three simple what-ifs will be used to illustrate how the AR predictive models can work. They are: (1) capping class sizes for existing course instances, (2) eliminating course instances with fewer than a certain number of enrollments, and (3) creating a new course instance in a particular semester or on a particular campus. Each requires modeling of enrollment redistribution, plus the new section counts, staffing needs, and direct costs of staff. Larger variations in enrollment can be simulated in the same way, but they also require that one consider variations in overhead costs.

Redistribution of Enrollments

Figure A.2 illustrates an input screen for enrollment capping. The upper panel shows the historical frequency distribution of class sizes for lectures in all the faculties of Australia University. Similar charts for the other class types are only a click away. These are useful references when deciding where to set the class size caps. Users input their class size caps into the boxes in the lower panel. Pursuant to the hierarchical scheme discussed in chapter 4, the illustrated figures (which aren't necessarily realistic) apply to the whole university. They become the default, but one can override them by entering new values on the line for a given faculty—as with lectures for engineering and science and seminars for arts and education, for example. Clicking on a faculty label lists all the schools for that faculty, and so on down to departments and even individual courses. A similar input screen can be called up for minimum class sizes, or a business rule developed to calculate and apply desired threshold figures.

As noted, the model uses internal rules to calculate the what-if effects. The key issue for this example is what to do with students who are displaced by the enrollment caps. The simplest rule-set provides just enough sections to accommodate them in the same semester, campus, and teaching mode: in other words, in the same course instance where the cap was applied. As is true throughout the model, users can change the rules if they want to.

The rules are more complicated for what-ifs that involve eliminating or adding course instances. Perhaps the best approach is to use the principles listed in the sidebar. (As discussed earlier, F2F

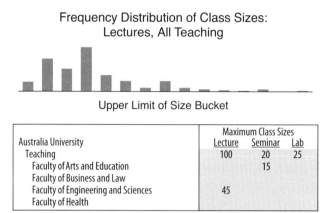

Frequency Distribution of Class Sizes:
Lectures, All Teaching

Upper Limit of Size Bucket

Australia University	Maximum Class Sizes		
	Lecture	Seminar	Lab
Teaching	100	20	25
Faculty of Arts and Education		15	
Faculty of Business and Law			
Faculty of Engineering and Sciences	45		
Faculty of Health			

Figure A.2. Input Screen for Capping Class Sizes

refers to courses taught in person, BL refers to blended learning, and DL refers to distance learning.) All students must be accommodated in the same course but not necessarily in the same semester or teaching mode, or, for distance learning, on the same campus. (This can be relaxed by changing principle 5.) The principles are not intended to be dispositive but rather to show the kind of thinking that can be brought to bear on the predictive model.

Adding a new instance is more complicated yet but still manageable. It requires that the model determine both the number of students to be attracted and where they will come from. This is harder than redistributing enrollments from an existing instance. Two approaches suggest themselves: a rule-based system like the one described earlier and direct input by the user. The simplest possible rule-set starts with a figure for the new instance's total enrollment and assumes that all students come from existing instances of the same course ("one hundred percent cannibalization"). Enrollment could be set at a fraction (e.g., three-quarters) of the maximum class size, for example. Then the five principles can be used to collect these enrollments from other course instances. This approach is likely to work best for policy-related what-ifs: for example, "We

Principles for Redistributing Displaced Students

1. F2F students will switch to BL and if necessary to DL, but BL students will switch only to DL. Distance students must stay in the DL mode.
2. Students will switch to another semester (in the same academic year) before they will switch teaching modes.
3. Campus-based students will switch only to F2F and BL instances on their own campus. Campus doesn't matter for DL instances provided they're in the same country (United States and Canada excepted).
4. If qualifying instances can be found in more than one semester, then the enrollments are split equally among them.
5. If no instance that meets the criteria can be found, then the original instance is not changed.

want every lower division F2F course to be offered in every semester including (or not including) summer."

The direct approach is appropriate for targeted additions: for example, when research suggests that lack of a course instance for a particular semester or campus inhibits student progression. Here the user would input the data for when, where, and how the instance is to be taught, *and* the number of enrollments it will draw from a specified list of existing instances in the same or related courses. The direct procedure also could replace the rule-set for deleting course instances. I don't know whether it has been implemented anywhere yet, but doing so would be straightforward.

Section Counts, Staffing, and Direct Costs

Two additional steps are needed to finalize these what-if predictions. The first calculates the number of class sections for each course instance. This is readily done with the formula

Section Count = Enrollment ÷ Maximum Class Size

rounded up to the next largest integer.

The second step determines the number and types of teachers needed for the new section configuration. The simplest method assumes that regular faculty will teach a specified number of sections with the difference being made up by adjuncts. The user can look at the resulting figures for faculty hours and adjunct usage to decide whether, and how, to change the faculty workloads and then rerun the simulation. Rules for automatically changing faculty numbers are available and may be preferred for some purposes, but the aforementioned often will suffice. The model's regular procedures now can calculate the direct costs of the new section and teacher configuration.

Variable Overhead Costs

Overhead calculations require more thinking than meets the eye. I noted in chapter 4 that some overhead costs depend on the university's scale of operations, and that the relationship is large enough to matter when the numbers of students, staff, and so forth vary by a significant amount. AR predictive models have used two different methods to estimate variable overhead: statistical analysis of time-series data and informed judgments about overhead structures.

Statistical analyses for time series tend to be top-of-mind for accountants and institutional researchers. One collects multiple years of data and then runs regression analyses of the form

$$Overhead = FC + VC_1 \times Driver_1 + VC_2 \times Driver_2 + \ldots$$

where $Driver_1$ is a scaling variable such as student or staff numbers, VC_1 is the variable cost for the ith driver, and FC is the fixed cost. Separate equations can be estimated to get the fixed and variable costs for collections of overhead elements.

The first AR predictive models were configured to run these regressions automatically, during the data update for each new year. The approach works fairly well from a technical standpoint, but it suffers from two drawbacks. First, one must wait at least four or five years from the historical model's original installation to get enough data points for a minimally stable analysis—and even then one must edit the coefficients to smooth out the inevitable anomalies. I do believe the analysis is worth doing in cases where there are sufficiently longtime series, if for no other reason than to build up experience for informing the judgmental approach to be described next.

I developed the judgmental approach at Stanford during my tenure as CFO. Looking carefully at our detailed chart of accounts, my staff made judgments about the fraction of cost in each category we believed to be variable with respect to particular drivers. Looking at payroll, for example, it was possible to distinguish between policy-making (fixed cost) and transaction processing (variable with the number of students, staff, etc.). Likewise, the cost of negotiating staff benefits and calculating rates was judged to be fixed while that of counseling and transaction processing was judged to be variable for reasonably expected changes in Stanford's operational scale. The process wasn't difficult given that we were content with rough approximations. Aggregating the results over all the overhead areas led us to conclude that about two-thirds of our overhead dollars were essentially fixed and the other one-third were variable with respect to one driver or another.[4] Users of modern AR predictive models can perform the analysis based on data like those described in chapter 5, and the model includes screens on which to input the results.

It's worth noting that, once implemented, the variable overhead structure can be applied automatically to all kinds of changes generated by the predictive model. This includes not only enrollment changes but also changes in faculty, staff, facilities, and sponsored research. As for so many areas of the AR model's usage, the university's fixed and variable overhead proportions eventually will become part of its planning DNA.

Strategies for Coping with Revenue Losses

Raise Net Tuition and Fees

Raising tuition and fees is often the top-of-mind response regarding losses of state support in US universities, and this has indeed been happening for many years. The situation is more complicated in Australia, where tuitions for domestic students are regulated, but rates can be adjusted for overseas students. The predictive model handles any specified tuition rate, across-the-board or varying for in-state versus out-of-state residence or even by program. Student fees can be adjusted down to the level of individual courses, if desired. Financial aid policies can be adjusted as well. One does not need a structural AR model to get the university's bottom line for overall tuition, fee, and financial aid adjustments, but it can be helpful to see the impacts by degree program, school, and department and then perhaps fine-tune the adjustments. The Australian leading universities' teams experimented with a number of tuition-raising strategies to get a feel for their impact in the two revenue-loss situations.

The higher-tuition strategy proved problematic for the worst-case situation. First, the revenue shortfalls were too large to offset with any reasonable student revenue adjustments. (In Australia, especially, it is the more risky overseas students who generate the largest margins.) Moreover, any effort to do so risked triggering substantial stakeholder opposition. "Why should the pocketbooks of domestic students be squeezed to solve problems in foreign markets?" At the very least, the model showed that the university should try to explore other strategies. Indeed, concerns about tuition rates and student debt recommended such exploration for the intermediate situation as well as the worst case.

Intensify Fund-Raising

Revenue shortfalls also produce calls for increased fund-raising. The first question, of course, is to determine the practical limits for such increases and how much of the revenue shortfall they could offset. Scenario development should include time for fund-raising officers and their consultants to describe and defend the realism of their plans. The new gift flow must be sustainable: the fund-raisers must commit to bringing it in year after year, which is a particular problem in Australia. The AR predictive model is not needed for these conversations, but the model becomes important at the next stage of analysis.

Fund-raising must contend with the problem of restricted gifts. Any professional will say that restricted money is easier to raise than unrestricted money. The problem is how much the restricted gifts will close the revenue gap. The predictive model can test the impact of money for endowed chairs in specific fields, and for library acquisitions, student financial aid, and similar restricted purposes. It also can test for support of general functions such as research and for organizational units like schools, departments, and programs—all at whatever level of detail one wishes to analyze. The new data will percolate through the model and produce new margin estimates for teaching and research, for schools, departments, programs, and so forth. It is what happens to these margins that determines whether the revenue gap is effectively closed.

Boost Class Sizes, Faculty Workloads, and Adjunct Usage

Planned or unplanned increases in class sizes, faculty workloads, and adjunct usage are common responses to revenue shortfalls. I've noted that class sizes and faculty workloads drift up as a result of enrollment increases without compensating additions to section counts or faculty lines. Enrollment reductions may force faculty FTE reductions, which again boost class sizes. The percentage of sections taught by adjuncts (or teaching assistants, etc.) rise as well, due to professors' desires to maintain departmental research. I began my research on course-level activity-based costing in the interest of illuminating and managing these situations.[5] AR historical models present all the data necessary to diagnose the problems when they have occurred. AR predictive models allow decision makers to anticipate them and take early remedial action.

As noted, the predictive model tries to manage class sizes within user-specified bounds and adjust faculty lines and adjunct usage accordingly. Following these recommendations ought to mitigate the problem, but to do so one must make enough changes elsewhere to maintain the university's financial viability. If necessary, decision makers can increase the model's class size limits or accept higher faculty workloads and adjunct percentages. The model enables and informs the conversations needed to navigate the complex array of alternatives.

Insight about the effect of faculty workload increases on research can be gained from the model's reports on the supply and demand for faculty effort. It seems likely that departmental research is something that will suffer as demand exceeds supply by increasing amounts. Teaching contact hours, preparation, and grading are less elastic in most situations because the tasks are more clearly defined, and because many students are quick to criticize what they see as shortfalls in performance.

Boost Enrollments in High-Margin Programs

This option is less threatening than the ones considered so far. The analysis begins by scanning summary enrollment, revenue, cost, and margin data for courses and programs across the university. The worst-case situation requires reductions in student numbers from the countries where demand is expected to decline before doing the analysis. Academic resourcing managers would search for the subset of profitable programs that have good market potential and align well with the university's academic objectives, and then test the effects of boosting enrollments in these programs. It's not necessary to consider capacity limits, because the scenario analysis will add faculty and other teaching inputs to maintain current resourcing ratios.

What follows is an iterative series of model runs where the analyst increments the enrollments of candidate programs, evaluates the effects, and makes further adjustments until margins reach the level needed to offset the assumed losses or the potential for market expansion has been exhausted. The predictive model will automatically determine course-by-course revenues, section counts, faculty requirements, costs, and margins for each assumed enrollment level. Models with robust classroom utilization data will be able to flag situations where room scheduling has become problematic; otherwise, judgments will need to be made based on one's sense of overall section counts and sizes. Variable overhead adjustments will be made where applicable. The iterative process is easy to describe, but its simplicity belies the massive amount of computation that's done under the hood of the predictive model. This level of detail matters, and it is completely impractical using spreadsheet analysis.

Close or Merge Courses, Programs, Departments, or Campuses

Having exhausted the opportunities for revenue replacement, cost reduction is the next logical area for consideration. One approach is to consider culling courses with small enrollment: for example, those that fail to break even on a fully loaded basis, as described earlier. Care must be taken not to undermine the department's learning goals, but unjustifiable small course instances should be challenged even in normal times.

The same approach can be applied at the program level. To simulate closure with total loss of students, one simply eliminates its enrollment and runs the predictive model to view the effects on courses, programs, and campuses. (The need to "teach out" such programs is handled at a later stage of the analysis.) Or one can assume the students transfer to other programs and adjust those programs' enrollments accordingly. Merging programs probably will require adjustments to the survivor's curriculum, which in turn will mean adjusting enrollments at the individual course level. Program elimination assumes the transferred students accept the target program's curriculum as is. I've already described the machinery for course-by-course enrollment adjustment, and there is no denying that it's a somewhat tedious operation. Still, program merger is such an important action that a considerable amount of analysis is justified.

Closing or merging departments or campuses is more complicated yet, but the predictive model can help here, too. As in the earlier example, one starts by making assumptions about the disposition of courses and enrollments. Courses and faculty can be assigned to other departments, for instance, or teaching operations assigned to alternative campuses. These changes are large enough that the predictive model's built-in variable overhead structure may have to be overridden. God is once again in the details, and the AR model includes the business rules needed to isolate and modify chunks of overhead when this becomes important.

Prune Overhead Areas

Overheads make up more than half of mainstream cost in many universities and a significant portion in all the rest. Every cost reduction exercise with which I have been associated has included a vigorous effort to improve the efficiency of administrative and support services. The AR models don't address overhead efficiency per se, but they can identify areas where expenditures are large enough for efficiency gains to materially affect the university's bottom line. Once identified, the savings can be plugged into the predictive model to see their effects on the cost allocations to teaching and research in particular schools and academic programs. But this is not the only way the model can be helpful. Even top efficiency in overhead provision begs the question of whether all the "services" supplied are, in fact, necessary. Members of the central administration should not be the sole arbiters of this question. Deans, in particular, have both the insight and motivation to contribute to the conversations. Never is this truer than during times of revenue shortfall.

Effective decanal participation in conversations about overhead requires more data than are available from conventional sources. "Why are the allocations to my school so large?" the deans ask, "and what can be done about them?" Answers to the first part of the question usually focus on accounting rules, cost drivers, and the like. Such explanations aren't satisfying to academics. What deans really want is not simply the logic of overhead allocation but to understand the activities and costs in enough detail to engage with central administrators about value for money in particular areas.

Table A.2, for the USA University College of Arts and Sciences, caters to this need. The stub of the table lists all the overhead areas

Table A.2. Overhead Allocations by Source (Dollars in Millions)

Area of Activity	Expense	Area of Activity	Expense
Academic Affairs	1.3	Legal	2.2
Admissions	3.4	Library	5.9
Athletics	3.1	Network Systems	3.4
Chief Financial Officer	1.1	Planning and Assessment	1.3
College Relations	4.1	President's Office	1.3
Communications	4.1	Purchasing	0.6
Controller Group	3.8	Registrar	1.3
Counseling and Wellness	1.1	Research Administration	0.3
Data Warehouse	0.6	Residential Life	10.5
Enterprise Systems	2.2	Security	0.8
Faculty/Staff Reporting Activities	(3.1)	Student Affairs	1.3
Facilities Conferencing	0.2	Student Services Administration	1.4
Facility Operations	10.3	Student Solutions Center	2.2
Financial Aid	1.6	Technology-Based Learning	0.8
Human Resources	1.1	VP for Development	2.0
Institutional Support	17.2	Enrollment Management	3.4

with material cost allocations to the college. (Some of the labels will seem opaque to outsiders, but they are well understood by the deans and their staffs.) The categories are fine enough to support conversations of the kind cited earlier. The drivers include student credit hours for different campuses and overseas operations, total college expenditures, FTEs for various faculty types, library expenditures, various IT expenditures, and the floor space utilized for faculty offices and other kinds of nonclassroom space. (Recall that classroom utilization is allocated as a direct cost, based on timetabled room numbers.) Another display (not shown) gives the size of the expense pools that are allocated by the drivers.

I observed a room full of USAU deans "having at it" with central administrators over the size of the overhead pools and how they are allocated to their schools. The data in the displays, coupled with additional information that can be supplied in response to questions, encourages substantive and constructive conversations instead of the often intense but usually ill-informed complaints that are so familiar in universities. Such meetings also provide administrators with opportunities to describe their efforts to contain or roll back costs in the various areas, the risks involved in doing so, and the possible impact of these actions on the services provided to schools.

The conversations provide needed pushback against the tendency of even the most well-meaning administrators to add capacity, and therefore cost, in the areas for which they are responsible. One reason for this is that an asymmetry of risks and rewards tends to reward risk-averse behavior. Another is what at Stanford we used to call "function lust": the tendency of administrative and support service managers to believe that excellence in their particular area is of disproportionate importance to the university (as well as to themselves). Empowering deans and their staffs will add powerful, savvy, and informed voices to the conversations about overhead. This will help level the playing field and mitigate administrators' risks by sharing the decisions to economize. Hopefully this will relieve the pressure for overhead costs to creep up as a fraction of total expense, or perhaps even roll back the percentage.

Scoring Market Data with Fuzzy Logic

The Gray Associates scoring system for market-related data that was discussed in chapter 7 is serviceable, but it can be improved in at least two ways. First, the categories aren't anchored in language that describes users' feelings about the marketplace. What do the abstractions "low" and "medium" really mean, for example? Second, why should the difference between, say, 2,000 and 2,001 inquiries change the score by two full digits (from 3 to 5), whereas moving from 2,001 to 2,002 means nothing? These issues aren't surprising given that the use of market data is in its infancy, but they will loom larger as time goes on. Users who are not natural innovators will relate more easily to grounded categories, and mitigating the "step function" problem will make it easier to see relations among scores and nonmarket variables. There are many approaches to mitigation, but I suggest one based on "fuzzy logic" principles. I don't propose this as settled science but rather as an approach that I believe is interesting and should be explored.

Fuzzy logic was invented in the 1980s and popularized in the 1990s with a best-selling book by computer scientist Bart Kosko.[1] It allows one to model constructs that are defined in natural language and involve nonlinear and interactive relationships that are hard to represent structurally. The most widespread applications have been in control system engineering: for example, for familiar consumer products such as thermostats and washing machines as well as highly technical defense and producer goods. The ideas also have been used in data and policy analysis, and some regard them as precursors of today's neural network algorithms for computer learning. There has been controversy about the philosophical underpinnings of fuzzy logic, and in particular how it differs from probability and networking theories, but that needn't concern us here. The important thing is that fuzzy logic offers a commonsensical, well-grounded, and inexpensive methodology for solving the problems described earlier.

Market mapping starts with the idea that each of the metrics being considered has some causal effect on market performance. For example, student inquiries indicate interest that potentially can be converted to applications and thus to matriculations. Percent of completions by degree level can affect student perceptions and the ability of faculty to offer the right kind of instruction, which in turn feeds back on completions and eventually on matriculations. It will be a long time, if ever, before these relationships can be described by structural mathematics. However, people familiar with how programs interact with the markets they serve often have well-formed ideas about them. The challenge of market mapping is to encode the ideas of these "experts," so they can be presented to people (e.g., program reviewers) for whom the data may elicit insights that lead to improvement.

Gray's approach is to encode the experts' ideas into buckets that indicate the variable's effects on market performance. I suggested previously that more expressive names than minimum, low, and the like should be used, and I will give an example shortly. However, the experts' ideas will be "fuzzy" no matter what the labels are. Precise demarcation lines don't mesh with how people think. Hence they spawn confusion, argument, and frustration. We need to define "fuzzy buckets" that can mimic the user's "fuzzy thinking."

To set ideas, let's consider the following fuzzy bucket labels, which might be applied to the student inquiries data for a particular program during a given year.

- *Hot.* Interest in this kind of program is really hot. There are plenty of inquiries to sustain our growth and even to accommo-

date new programs should they enter the market (or our program if we are the potential new entrant).

- *Sustainable.* Interest is sufficient to sustain our program, but
  there isn't a lot of slack. Entry of new competitors or modest
  shifts in student preferences would seriously affect our application rates.
- *Questionable.* Interest is questionable. We may be able to spur it
  through outreach programs, but this could well be an uphill
  effort that's vulnerable to competitive countermeasures.
- *Problematic.* Interest is marginal or worse. We need to look
  carefully at the market for our program (or look elsewhere if
  we're considering a new market entry).

This is consistent with the four-category scheme used in table 7.1,
but it conveys the experts' thinking better than simple descriptors
do. Once again, the assignments will be informed by the market
percentile data as interpreted in light of the program's specific characteristics. But the step function problem remains.

How can we reflect the "fuzzy bucket" idea as opposed to the sharp
demarcation lines of 500, 2,000, and so on? A little reflection shows

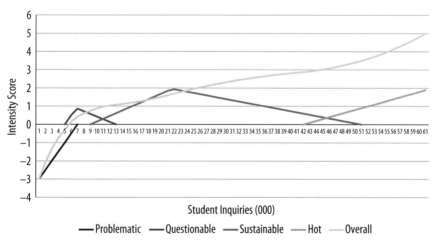

Figure B.1. Illustrative Fuzzy Scoring Scheme

that even experts don't really know how well each description applies to any given level of inquiries. The best they can do is approximate their feelings in terms of vague and often overlapping regions: what I've called fuzzy buckets. Figure B.1 shows how such an approximation might work. It displays student inquiries on the horizontal axis and intensity of the experts' feelings on the vertical one.

Notice that the sharp demarcation lines have been replaced by overlapping triangles. For example, the highlighted triangle near the middle of the diagram depicts the sustainable region. Its apex is 2,000, which implies that the medium score in Figure B.1 is considered most likely to represent sustainability. However, the range of uncertainty (fuzzy bucket) runs from 700 to 5,000. Any score in that range might turn out to be sustainable. The small triangle to the left (with apex at 500) depicts the questionable region, and the two triangles with apexes at the left and right of the diagram depict the problematic and hot regions.

The remaining task is to calculate a summary score for each level of inquiries: in effect, a weighted average of the experts' feelings about the various categories.[2] This is depicted by the dashed curve in the figure. The scheme replicates the earlier result, but in a smoother and more believable fashion.[3] The four-quadrant display illustrated back in table 7.1 requires only a little modification to take account of the anchored and fuzzy bucket scoring system.

More on Not-for-Profit Models

Elaboration of the Not-for-Profit Paradigm

Chapter 8 described the not-for-profit paradigm that underpins the use of AR models by academic staff and faculty rather than simply by financial staff. This section elaborates on that discussion under the rubrics of "the importance of mission" and "the deeper meaning of margin."

The Importance of Mission

Table C.1 sums up the important differences between for-profit and not-for-profit behavior that were discussed in the text. The first line reiterates the all-important difference in how surpluses are distributed. The second presents the decision rule for determining output levels. Elementary economics courses teach us that, to maximize profits, an entity should boost a program's or product's output so long as marginal revenue (ΔR, which depends on market demand) is greater than its marginal cost (ΔC): that is, until the incremental output ceases to produce a profit. In not-for-profit entities, this relation is buffered by adding "Δ Value" (i.e., contribution to mission) to the revenue side of the equation. This says universities should expand programs for which the sum of mission contribution and marginal revenue exceeds incremental production cost, and should downsize those where the opposite is true. Putting a number on Δ Value is challenging, though chapter 8 does present a scheme for doing so. Yet the principle is of great practical importance. Not-for-

Table C.1. Key Implications of the Not-for-Profit Difference

	For-Profit	Not-for-Profit
Decision rule for expanding programs	$\Delta R > \Delta C$	Δ Value $+ \Delta R > \Delta C$
Cross-subsidizing programs	Never on a permanent basis	Often: Reflects academic values
Incentives to raise prices (tuition)	Strong: Limited by the market	Strong: Limited by the market
Efficiency and productivity improvement	Important: Savings drop to the bottom line	Important: Savings drop to cross-subsidies
Effect of extreme financial stringency short of bankruptcy	Low share price, increased likelihood of hostile takeover	Mission becomes less important relative to money

profits should make the best judgments they can about mission contribution and not base their decisions on market or money alone.

While not shown in the table, the relative importance of the Δ Value
and ΔR terms depends on the university's financial situation, especially the amount of discretionary fixed revenue at its disposal. This
is unrestricted income that does not depend on the volume of any
particular output. Examples include unrestricted gifts and endowment returns, and, for public universities, the amount of general (as
opposed to enrollment-determined) subsidy received from the government. Variable revenue does depend on the level of one or another
output. It pulls the university toward producing more of that output
while at the same time improving its overall financial situation. Discretionary fixed revenue does not favor any activity and thus provides the most opportunity for the university to assert its values.

The second line of the table states a key corollary to the aforementioned: namely, that it's perfectly fine (not to mention common) when
not-for-profit entities subsidize money-losing programs using discretionary fixed revenue or cross-subsidize them with the profits from
moneymaking programs. (The two cases are economically indistin-
guishable.) For-profits never do this on a permanent basis (though it

can happen when losses are believed to be temporary) because out-side shareholders claim the proceeds from profitable activities. With not-for-profits, however, the institution itself is the "shareholder" and the disposition of profits should reflect its mission-related values. Eschewing cross-subsidies is tantamount to saying that the market, and only the market, should determine the relative importance of programs. This is equivalent to banishing mission contribution from conversations about academic resourcing decisions.

The next two lines in the table say that boosting the pool of funds available for cross-subsidies will give the not-for-profit greater lati-tude to further its mission. This provides an incentive to raise prices as much as the market will bear, and also to improve operating effi-ciency and productivity. These incentives are the same as in for-profit entities, which should not be surprising given that the not-for-profit cross-subsidy pool plays the role of profits in business firms. Unfor-tunately, though, we'll see that these incentives are not as strong as those in the for-profit sector.

The last line describes what happens when there is a sustained period of extreme financial stringency, but not to the point where the entity must actually declare bankruptcy. (Bankruptcy is essen-tially the same for both for-profits and not-for-profits: the entity either ceases functioning and sells its assets or merges with another entity.) Financial hard times drive down the for-profit's stock price, which increases the likelihood that a corporate raider will persuade disappointed shareholders to approve a hostile takeover. Hostile takeovers can't happen to not-for-profits, but the equivalent of a low share price is a depleted cross-subsidy pool—which amounts to a bankruptcy of academic values. Cash-strapped universities must behave like a business by catering to the market and only to the market. Money is king, and mission primacy is lost. Maintaining a reasonable degree of financial health is necessary for asserting one's mission. Most colleges and universities are still able to do that, but it can no longer be taken for granted.

The Deeper Meaning of Margin

The text asserts that, in addition to its implications for financial health, margin provides insight about a well-run university's values. This derives from line 1 of table C.1: the decision rule for determining outputs in a well-run traditional university. Universities that are not well run aren't guided by the decision rule, which means there is no relation between margin and mission. The decision rule is:

$$\Delta\ Revenue + \lambda\Delta\ Value = \Delta\ Cost, \text{ for each program (the decision rule)}$$
$$\text{and}$$
$$Cost = Revenue \text{ overall (the financial constraint)}$$

The theory shows that $1/\lambda$ is the extra value that can be obtained by reoptimizing the mix of programs with an extra dollar of income or one fewer dollar of cost in the financial constraint. Economists would call $1/\lambda$ the "marginal value of money." It's possible to prove that $1/\lambda$ becomes infinite as the entity teeters on the edge of bankruptcy.[1] This means that λ itself becomes zero, so the value term drops from the decision rule. This means the not-for-profit entity is behaving like a for-profit one, which is to be expected if it's sacrificing mission in a desperate search for dollars.

To simplify, let's define "Δ Effective Value" as $\lambda\Delta\ Value$. This quantity tends to be large for affluent institutions and smaller or less-affluent ones. Now we rearrange the first equation slightly to get:

$$\Delta\ Effective\ Value = \Delta\ Cost - \Delta\ Revenue,$$

which produces the following decision rule:

$$\Delta\ Effective\ Value = -\Delta\ Margin$$

This equation will hold, approximately, for each academic program in a well-run university. If it doesn't, academic resource managers will be motivated to upsize or downsize programs until the equation comes closer to balance—all the while maintaining a balanced budget. *Reengineering the University* provides more details on page 23 and in appendix G.

It's worth noting that the previous discussion deals with *incremental* mission contributions and margins, not *overall* mission contributions and margins. The not-for-profit decision rule describes tradeoffs made on what might be called the "value frontier" of the relation between mission contribution and margin, which is where the inverse relation between the two must hold. It's perfectly possible for an option to have a positive overall mission contribution *and* to make money, but such options would not be on the value frontier.

Value Function Analytics

The judgmental Constrained Choice Tool discussed in chapter 8 operates as a freestanding Excel app. However, data accumulated during its use can inform a suite of value analytics that make it easier to prepare new budgets if the spending limit is changed; options are added, eliminated, or reranked; or the market or financial data shift. The analytics also can enhance the judgmental tool itself, by using the choices on prior iterations to provide guidance for the next one. Only experience can show whether the guidance is valuable or distracting, but the ability to change data without totally redoing the judgmental choice process does represent an unequivocal advantage.

The analytics rely on two procedures: one that assesses the budget group's value system as revealed by choices made using the judgmental choice tool and a second that applies these assessments to quickly revise the resulting budget selections when conditions changed. Users need not grapple with the specifics of the procedures, but their operation and interpretation does require more analytical prowess than is needed for the judgmental choice process itself.

Quantifying the Value System

Like most analyses of choice behavior, value quantification assumes that the budget group's decisions, though highly subjective, tend to follow an underlying preference pattern—a so-called value function.

What is it, in generic terms, that the university looks at when making choices? Chapter 1 of *Reengineering the University* argues that traditional institutions concern themselves with two "value propositions": intrinsic values derived from their own mission and so-called customer values as revealed in the marketplace.[2] This suggests the value function should include a term for each type of value. A weighted average provides the simplest possible way of combining the two effects:

Value Function: $\text{Value} = v_p \times \text{Intrinsic Value}$
$+ v_m \times \text{Customer Value}$

It's no coincidence that the two terms correspond to the mission and market variables of the constrained choice model, there called "Preference Ranking" and "Market and Brand." Economists would say the parameters reflect the budget group's "revealed preference" because they are estimated from data accumulated during the judgmental choice process.

What to do with the third variable, "Adjusted Margin," is not resolved by the aforementioned. It doesn't enter the value function because it's a means for *creating* valued ends rather than an end in itself, yet it looms large in the choice process when there is a binding budget limit. Choosing a costly option rules out other options and choosing a moneymaking one opens up other possibilities. Either way, adjusted margin needs to be included in the analysis of revealed preference.

This extends the value function to form the following decision rule for differentiating the best option from the available alternatives at any iteration of the choice process.

Decision Rule:
$\text{Dollar-Adjusted Value} = v_p \times \text{Preference Rank}$
$+ v_m \times \text{Market \& Brand}$
$+ \lambda \times \text{Adjusted Margin}$

where λ stands for "marginal value of money," as in the previous section. (Actually, the two versions of λ may differ by a proportionality factor.) Knowledge of w and λ enables calculation of each option's dollar-adjusted value. The option with the highest dollar-adjusted value should be selected at each iteration, which is why we call this equation a decision rule.[3]

Parameter Estimation

The three parameters are estimated by forming paired comparisons from data generated by successive iterations of the judgmental choice process. How this works can be seen by looking at the second column of table 8.5, for iteration 2 of the illustrated choice process. Option 3 was chosen in preference to options 1, 2, 6, 7, 8, and 13—all of which were available. This implies that the estimated dollar value for option 3 was greater than for any of the six that were passed over, and that failure on any of these comparisons represents an "inversion error." The value function parameters are estimated in a way that minimizes these errors.

Data generated from successive iterations of the judgmental procedure are accumulated in a hidden file and used to estimate the decision rule's parameters. Each iteration generates $n-1$ new data points, where n is the number of available options at that iteration. The estimator normalizes the variables and then uses linear programming to minimize the sum of the inversion errors that arise from cases where the chosen option does not have the largest calculated dollar-adjusted value.

Suppose the estimation is to be performed after the second iteration of the heuristic procedure. There will be $N = n_1 + n_2 - 2$ data points in this case (n_i is the number of available options at iteration i, which takes the values 1 and 2). For each data point, we define the difference between the selected item and the comparator item:

$$\Delta\{\theta\} = Value\{Selection|\theta\} - Value\{Comparator|\theta\}$$

where θ is the vector of unknown parameters. Negative values of Δ represent inversion errors. The formula's inputs are extracted and stored after each iteration of the heuristic procedure.

We want to find the positive values of θ that minimize the sum of these errors over the N data points, subject to the requirement that the coefficients of MBD and NPV, and dR/dV be nonnegative. This requires defining a set of N nonnegative auxiliary variables: Z_1, Z_2, Z_3, ..., Z_N, to represent the inversion errors. Combining these with the aforementioned nonnegativity requirements on the parameters produces the following minimization problem:

Minimize $B = \sum_i Z_i$ with respect to θ,

subject to

$$Z_i \geq 0 \text{ for } i = 1, N \text{ data points}$$
$$Z_i + \Delta\{\theta\}_i \geq 0 \text{ for } i = 1, \dots \text{ data points}$$
$$\frac{dX_{1,k}}{dR_k} \geq 0 \text{ for } k = 1, \dots \text{ candidate items}$$
$$\theta_j \geq 0 \text{ for } all \ j$$

Minimization is accomplished using the Simplex method of linear programming.

The Inversion Errors Ratio given in the following table divides the total inversion error by the sum of decision rule results for all comparisons. This is a variant on the so-called LINMAP procedure long used by market researchers for consumer preference analysis.[4] The percentage of inversion errors after estimation provides a measure of how well the value function fits the user's underlying preference pattern.

Estimated decision rule parameters based on the illustrated choice process, where the sixteen iterations generated seventy paired comparisons, are shown in the following table.

Intrinsic Value (v_p)	Market and Brand (v_m)	Adjusted Margin (λ)	Inversion Errors Ratio
2.78	0.18	0.06	3.2%

The estimates suggest that Adjusted Margin has about the same effect as Market and Brand, and that both are considerably less important than Intrinsic Value. The small inversion error ratio (3.2%) indicates that the model fits the data very well. In fact, only eight of the seventy data points produced inversion errors, and all of them were near the noise level.

The estimates of v_p and v_m can be interpreted as parameters of the value function as well as the decision rule. It tells us that, in this case, the budget group considers mission to be a great deal more important than market. The not-for-profit model discussed in chapters 1 and 8 says the relative importance of mission and market should depend on a school's discretionary resources. Mission, as represented by intrinsic value, is expected to dominate for affluent universities, and market forces are expected to dominate for universities facing financial stringency. The theory predicts that λ will be larger in cases of financial stringency, but it supplies no benchmark for judging "how large is large?"

Guidance during the Choice Process

The decision rule can be estimated after each iteration of the judgmental choice process. This allows guidance to be given during the process rather than only at the end. Figure C.1 shows the value analytics screen as it appears at the end of the illustrated process. The figure is divided into three sections:

1. *Dollar-Adjusted Value*: numeric estimates for each of the options using parameters from the preceding iteration. This and the following display are refreshed at every iteration. Figures for currently available options (only) are provided to decision makers in a column adjacent to the status tableau when the value analytics feature is active. Selecting the available option with the highest dollar-adjusted value guarantees that the next choice will be consistent with the previous ones. One must be careful not to be led astray, however, because aberrations introduced at early iterations are carried forward to the rest of the analysis.

2. *Value Contributions*: stacked bars that show the contribution of each variable to the dollar-adjusted values. (For clarity, this

graph assumes all three coefficients to have the same value; the coefficients actually estimated give too small an effect for market and margin to properly illustrate the chart.) Notice that an option's contribution will be negative if, as may be true for some adjusted margins, the underlying datum is negative.

3. *Selection Consistency History*: feedback on where each choice fell on the spectrum of dollar-adjusted value figures (normalized to a range of 0–100) for each iteration prior to the current one. Consider the topmost bar, which is for iteration 2 because the decision rule can be calculated only after the first iteration. This bar is divided into four sections. Reading from left to right:

   1. The leftmost (dark) bar depicts the range of values for low-valued options that *were not* available at iteration 1.
   2. The second (lighter) bar depicts the range for options that *were* available and had values less than that of the option actually chosen.
   3. The third (lightest) bar depicts the range for available options with values greater than that of the chosen option.
   4. The rightmost (dark) bar depicts the range for options that were not available and had values higher than the available ones.

In other words, the dark bars bracket the channel of values for the available options, and the breakpoint between the two lighter bars shows where in the channel the choice was made.

A new bar is added at each iteration, which means the presentation evolves as the choice process proceeds. Appearance of the lightest bar (the one for available options that were valued more than the chosen one) tells users that their latest choice has not been consistent with their previous ones. This is illustrated in the topmost bar, where the best option's dollar-adjusted value was in the high seventies and the chosen one's was less than twenty. (Recall my comment that the budget group "looked ahead" to the prospect of choosing option 1.) Notice that the bars end after iteration 16, which was the stopping point of the illustrated choice process.

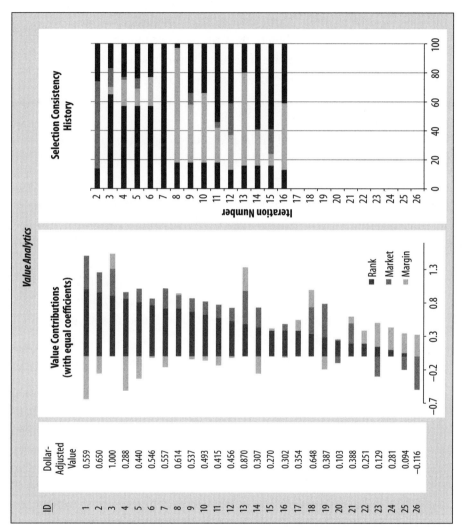

Figure C.1. Value Assessment Analytics

The value analytics screen changes at each iteration of the constrained choice process. Each iteration generates its own parameter estimates, and each set depends on the user's iteration history to that point. This differs from the situation for judgmental choices, where it's only the ending point that matters. After watching many estimations, however, I've concluded that the sequencing effects aren't likely to be material once the successive estimates have stabilized. This usually is after the first dozen or so iterations.

Quick What-If Budget Analysis

The parameters described in the previous section also can be used for quick what-if analysis, which is implemented by the value optimization tool described in this section. As noted, the tool can be used to test a new spending limit, when an option is added or eliminated, or when an option's attribute data change. The analysis involves maximizing the value function estimated earlier, subject to the chosen spending limit, with respect to the options that will be included in the budget. The well-established mathematical optimization procedure described later on can be used to accomplish this. Issues related to dominance and the effect of each option's inclusion or exclusion on the affordability of other options are handled automatically, although a constraint that prevents options determined to be unacceptable from entering the solution can be invoked, if desired. The what-if model allows one to bypass the labor-intensive process of making judgmental choices once the value function has been estimated with an acceptable degree of accuracy.

The optimization tool's mathematical algorithm finds the list of options that produces the largest possible mission contribution given the university's available funds. It maximizes the sum of the estimated value contributions of the selected alternatives, subject to the budget limit and precedence relations. Management scientists call this a "knapsack problem," in which one wants the chosen items' total contribution to be as large as possible without exceeding the knapsack's capacity or any precedence relations. Our problem differs from the classic knapsack one because the contributions and margins can be negative as well as positive, but that poses no difficulty.

Implementation proceeds by defining each decision budget item as a binary variable that equals 1 if chosen and 0 if not, then maximizing the sum of the chosen contributions subject to the budget limit and precedence relations. Then the optimization can be formulated by means of the following integer programming problem.

Define:

i the *index* of the candidate budget item

X_i the item's *decision variable*: $X_i = 1$ if the option is included in the optimized budget and $X_i = 0$ if not

v_i the item's *mission contribution* as determined by Value[θ] as estimated earlier

m_i the item's up-front *margin*

P_i the item's *precedence variable*, if any: $P_i = X_j$, where X_j refers to the package pointed to by i's precedence relation and $P_i = 1$ if i has no precedence relation

Q_i identifies the items that remain *unselected at early termination*; $Q_i = 1$ in this case, and 0 for all other cases

B the budget limit

Maximize $\Sigma_i \{v_i \times X_i\}$ with respect to the X_i

Subject to the constraints

X_i is Integer	*To prevent fractional choices*
$0 \leq X_i \leq 1$ *(all i)*	*Upper and lower limits for the integer definitions*
$X_i \leq P_i$ *(all i)*	*Precedence requirements*
$Q_i \times X_i \leq 0$ *(all i)*	*Locks out the excluded items*
$\Sigma_I \{-m_i \times X_i\} \leq B$	*Budget limit*

This maximizes the sum-product of the decision variables (X_i) multiplied by their contributions (v_i), subject to the five constraints. The first two constraints enforce the variable definitions. The third keeps X_i at 0 unless (1) the package preceding it already has been selected or (2) it has no precedence relation. ($P_i = 1$ in either of these cases, whereas $P_i = 0$ if there is a precedence relation and it's not in the budget.) The fourth constraint enforces the user's decision about early termination as discussed in the text. The fifth constraint ensures that the sum of the margins for the chosen alternatives does not exceed the available budget.

Running the optimizer on the dataset used to generate the judgmental result produced a good but not perfect correspondence. Option 1, "Launch a major research innovation," was left out of the optimizers' solution even though it was in the judgmental one. This saved enough money to allow the optimizer to fund options that were excluded from the judgmental result: specifically, option 4, "Reduce faculty teaching loads" and option 16, "Add a part-time vice provost for student diversity." Putting these discrepancies in context, the overall score was fifteen options classified correctly and three classified incorrectly—with all three discrepancies stemming from the change in outcome for option 1.

The main reason why one should not expect perfect correspondence between the two solutions lies in the use of a linear value function. The function ascribes the same change in value to every pair of rankings: for example, the incremental value going from option 2 to option 1 is the same as that for the move from option 3 to option 2 and, for that matter, for going from option 26 to option 25. The judgmental process imposes no such limitation. In the example, it appears that the hypothetical budget group valued the research initiative more highly than would be expected from the difference in ranking between it and the next lower-ranked option. Once the optimizer result is known, it would be possible to adjust the value scale to increase this difference and then run the optimizer again. This is something of an ad hoc approach, however, and I did not pursue it. Nor did I test the optimizer with different budget limits, though that would be a logical thing to do with a larger and more realistic dataset.

The motivation for the "quick what-if procedure" is to provide decision makers with an intuitive sense of how changes in the budget limit, options list, and other data affect the affordable budget. No one should be expected to accept the results uncritically, but they do provide the starting point for further judgments. Moreover, staff members with management science experience would be able to force any chosen set of options into the solution, or keep them out of the solution, and see what happens to the rest of the solution. Such analyses are easy to do, and they would provide managers with additional insights.

Notes

Prologue. Preview of Applications

1. Anguiano et al. (2017), p. 12, scenario 1.
2. Robert Zemsky, personal communication.
3. Based on Anguiano et al. (2017), p. 13, scenario 3.
4. Dickeson (2010), p. xiii.
5. Dickeson (2010), p. xiii.

Chapter 1. Changing the Conversation

1. Closely paraphrased from Patrick Methvin, "Help Wanted: Supporting Colleges and Universities on the Road to Transformation." Bill and Melinda Gates Foundation, January 23, 2019.
2. Massy (2007). See also Massy (1996, 2016).
3. Zemsky and Massy (1990).
4. To avoid confusion, I am using RCB rather than RCM (responsibility center management) because the former was adopted by the National Association of College and University Business Officers (NACUBO) in its authoritative volume on budgeting. Goldstein (2019), p. 205.
5. I reported this in chapter 4 of Massy (2003) and see no evidence that it has changed.
6. Kegan and Lahey (2016), p. 125. The authors stress the importance of maintaining a "trustworthy environment, one that tolerates—even prefers—making your weaknesses public so that your colleagues can support you in the process of overcoming them" (p. 5). That certainly comports with parts of the academic culture as it pertains to research and scholarship, but it may be something of a stretch when it comes to academic resourcing. Still, engaging in deep and evidence-based AR conversations is a good way to get feedback about whatever blind spots you may have about resourcing.
7. Schumpeter (1942).
8. Kegan and Lahey (2016), p. ix.

9. The quotations throughout this section come from John P. Kotter with Professor Richard Boyatzis and from Russell Raath, Celia Kirwan, Gaurav Gupta, Rachel Rosenfeldt, and David Carder, "Survive + Thrive," working paper, Kotter International, 2018.

10. See especially chapter 2 of Kotter (2014).

11. This observation emerged from my own experience. For a scholarly justification and window on the literature, see Zaffron and Unruh (2018).

12. Massy (2007).

13. Mitchell and King (2018), p. 16.

14. Massy (2003), p. 285, after Hoenack (1983).

15. For an extended discussion of the three types of budgeting mentioned in the text, see chapter 12 of Massy (1996).

16. Massy (2016), p. x.

17. Carlson (2018), p. 15.

18. Morson and Schapiro (2017).

19. Snow (1959).

20. One also hears concerns that artificial intelligence (and, it seems, by implication all computer models) reinforces past relationships and focuses users too strongly on the past. However, that is not true for decision support models of the kinds discussed in this book. These models present the historical record in a way that invites changes for the future.

Chapter 2. Getting into AR Models

1. See National Research Council (2012) for further discussion.

Chapter 3. Building Trust in Your AR Model

1. Agrawal et. al (2018), chapter 6.

2. Agrawal et. al (2018), p. 58.

3. Agrawal et. al (2018), chapter 5.

4. Agrawal et. al (2018), p. 59.

5. Agrawal et. al (2018), chapter 2.

6. Hopkins and Massy (1981) analyze the early failures and describe the successful modeling efforts that took place at Stanford in the 1970s, for example.

7. See Massy (2016) for differences between classic and modern ABC.

8. Anguiano (2013). The University of California, Riverside, had just finished installing the Pilbara Model when the paper was written.

9. https://ire.udel.edu/descriptive-summary/.

10. Morson and Schapiro (2017), p. 66.

11. Morson and Schapiro (2017), p. 66.

12. Hopkins and Massy (1981), p. 51.

13. Rogers (2003) and Massy (1960).

14. For example, "trust" does not appear in the index of Rogers (2003), the landmark book on innovation adoption, even though many of his examples can be interpreted with that in mind. This section draws heavily on his work.

15. Rogers (2003), starting at p. 169.

16. Rogers (2003), p. 175.

17. Rogers (2003), p. 281.

18. Rogers (2003), p. 284.

Chapter 4. Pilbara's Full-Function AR Model

1. I'm grateful to chief executive officer Lea Patterson and his colleagues for giving me unfettered access to the model and supporting my involvement with their clients both in the United States and Australia.

2. Universities that place less emphasis on research will use a different set of numbers, but the important thing for present purposes is that the expectations be reasonably well spelled out.

3. Critics sometimes point out that room numbers may be subject to unrecorded last-minute changes. These changes usually involve seating capacity, which can affect the enrollment slack and marginal cost calculations. The university should improve the accuracy of last-minute recording if the problem proves material.

Chapter 5. Historical Models and Operating Decisions

1. The numbers were taken from table 5.2 because the USAU demonstration files contain only one year of data.

2. The data from the institution in question have been displaced somewhat to protect proprietary information, so these results should not be taken as typical.

3. Zemsky and Shaman (forthcoming).

4. The delivery mode analysis was not included in the dashboards originally constructed for USAU, but it took me only a few minutes to prepare it—even though I am far from expert in the use of PowerBI. This illustrates the AR model's ability to inform many different kinds of inquiries, even those that were not anticipated during the original design process.

5. This important idea didn't originate with me. It goes back to Cyert and March (1963).

6. See also Massy (2016), p. 159, on student segment analysis.

7. The technical problem lies with what are called online analytical processing (OLAP) data cubes, where the number of variables and categories must be limited in order to avoid explosive growth in dimensionality. Conventional SQL (structured query language) systems avoid this difficulty, but they are not fast or flexible enough to directly drive dashboard-style reporting. The "data lake" approach now being offered by Microsoft and other database

vendors appears to provide the needed way forward, and we may expect to see them adopted in AR models soon.

8. However, see National Research Council (2012), pp. 78–79.

9. Hemelt et al. (2018).

Chapter 6. Predictive Models and Scenario Planning

1. Chermack (2011), p. 108.

2. See Isaacson (2015a, 2015b).

3. See, for example, Hopkins and Massy (1981).

4. Gray Associates, "Program Portfolio Strategy: Deciding Which Programs to Start, Stop, Sustain, or Grow." https://www.grayassociates.com.

5. https://www.grayassociates.com.

6. I'm referring to leadership programs in academic resource management run by the L. H. Martin Institute at the University of Melbourne in conjunction with the Pilbara Group. Pilbara's AR predictive model has been installed on a number of client campuses, but their work with it has tended to be proprietary.

7. See Chermack (2011) and Van der Heijden (2005).

8. "Scenario planning," *Economist*, September 1, 2008, "Idea" section.

9. Van der Heijden (2005).

10. Chermack (2011), p. 10.

11. Rieley (1997), pp. 2–3.

12. Chermack (2011), p. 129.

13. Massy (2016), beginning on page 159.

14. Gray Associates, "Program Portfolio Strategy."

15. The principles behind the development of the needed financial planning models can be found in figure 5.3 of Massy (2016) and the ensuing discussion.

16. Massy (2016), pp. 175–186. The study is described in Tough (2014).

17. See, for example, Massy (2016) and Hopkins and Massy (1981).

18. Massy (2016), pp. 181–184; see also Hopkins and Massy (1981), chapter 6, and Massy (1990). The three requirements are: (1) income must equal expense after taking account of all needed transfers and other adjustments, (2) the growth rate of income needs to be approximately equal to the growth rate of expense, and (3) there are no hidden liabilities and all significant obligations have been taken into account. The endowment spending rate depends mainly on the second requirement.

19. Massy (2016), pp. 192–194. See chapter 9 of Goldstein (2019) for a slightly different classification.

20. An AR model applied to a single RCB school could treat the charge-out rate simply as a price, but this begs the question of what the year's actual overhead allocation should be.

21. Massy (1996), chapter 12.

Chapter 7. Comprehensive Program Review

1. Dickeson (2010), p. 59.

2. Western Association of Schools and Colleges (2002), p. 3. I have worked with WASC over the years, and have high regard for their processes and thinking.

3. Northwestern University website: https://www.adminplan.northwestern.edu/program-review/. This website provides a good overview of a well-managed program review process. I served as a reviewer for the university's program review oversight unit, then managed by Marilyn McCoy, in the early 1990s, and came away very impressed. I also served on Yale's University Council, which oversees their program review process, during the 1980s.

4. Western Association of Schools and Colleges (2002).

5. Zemsky et al. (2001).

6. See Dill (1992) and Van Vught (1995); quotation in Van Vught (1995), p. 13.

7. Massy et al. (2007), p. 27; emphasis original.

8. Bok (2013).

9. NCPI was a Department of Education–funded cooperative research effort, during the 1990s, at Stanford, the University of Pennsylvania, and the University of Michigan.

10. Zemsky and Shaman (forthcoming).

11. I would like to thank C. Jackson Grayson, then director of the American Productivity and Quality Center, for giving us unrestricted access to the center's extensive library and Stanford colleague Andrea Wilger for her brilliant work on distilling the material.

12. Massy et al. (2007), beginning on p. 32.

13. Massy et al. (2007), figure 1.1.

Chapter 8. Universities as Mission-Driven Enterprises

1. See Massy (2016), p. 18, and Massy (2004) for other descriptions.

2. This assumes that marginal revenue declines as more units are sold (e.g., due to the lower prices needed to increase sales), and/or that marginal costs increase (e.g., due to growing inefficiencies). Notice that situations where marginal revenues decline but marginal costs remain constant satisfy the condition. These conditions generally are realistic, and they apply to not-for-profit entities as well as to for-profit ones. Additionally, although one might argue that the financial condition is that revenue should equal or exceed cost, the equality will hold as a practical matter because maximizing value always will exhaust the available funds.

3. Massy (2016), pp. 33–38.

4. Another commonsense notion, that market forces will limit expansion, comes into play via the margin term itself. Most markets permit the generation

of more sales if price is lowered, but this will invariably reduce margin. Hence the statement in the text is correct, even though it does not directly reference market constraints.

5. The curve ignores the possibility of "increasing returns to scale" for program sizes that have yet to achieve critical mass.

6. Massy (2016), p. 28.

7. The approach described here extends the one in *Reengineering the University*. I demonstrated that version to academic and financial decision makers in the United States and Australia, and the responses have been encouraging.

8. Adapted from Massy (2016), p. 200.

9. See Massy (2016), p. 194, for a discussion of how to set the budget limit.

10. For a detailed discussion of this and the other concepts that guided development of the choice model, see Massy (2016), especially pp. 17–23, pp. 207–215, and appendix G.

11. These so-called knapsack problems are solved by integer programming.

12. See Hopkins, Larréché, and Massy (1977), and Hopkins and Massy (1981, p. 416).

13. This is a variation on the so-called Delphi procedure for pooling judgments in a group setting.

14. Some of this may come from payments to the revolving fund after the NPV time horizon, although universities also might wish to reduce the budget base when the horizon is reached.

15. The engineered procedure may look complicated, but it's not outside the norms of what's done routinely by financially sophisticated entities. For example, its derivation is at a level that might well be considered homework in an MBA finance course.

16. The "Dominance Principle" is called the "Pareto Principle" by economists. Notice that ties don't count when determining dominance.

17. The justification for this assertion lies in the mathematics of optimization subject to constraints. These algorithms begin by finding any feasible solution and then make feasible upward-moving steps until no more such steps can be found.

18. We shouldn't take the numbers too literally, since the expected savings from downsizing history and the expected cost of reducing adjuncts reflect judgments about how far to go in each area, which means they are subject to modification as the budget process proceeds. The figures do illustrate the trade-off between pain and gain, however.

19. Recall that the discussion in appendix C concerned incremental mission contributions and margins, not overall mission contributions and margins. It's perfectly possible for an option to have a positive overall mission contribution *and* to make money.

20. It's possible to expand the model to include more than one set of preference rankings, which would allow the dominance and affordability principles to be used to balance the views of multiple participants.

Conclusion. The Way Forward

1. Christensen (1997).

2. Heifetz and Linsky (2017), especially chapter 1.

3. Kotter (2014).

4. The headlines are quoted and the discussion is paraphrased from Kotter (2014), beginning at p. 23.

5. Once again, the headlines are quoted and the discussion is paraphrased from Kotter (2014), beginning now at p. 27.

6. Hemelt et al. (2018). The paper uses data from the Delaware Cost Study, but, as noted in chapter 3, more information would be available from AR models.

7. "NACUBO's Strategic Priorities." https://www.nacubo.org/who-we-are/strategic-blueprint.

8. I had planned to create such a program at Stanford in the early 2000s. However, I failed to get the business model right and eventually took early retirement and went into private consulting.

Appendix A. More on Full-Function AR Models

1. The identity in the text can be restated as the following:

$$Hours = Sections \times HrsPerSection + Enrollment \times HrsPerEnr$$

The current AR model uses *hours* as defined earlier as the driver for distributing the faculty and adjunct cost pools to courses. The calculation of *hours* from enrollment is nonlinear due to the step function for *sections*, but the allocation of cost on the basis of *hours* is linear. This makes the two models equivalent, and thus the AR teaching module is, in fact, a structural model. Pilbara's full-function model contains a generalized capacity for applying a user-created, nonlinear mathematical function as the driver for any variable.

2. Light et al. (n.d.).

3. This is a classic example of decision-making under uncertainty, also known as Bayesian decision analysis. See any business school text on quantitative decision-making.

4. My memory of this figure goes back more than thirty years, but I believe it to be approximately correct. Unfortunately, I do not have any written record of the analysis.

5. See the English department example in Massy (2016), chapter 4, for example.

Appendix B. Scoring Market Data with Fuzzy Logic

1. Kosko (1993) provides a readable and interesting description of fuzzy logic principles and why they are important.

2. The procedure adds up the fractions of the triangles' areas that lie below the given inquiry level. An explanation and Excel macro can be found on the publisher's website page for this book.

3. Readers familiar with Bayesian decision analysis may recognize the triangles as akin to subjective probability distributions. As noted, they encode expert judgment into a form suitable for analysis. This suggests that two variables (e.g., the level and growth of inquiries), or more, might be combined by multiplying their single-variable scores. Doing so would require calibrating the variables. Two points are sufficient for the calibration, so this might be done by equating the apexes for sustainable and questionable regions on the two scales.

Appendix C. More on Not-for-Profit Models

1. The underlying mathematics can be found in Hopkins and Massy (1981), pp. 86-94.

2. Massy (2016), pp. 29-38.

3. Knowing two of the three values would suffice, since any of them can be calculated from the other two. However, the algorithm used here estimates all three.

4. See Srinivasan and Shocker (1973) and the large follow-up literature.

Bibliography

Agrawal, Ajay, Joshua Gans, and Avi Goldfarb. (2018). *Prediction Machines: The Simple Economics of Artificial Intelligence.* Boston: Harvard Business Review Press.

Anguiano, Maria. (2013, December). "Cost Structure of Post-Secondary Education: Guide for Making Activity Analysis Meaningful and Practical." Policy Paper from the Bill and Melinda Gates Foundation: Post-Secondary Education Success.

Anguiano, Maria, Paul D'Anieri, Matthew Hull, Ananth Kasturiraman, and Jason Rodriguez. (2017). "Optimizing Resource Allocation for Teaching: An Experiment in Activity-Based Costing in Higher Education." White Paper from the Office of the Provost, University of California, Riverside.

Bok, Derek. (2013). *Higher Education in America.* Princeton, NJ: Princeton University Press.

Carlson, Scott. (2018). "Sustaining the College Business Model: How to Shore up Institutions and Reinvent Them for the Future." White Paper from *The Chronicle of Higher Education.*

Chermack, Thomas J. (2011). *Scenario Planning and Organizations: How to Create, Use, and Assess Scenarios.* San Francisco: Barrett-Koehler Publishers.

Christensen, Clayton M. (1997). *The Innovator's Dilemma: When New Technologies Cause Great Firms to Fail.* Boston: Harvard Business School Press.

Cyert, Richard M., and James G. March. (1963). *A Behavioral Theory of the Firm.* New York: Wiley-Blackwell.

Dickeson, Robert C. (2010). *Prioritizing Academic Programs and Services: Reallocating Resources to Achieve Strategic Balance.* Revised Edition. San Francisco: Jossey-Bass.

Dill, David D. (1992). "Quality by Design: Toward a Framework for Academic Quality Management." In J. Smart (ed.), *Higher Education: Handbook of Theory and Research* (Vol. VIII, pp. 37–83). New York: Agathon Press.

Goldstein, Larry. (2019). *College and University Budgeting: A Guide for Academics and Other Stakeholders*. Fifth Edition. Washington, DC: National Association of College and University Business Officers.

Isaacson, Walter. (2015a). *Steve Jobs*. New York: Simon and Schuster.

———. (2015b). *The Innovators*. New York: Simon and Schuster.

Heifetz, Ronald, and Marty Linsky. (2017). *Leadership on the Line: Staying Alive through the Dangers of Change*. Boston: Harvard Business Review Press.

Hemelt, Steven W., Kevin L. Strange, Fernanda Furquim, Andrew Simon, and John E. Sawyer. (2018). "Why Is Math Cheaper Than English? Understanding Cost Differences in Higher Education." Working Paper 25314, National Bureau of Economic Research (Cambridge, MA), November 2018.

Hoenack, Stephan A. (1983). *Economic Behavior within Organizations*. Cambridge: Cambridge University Press.

Hopkins, David S. P., and William F. Massy. (1981). *Planning Models for Colleges and Universities*. Stanford, CA: Stanford University Press.

Hopkins, David S. P., Jean-Claude Larréché, and William F. Massy. (1977). "Constrained Optimization of a University Administrator's Preference Function." *Management Science* 24: 65–377.

Kegan, Robert, and Lisa Laskow Lahey. (2016). *An Everyone Culture: Becoming a Deliberately Developmental Organization*. Boston: Harvard Business Review Press.

Kosko, Bart. (1993). *Fuzzy Thinking: The New Science of Fuzzy Logic*. New York: Hyperion.

Kotter, John P. (2014). *Accelerate*. Boston: Harvard Business Review Press.

Light, Richard, et al. (n.d.). "Reducing Class Size: What Do We Know?" Working Paper at the Harvard Graduate School of Education.

Massy, William F. (1960). "Innovation and Market Penetration." Unpublished PhD thesis, Department of Economics, Massachusetts Institute of Technology.

———. (1990). *Endowment: Perspectives, Policies, and Management*. Washington, DC: Association of Governing Boards of Universities and Colleges.

———, ed. (1996). *Resource Allocation and Higher Education*. Ann Arbor: University of Michigan Press.

———. (2003). *Honoring the Trust: Quality and Cost Containment in Higher Education*. San Francisco: Jossey-Bass.

———. (2004). "Collegium Economicum: Why Institutions Do What They Do." *Change* 36, no. 4 (July-August): 26.

———. (2007). "Using the Budget to Fight Fragmentation and Improve Quality." In Joseph C. Burke (ed.), *Fixing the Fragmented University: Decentralization with Direction*, pp. 122–144. Bolton, MA: Anker Publishing Company.

———. (2016). *Reengineering the University: How to Be Mission Centered, Market Smart, and Margin Conscious*. Baltimore: Johns Hopkins University Press.

Massy, William F., Steven W. Graham, and Paula Myrick Short. (2007). *Academic Quality Work: A Handbook for Improvement*. Bolton, MA: Anker Publishing Company.

Mitchell, Brian C., and W. Joseph King. (2018). *How to Run a College*. Baltimore: Johns Hopkins University Press.

Morson, Gary Saul, and Morton Schapiro. (2017). *Cents and Sensibility: What Economics Can Learn from the Humanities*. Princeton, NJ: Princeton University Press.

National Research Council. (2012). *Improving Measurement of Productivity in Higher Education*. Panel on Measuring Higher Education Productivity: Conceptual Framework and Data Needs. T. A. Sullivan, C. Mackie, W. F. Massy, & E. Sinha (eds.). Committee on National Statistics and Board on Testing and Assessment, Division of Behavioral and Social Sciences and Education. Washington, DC: National Academies Press.

Rieley, James B. (1997). "Scenario Planning in Higher Education." Paper Presented at the Sixth Annual International Conference for Community and Technical College Chairs, Deans, and Other Organizational Leaders; Reno, Nevada, February 12–15; ERIC 970 207.

Rogers, Everett M. (2003). *Diffusion of Innovations*. Fifth Edition. New York: Free Press.

Schumpeter, Joseph A. (1942). *Capitalism, Socialism and Democracy*. New York: Harper and Brothers.

Snow, Charles Percy. (2001, 1959). *The Two Cultures*. London: Cambridge University Press.

Srinivasan, V., and A. D. Shocker (1973). "Linear Programming Techniques for Multidimensional Analysis of Preference." *Psychometrica* 38:337–342.

Tough, Paul. (2014). "Who Gets to Graduate?" *New York Times Magazine*, May 18, 28–33.

Van der Heijden, Kees. (2005). *Scenarios: The Art of Strategic Conversation*. Second Edition. New York: Wiley.

Van Vught, Frans. (1995). "A New Context for Academic Quality." In D. D. Deal & B. Sporn (eds.), *Emerging Patterns of Social Demand and University Reform: Through a Glass Darkly*, 194–211. New York: Elsevier.

Western Association of Schools and Colleges (WASC). (2002, September). "WASC Resource Guide for 'Good Practices' in Academic Program Review." https://www.csun.edu/sites/default/files/wasc_program_review _resource_guide_1.pdf.

Zaffron, Steve, and Gregory Unruh. (2018). "Your Organization Is a Network of Conversations." *MIT Sloan Management Review* blog. July 10. https://sloanreview.mit.edu/article/your-organization-is-a-network-of -conversations/.

Zemsky, Robert, and William F. Massy. (1990). "Cost Containment: Committing to a New Economic Reality." *Change* 22, no. 6 (November/December): 16–22.

Zemsky, Robert, and Susan Shaman. (Forthcoming). *Making Sense of the College Curriculum.* Baltimore: Johns Hopkins University Press.

Zemsky, Robert, Susan Shaman, and Daniel B. Shapiro. (2001). *Higher Education as Competitive Enterprise: When Markets Matter. New Directions for Institutional Research* 2001, no. 111 (Special Issue). New York: Wiley.

Index

Page numbers in *italics* refer to tables and figures.

for-profit paradigm, 44; contrast with not-for-profit paradigm, *218*, 220–22; decision rule, 219

Forum for the Future of Higher Education, xv

full-function (level III) AR models, 96, 111; core engine data hierarchy, 99, 118, *119*; interactive dashboards, 95, 99, 116, 118–22, *119*, *121*

function lust, 262, 296

fund-raising, 165

fuzzy logic, 297–98, 324n1 (app. B); use in scoring market data, 298–300

Gans, Joshua, 73

Gates Foundation, xv, 19, 33

Goldfarb, Avi, 73

Graham, Stephen W., 202

Grant Thornton LLC, 68

Gray Associates, xiv, 18, 47, 167, 193

Gray Program Economics Model, 18, 30, 48–58, *53*, 64, 70, 257; as level II AR model, *58*; in program portfolio analysis, 61, *213*

Gray Program Evaluation System, 91, 155, 186, 194, 257; scoring system, 194, *194*, *196*; use in program portfolio analysis, 212, *213*

Grayson, C. Jackson, 321n11

growth by substitution, 21, 32

hard and soft management, 37–38, 201, 259

Heifetz, Ronald, 32, 261

historical models. *See* AR models

holistic thinking: about AR, 257; about market data, 187; in program review, 203; regarding mission, market, and margin, 2; in scenario planning, 175

Hong Kong University Grants Committee (UGC): Quality Assurance Council, 202; quality process review, 201

Hopkins, David S. P., 84

Ikenberry, Stanley, 13

improving the higher education sector, 270–76

incentives: for change, 41, 79; impact of AR models on, 259; for raising price, *302*, 303; in university's internal economy, x, 20–21, 31, 38

increasing returns to scale, 322n5

incremental cost. *See* marginal cost

incremental revenue. *See* marginal revenue

indirect cost, 4, 8, *59*, 112–116; categories of, *113*; handling of, in AR models, *58*

initiatives: AR model usage, 254; budget reduction, 233; organizational change, 19, 268; quality improvement, 204, 209–11, *210*, 259; research, 82, 109; revenue growth, 37; strategic, 157

innovation: adoption of, 83–91; in university cost structures, 79

integer programming, 313

internal economy, of the university, 22, 146, 164, 184; invisible hand of, 32; in program review, 197; as represented in AR models, 25, 48, 186, 254, 256

IPEDS (Integrated Postsecondary Education Data System), 80, 150, 155, 187–88, 190–91

IT department, 10, 108; iterative development, 63, 263; legacy systems, 65; planning and data readiness, 63–64, 262

Jobs, Steve, 137, 153, 155

joint production, 100, 134

judgments: about academic quality process maturity, 208–9; about inputs to AR models, 4, 23, 76–77, 81–83; about mission contributions, 226–27; role of deans in, 101, 106; about student performance, 205. *See also* constrained choice model

Kasparov, Garry, 75

Kennedy, Donald, 262

Kennedy, John F., 98

King, W. Joseph, 38

knapsack problem, in optimization, 312, 322n11

Kotter, John, 33, 88, 265

last mile problem. *See* constrained choice model

levels: of AR models, 10, 18, 57–58, 62; within AR models, 48, 60, 93, 101, 120, 125, 140, *141*, 188, 281; degree, 192–93, 298; experience, 105; organizational, 23, 114, 133, 264, 267, 279; of students, 59, 120